MAINSTREAMING YOUNG CHILDREN

Bernard Spodek
University of Illinois

Olivia N. Saracho
University of Maryland

Richard C. Lee
University of Wisconsin—Whitewater

Wadsworth Publishing Company
Belmont, California
A Division of Wadsworth, Inc.

Education Editor   Bob Podstepny
Production Editor   Robin Lockwood
Designer   Lois Stanfield
Copy Editor   Sandra Sailer
Illustrator   Brenda Booth
Cover   Lois Stanfield

Printed in the United States of America

1 2 3 4 5 6 7 8 9 10—88 87 86 85 84

ISBN 0-534-02803-9

Library of Congress Cataloging in Publication Data

Spodek, Bernard.
  Mainstreaming young children.

  1. Handicapped children—Education—United States.
2. Mainstreaming in education—United States.   3. Education, Preschool—United States.   4. Education, Primary—United States.   I. Saracho, Olivia N.   II. Lee, Richard C., 1952–   III. Title.
LC4031.S75   1983   371.9'046   83-12544
ISBN 0-534-02803-9

CONTENTS IN BRIEF

CONTENTS

ABOUT THE AUTHORS

Bernard Spodek is Professor of Early Childhood Education at the University of Illinois, Urbana-Champaign. He received his doctorate from Teachers College Columbia University in 1962. Previously he was on the faculty of the University of Wisconsin-Milwaukee and has taught at the nursery, kindergarten and elementary school level. He has written extensively in the field of early childhood. Among the books he has authored and edited are *Teaching in the Early Years, Early Childhood Education* and *Handbook of Research in Early Childhood Education*. He has been extensively involved in professional associations and served as president of the National Association for the Education of Young Children.

Olivia N. Saracho is Associate Professor in the Reading Center at the University of Maryland. She completed her Ph.D. in early childhood education at the University of Illinois in 1978. She also served on the faculty of Pan American University and taught Head Start, preschool, kindergarten and elementary classes. She has authored numerous articles on early childhood education and teacher education and is co-editor of *Understanding the Multicultural Experience in Early Childhood Education* (forthcoming).

Richard C. Lee is Assistant Professor in the Department of Special Education at the University of Wisconsin at Whitewater. He received his Ph.D. from the University of Illinois in 1979 in early childhood education of the handicapped. He previously served on the faculty of the University of Maryland and has co-authored several articles on early childhood education of the handicapped.

PREFACE

My first job in early childhood education, more than thirty years ago, was related to integrating a handicapped child in a regular classroom setting. The school had agreed to accept an autistic child for a two week trial. I had been an observer/participant in the classroom for a college class and I was asked to work as an extra adult.

In the years that followed I had children enrolled in my classes with visual handicaps, orthopedic problems, and a range of psychological and physiological difficulties as well as gifted children. Although early childhood special education was in its infancy in those days, early childhood educators strove to educate *all* children, regardless of their personal strengths and weaknesses while responding to individual differences among children.

We have learned a great deal since those days about the nature of young children, and about how they grow, learn and develop. We have learned a great deal about handicapping conditions, their causes, the remedies that are available and the ways in which we can help children to make maximum use of their capacities. We have also learned new ways to provide educational programs for both normal and handicapped children, and have developed a range of techniques for organizing classrooms and supporting positive interactions with materials and with other children within those classrooms.

Unfortunately as the fields of early childhood education and special education have developed, they have grown progressively isolated from one another. Handicapped children have been educated in segregated settings and the methods used in working with the handicapped have become progressively specialized. The move to mainstream children, to educate mildly and moderately handicapped children in regular classrooms, has reversed that trend to some extent. Regular classroom teachers and teachers of the handicapped are collaborating together in the best interests of all children. And in the process regular and special educators have been learning from one another.

This book is an extension of the move to lessen segregation. It is designed for use by teachers and those preparing to be teachers who will work in regular classes in which some handicapped children are enrolled. It is the result of a collaboration of specialists in early childhood education for normal children and in early childhood education of the handicapped. It is designed to provide teachers with the information they need to know about handicapped children and their educational needs as well as about ways to modify their program to respond to the extended range of individual differences they will find when children with handicapping conditions are included in their classes.

The book is divided into three sections. The first section, *Foundations of Mainstreaming*, contains information on the situation that has led to the policy of educating handicapped children in the least restrictive setting, and has resulted in increased numbers of children being taught in integrated classes. The second chapter describes various handicapping conditions teachers are likely to encounter in children in these classes.

The second section, *Planning, Organizing, and Collaborating for Mainstreaming*, describes procedures by which handicapped children are identified and assessed as well as procedures for developing Individualized Educational Programs, for modifying classroom settings, and for enhancing the social environment when hand-

icapped children are present. A special chapter in this section deals with working with parents, an aspect of teaching that takes on increased importance with handicapped children.

The third section, *Modifying Classroom Programs for Young Handicapped Children*, deals with ways to adapt the existing curriculum for children with varying handicaps. Each curriculum area is dealt with in a separate chapter or section of a chapter, and specific examples are provided relating to each specific handicapping condition. The chapter on play is particularly important, since education through play is so vital a part of early childhood education programs.

Throughout the book specific examples are given to illustrate the text. In addition, resources are listed in the area of identification and assessment so that teachers will have knowledge of some of the instruments they can use for these purposes. Photographs of actual classes as well as drawn illustrations are also used to make meanings more available to the reader.

Reflected throughout this book are the basic values of early childhood education: respect for each child and his particular pattern of development; concern for comprehensive education related to all areas of human development and grounded in personal expression and creativity; concern for the autonomy and freedom of the individual; a belief that education should be relevant to the current life of the young child as well as preparatory to later life; and a view that children's educational experiences be joyful ones.

In addition the field has consistently viewed the teacher as the focal element in the education of young children. It is to the individual teacher in the regular early childhood classroom and to those who are preparing to be teachers of young children that this book is addressed. It brings together a wealth of information about the education of young children, culled from the experiences of practitioners as well as the experiments of researchers. It provides examples of ways to modify classroom environments and educational activities in response to the needs of individual children as well as the theory underlying those modifications. To the task we have brought years of experience in teaching children, both normal and handicapped, in working with teachers of young children, and in studying teaching and learning.

There are many people, colleagues, students and practitioners to whom we are grateful for help, advice and support—too many to individually acknowledge them all. Special thanks needs to be given, however, to Jeanette Walker, Mark Levine and Linda Rubinowitz, for their careful review of earlier versions of the manuscript as well as the staff, children and parents of Chiaravalle School in Evanston, Illinois, for allowing us to take pictures of children, parents and staff of a mainstreamed school. All the photographs in the book were taken at the school. All, with the exception of the one on page 217 taken by Linda Rubinowitz, were taken by me. James B. Donnelly provided the original sketches for the artwork.

I would like to thank the following reviewers for their helpful comments: Richard L. Shick, Mansfield University; Rosemarie Slavenas, Northern Illinois University; Marjorie W. Lee, Howard University; Kevin J. Swick, University of South Carolina; Phyllis Weisberg, Trenton State College; Carol Cartwright, The Pennsylvania State University; Samuel J. Meisels, University of Michigan; Ron Colarusso, Georgia State University; Dennis Moore, Sinclair Community College.

My coauthors and I would also like to acknowledge the encouragement and support provided by our families and our friends during the development of this book. Heartfelt thanks go to Francisca S. and Pablo J. Villareal, to Saul M. Villareal and Lydia Gonzales, to Lexene and Dan Zolfo, to Joyce Lee, and to Prudence Spodek.

Bernard Spodek

Part One

FOUNDATIONS OF MAINSTREAMING

One

INTRODUCTION

Mainstreaming means helping people with handicaps live, learn, and work in everyday settings where they will have the greatest opportunity to become as independent as possible. . . . It gives handicapped children the chance to join in the "mainstream of life" by including them in the regular preschool experience, and gives nonhandicapped children the opportunity to learn and grow by experiencing the strengths and weaknesses of their handicapped friends.

However, mainstreaming does not simply involve enrolling handicapped children in a program with nonhandicapped children. Definite steps must be taken to ensure that handicapped children participate actively and fully in classroom activities (Hayden, Smith, von Hippel, and Baer, 1978, p. 4).

Not too many years ago children regarded as "special" were not educated in public schools. In many schools before the 1950s, for example, a child not considered ready for kindergarten, was sent home and allowed to stay there another year to mature. And a child unable to navigate a school's stairways and corridors because of an orthopedic problem was educated in a separate school or at home. Few resources were made available in public schools to help children with vision or hearing problems or with behavior problems.

Many changes have taken place since those days. Some of these changes have resulted from new laws and regulations providing resources for teaching handicapped children and requiring that these children be educated in public schools. Other changes were stimulated by litigation in which courts ruled that the denial of educational opportunity to any child is the denial of equal protection by the law. As a result, schools have increased the educational opportunities provided to all handicapped children over the years.

It is to the full and active participation of handicapped children in regular classes, particularly those between the ages of three and eight, that this book is addressed.

3

Its focus is on young children who for some developmental, physical, or psychological reason are different from the normal child in a way that makes it difficult for them to cope with and benefit from the regular educational program without special help. These handicapping conditions include behavioral disabilities, learning disabilities, mental retardation, visual impairment, hearing impairment, communication disorders, and physical and health impairments. The characteristics of children with these handicaps are discussed in Chapter 2.

When programs for handicapped children were first implemented in schools over a quarter of a century ago, the general pattern was to educate them in separate classes or facilities. It was felt that this way programs could be designed specifically to meet their needs and that teachers could use special educational methods with them without having to divide their attention between normal and handicapped children. Blind children could be offered a special program with language arts activities provided in braille, while mentally retarded children could be offered a program geared to their learning abilities—a program that would not allow invidious comparisons to be made with children who learned more easily. In addition, special education funds could be allocated in such a way that children who most needed those particular resources would benefit from them rather than diluting the resources by making them available to all children.

RATIONALE FOR MAINSTREAMING

The integration of handicapped and nonhandicapped persons of all ages in educational settings is a sound and ethical policy. Bricker (1978) has identified social-ethical, legal-legislative, and psychological-educational arguments on behalf of the educational integration of preschool children that hold for older children as well. These arguments relate to the possibility of altering societal attitudes toward the handicapped, to the negative effect on handicapped children of educational segregation, and to the increased efficiency of allocating resources to all children through integrated programs.

Over the last decade or so, a number of legal decisions have supported mainstreaming, providing (1) the right of all handicapped children to a free public education, (2) the right of handicapped children to be educated in the least restrictive environment possible, and (3) the right of parents to review educational decisions relevant to their handicapped children.

In earlier times, programs for the handicapped were generally designed for children who had reached the age of compulsory school attendance (usually six or seven years). Research, however, has suggested that for some children there is a greater possibility of overcoming educational deficits if these are addressed before kindergarten or the primary grades. Early intervention programs have been found, for example, to have pervasive and long lasting effects on children who are educationally disadvantaged, increasing their success in school and decreasing the need for special educational services (Consortium on Developmental Continuity, 1977). Early education experiences have also been found to be effective with mentally retarded children (Kirk, 1958). In addition, early experiences help children make the best use of their personal resources and capabilities even when there can be no developmental reversal of the disability.

While many handicapped children must be educated in isolation, educating children in segregated settings has a number of shortcomings. By its very nature it is an unequal form of education. This principle has been articulated for children from cultural minorities, but it is equally valid for children who are handicapped. It deprives them of many informal incidental learning opportunities that result from interacting with other people within a normal physical environment. Knowledge and skills gained in segregated settings are often less transferable to normal life settings than those gained in integrated settings. In addition, serious questions have been raised about the effectiveness of segregated special educational programs for handicapped children. A number of studies, as a matter of fact, have shown that in certain areas of education, handicapped children educated in normal settings do as well as or better than those educated in special classes. Thus, the call for mainstreaming—educating children in integrated settings with their normally developing peers—has been mounted, and all handicapped children are required to be educated in the least restrictive educational setting.

Two court cases were particularly important in establishing the rights of handicapped children to an appropriate education. In the 1971 case of *Pennsylvania Association for Retarded Children* v. *Commonwealth of Pennsylvania*, the right of a previously excluded group of retarded children to a free public education was ensured. The state also acknowledged the right of handicapped children to education in the least restrictive environment possible, separated from their peers only to the degree that is necessary for educational purposes. Although this was a landmark case, it only covered the rights of mentally retarded children. In a similar ruling, handed down in 1972 in the *Mills* v. *Board of Education of the District of Columbia* case, these rights were extended to all handicapped children. In addition, lack of school funds was declared to be an unacceptable reason for excluding handicapped children from public schools.

At about the same time a number of states, including Tennessee and Wisconsin, were enacting legislation intended to promote the education of school-age handicapped children in the most appropriate educational placement. Most of that legislation reflected the basic rights of handicapped children and guaranteed due process procedures for their parents. These rights were extended to all handicapped children in the United States when Congress enacted the Education for All Handicapped Children Act (Public Law 94-142). The result of these mandates is that integration of handicapped children into educational programs with nonhandicapped children is no longer the exception; it is the rule.

Educational research findings supported this move and provided a rational base for the actions of the courts and the legislatures. The reviews of research by Cegelka and Tyler (1970), and by Semmel, Gottlieb, and Robinson (1979), for example, found the issue of placement of mentally retarded children to be far from settled, with a number of studies showing no advantage of segregated placement in relation to academic achievement. As far as social behavior is concerned, studies by Gambel, Gottlieb, and Harrison (1974), and by Goodman, Gottlieb, and Harrison (1972) show that the social behavior of mentally retarded mainstreamed children tends to resemble that of their normal classmates and has increasingly less in common with their segregated peers as they stay in normal classes.

Nonhandicapped children also benefit from contact with the handicapped. They develop increased understanding of and sensitivity to individual differences and benefit academically from integrated programs to at least the same degree as would be expected had they attended nonintegrated preschools. The work of Bricker and Bricker (1971) demonstrated this for very young children. It can be assumed that the process occurs with older children as well.

Thus, growing out of the thrusts of legal decisions and research knowledge has come the move to mainstream: to educate handicapped children within the regular classroom with their normally developing peers. This policy is in effect for children in public schools and has impacted the preschool area as well. In Head Start pro-grams the policy since 1972 has been that at least 10 percent of the children enrolled be handicapped. In 1977–1978 it was estimated that 94 percent of school-age handicapped children received educational services in regular public schools (Dickerson & Davis, 1981).

Although the move to educate handicapped children in regular classrooms received great impetus from the passage of Public Law 94-142 (the Education of All Handicapped Children Act), the impact of this law has been more limited for children of preschool age. The act, which provides for the education of all handicapped children between ages 3 and 21, relieves the states of responsibility for educating handicapped children aged 3 to 5 and 18 to 21 if normal children in these age ranges are not served by a state's public schools. Even when handicapped children of those ages are enrolled in public schools, however, they may not be educated in classes with their normal peers. If only handicapped children below school age are educated in the public schools while normal children of that age are excluded (as is the case in Illinois, for example), then these handicapped children cannot be educated in the least restrictive educational environment. Thus preschool children may be excluded from mainstreamed classes even though mainstreamed classes are available for children in the elementary and secondary grades (Cohen, Semmes, & Guralnick, 1979).

Many handicapped preschool children are provided with an early educational experience through nonpublic school agencies, however. Head Start enrolls a number of handicapped children and will often have special educational personnel and other resources for the handicapped available. Many nonpublic nursery schools and day care centers also enroll handicapped children. In many cases public school and other community resources are provided to ensure the best possible services to these children.

Least Restrictive Environments

Not all handicapped children can be integrated into regular classes. The idea of mainstreaming is primarily intended for mildly and moderately handicapped children. Even with these children, special resources and additional services need to be provided along with special adaptations of regular classroom programs. For some handicapped children, however, the most appropriate educational placement is outside the regular classroom. The key criterion for placing handicapped children is providing education service in the least restrictive environment, that is, educating children in a manner as close as is appropriate to that provided for normal children. Regular classroom teachers cannot provide all the services some handicapped children require, and the regular school may be an inappropriate setting for the education of certain handicapped children. A determination should be made as to the needs of a particular child and the educational environment best suited to providing for those needs. Evelyn Deno (1970) has identified a hierarchy of placements for handicapped children:

1. Regular classroom assignment, possibly with classroom modification and supportive services provided

2. Regular classroom assignment plus supplementary instructional services (a resource room or itinerant teacher might provide these)

3. Part-time special classes with the balance of the day spent in a regular class or resource room

4. Full-time special class with the child segregated into a separate class in a conventional school

5. Special day school

6. Homebound instruction

7. Institutional or residential assignment

Each succeeding placement on the continuum provides a more segregated and therefore less normal educational environment for the handicapped child. Only the first three of these levels can be considered as mainstreaming.

IMPLICATIONS OF MAINSTREAMING FOR CLASSROOM TEACHERS

Enrolling handicapped children in a regular class does not require that the teacher of that class become a special educator since the purpose is to allow the child to experience as normal and regular an educational program as possible. On the other hand, the classroom teacher cannot take a business-as-usual attitude either. Classroom teachers know a great deal about children and about teaching that is as relevant to the education of handicapped children as it is to the education of normal children. As a matter of fact, there is much that special educators can learn from regular classroom teachers and teaching (Spodek, 1982). However, classroom organization and practices must be adapted to accommodate the extended range of individual differences to be found in a class when handicapped children are integrated into it. Teachers who have handicapped children in their classes have to work with a wider range of educational personnel (including resource teachers and evaluation and education specialists) than they would otherwise be required to work with. They have to develop different relationships with parents, some mandated by due process procedures, others by the particular needs of the parents. They have to be involved to a greater degree in team efforts in the interest of the handicapped children in their class. They have to use different assessment techniques, plan programs for children more systematically and possibly more formally, and review their own classroom procedures to determine if they are equally effective for all children in their classes. Teachers of mainstreamed classes have to learn more about children's normal and exceptional patterns of development, about different ways of learning that are effective for different children, and about ways of teaching that support each form of learning.

Classroom teachers must assume some responsibility for identifying handicapped children in the school and in the community, although the total responsibility will seldom fall on them. Sometimes children enrolled in regular classes are identified as handicapped only after being observed by the teacher in relation to other children of a similar age. In such cases, it is the teacher's responsibility to set in motion the process of assessing the nature and extent of a child's handicap and determining the appropriate methods for working with that child. In other instances, teachers will work along with other school personnel to identify children with handicapping conditions in the community before they enter school. Even when minimally involved in the process of identification and assessment, the classroom teacher must be aware of the work of the interdisciplinary team as well as of the actions taken in relation to specific children.

Once a child is identified as handicapped, the nature and extent of the problem must be assessed. A range of specialists, including psychologists, social workers, and speech and language specialists, help determine the child's needs and plan appropriate educational treatment. In this process, too, the classroom teacher should play a crucial role. Often only the classroom teacher has observed the child in the context of interpersonal relations and in the process of coping with the demands of everyday life. This knowledge is important in determining the appropriate educational treatment for a child and may in fact be a critical factor in decisions that must be made.

The program developed as a result of an assessment must be recorded in a formal document called an **Individual**

Educational Program (IEP); this is required by law. Parents must then be informed of the program established for their child and, if possible, should be involved in its development. They are also expected to approve the program established for their child. Often the teacher is the one who has the best relationship with parents and is in the best position to interpret the IEP to them, although social workers and parent liaison workers may assume responsibility for that role. If parents disagree as to the appropriateness of the plan, reviews must be made available to them, including due process appeals, and the teacher must inform parents of their options.

Much of the individual educational programs designed for most handicapped children will be implemented in the regular classroom. Many times children are removed from the regular classroom to a separate room within the school where they are provided with special services or instruction in academic skills basic to their education. This separation of the child for special instruction has been characterized as a pull-out program. Although the pull-out strategy is often used, we know little of its educational effectiveness. No studies have been done on the impact of such programs on handicapped children, but an interesting analysis of analyses, or meta-analysis, of a range of similar pull-out programs has been done in relation to research on children who are also in need of remediation and who are in programs supported by Title I of the Elementary and Secondary Education Act. After reviewing and reanalyzing studies of such programs, Glass and Smith (1977) concluded that the pull-out procedure per se has no clear academic or social benefits and, in fact, may be detrimental to pupils' progress and adjustment to school.

These conclusions, derived from remedial education, strongly suggest a need for studies of pull-out programs used for mainstreamed children. Such sessions may not be the best way to provide for the mainstreamed child's special needs. An alternative to pull-out programs is to have the special educator or resource consultant teacher work directly with the child in the regular classroom. In this way the special educator can become more aware of what is happening in the classroom and thus be in a better position to integrate the special activities with the ongoing classroom program. Resource teachers can also serve as consultants to the regular classroom teacher, providing additional resources and materials and suggesting procedures that might be effective in working with the handicapped child. The appropriateness of the option depends on the characteristics of the handicapped child, on the ability of the regular teacher to cope with the responsibilities of the regular class as well as the needs of the handicapped child, and on the nature of the relationship that develops between the regular teacher and the specialists in the school.

In any case, it is likely that modifications will be made in the way a regular class functions when a handicapped child is integrated within it. Mainstreaming handicapped children in the regular classroom also requires additional work for the teacher. The necessary schedule changes, the additional conferences with resource people, the formal evaluation and record keeping, the selection and use of special supplies and equipment, and the need to work more intensely with parents, place additional demands on the regular teacher. Many schools recognize this burden and compensate by providing smaller classes or a classroom aide. Others assign as much responsibility as possible to the special education resource teacher or to a coordinator. No matter how the responsibility is shared, however, knowledge of children and of educational practice must be brought to bear to respond to the range of differences found among the children in the class and to provide the best possible educational program, not only for the handicapped child but for all of the children in the classroom.

This book is addressed to early childhood teachers and those preparing to be teachers who have or will have handicapped children integrated in regular preschool, kindergarten, and primary classrooms. Part I, *Foundations of Mainstreaming*, provides background information for the teacher. In addition to this first chapter, which gives a historical and theoretical perspective to practice, the second chapter provides descriptions of characteristics of handicapping conditions found in children. The descriptions provided are generalized ones; children will manifest these conditions in somewhat different ways, or a child may suffer from a number of handicapping conditions at the same time. The information is presented to provide teachers with a background for understanding handicapped children who may enter the regular classroom and to serve as the beginning point for individual identification and assessment.

Part II, *Planning, Organizing, and Collaborating for Mainstreaming*, discusses the many professional activities in which a teacher must engage before, after, and while teaching handicapped children in a regular classroom. Identifying handicapped children, planning for their educational needs, modifying classroom organization, preparing a social environment, assessing children's needs and program outcomes, and working with parents are all a necessary part of the educational process. Because handicapped children may have specific difficulties in dealing with a learning environment, and because of particular laws and regulations that apply to them, these processes, so important in the education of all children, must be dealt with more explicitly.

Part III, *Modifying Classroom Programs for Mainstreamed Children*, presents background information and suggestions for helping handicapped children deal with the content of early childhood education. Each subject area is analyzed in relation to procedures to be used to help all children achieve those goals that are appropriate to them. Particular attention is given to the expressive arts and to the area of play, both of which are critical to a sound education in the early childhood years. We believe this will be a useful resource to teachers working at integrating handicapped and nonhandicapped children into a sound educational program within regular classrooms.

REFERENCES

Bricker, D. D. A rationale for the integration of handicapped and nonhandicapped preschool children. In M. J. Guralnick (Ed.), *Early intervention and the integration of handicapped and nonhandicapped children*. Baltimore, Md.: University Park Press, 1978.

Bricker, D. D., and Bricker, W. A. *Toddler research and intervention project report: Year I*. IMRID Behavioral Science Monograph 20. Institute on Mental Retardation and Intellectual Development. Nashville, Tenn.: George Peabody College, 1971.

Cegelka, J. J., and Tyler, J. L. The efficacy of special class placement of the mentally retarded in proper perspective. *Training School Bulletin*, 1970, *67*, 33–68.

Cohen, S., Semmes, M., and Guralnick, M. J. Public Law 94-142 and the education of preschool handicapped children. *Exceptional Children*, 1979, *45*, 279–285.

Consortium on Developmental Continuity. *The persistence of preschool effects*. Department of Health, Education and Welfare publication #(OHD) 78-30130, 1977.

Deno, E. Special education as developmental capital, *Exceptional Children*, 1970, *37* (3), 229–37.

Dickerson, M. D., and Davis, M. D. The developmental approach: A successful way to mainstream young children. *Childhood Education*, 1981, *58*, 8–13.

Gambel, D. H., Gottlieb, J., and Harrison, R. H. Comparison of classroom behavior of special-class EMR, integrated EMR, low IQ, and nonretarded children. *American Journal of Mental Deficiency*, 1974, *79*, 16–21.

Glass, G. V., and Smith, M. L. *"Pull-out" in compensatory education*. Paper prepared for the Office of the Commissioner, U.S. Office of Education. November 2, 1977.

Goodman, H., Gottlieb, J., and Harrison, R. H. Social acceptance of EMRs integrated into a nongraded elementary school. *American Journal of Mental Deficiency*, 1972, *76*, 412–417.

Hayden, A. H., Smith, R. K., von Hippel, C. S., and Baer, S. A. *Mainstreaming preschoolers: Children with learning disabilities*. Washington, D.C.: U.S. Department of Health and Human Services, 1978.

Kirk, S. A. *Early education of the mentally retarded: An experimental study*. Urbana: University of Illinois Press, 1958.

Mills v. *Board of Education of the District of Columbia*, 318 F. Supp. 866 (D.D.C., 1972).

Pennsylvania Association for Retarded Children v. *Commonwealth of Pennsylvania*, 343 F. Supp. 279 (E.D. Pa. 1972).

Semmel, M. I., Gottlieb, J., and Robinson, N. R. Mainstreaming: Perspectives on educating handicapped children in the public school. In D.C. Berliner (Ed.), *Review of Research in Education*, Vol. 7, 1979. Itasca, Ill.: F. E. Peacock, 1979.

Spodek, B. What special educators need to know about regular classes. *Educational Forum*, 1982, *66*, 295–307.

Two

CHARACTERISTICS OF YOUNG HANDICAPPED CHILDREN

All children, handicapped or nonhand-icapped have special educational needs and should be dealt with in a personal manner. There are, however, distinct groups of children with particular characteristics for whom education in the regular classroom must be specially adjusted. Such children have been in-dividually diagnosed and described as handicapped.

This chapter describes handicapped children according to their characteris-tics and suggests general classroom modifications for their education. For convenience, each type of handicap is presented here as a separate category, but it must be remembered that categories are of limited use in plan-ning for children, who must be seen and treated as individuals. Seven categories are discussed: behaviorally disordered, learning disabled, mentally retarded, visually impaired, hearing impaired, those with communication disorders, and physically and health impaired. Each of the following sec-tions is devoted to one of these classifications.

BEHAVIORALLY DISORDERED CHILDREN

Behavioral disorders, also called emo-tional disturbances, may be defined as deviations from age-appropriate behav-ior that significantly interfere with the child's own development or with the lives of others. Children with such dis-orders may be very aggressive or very withdrawn, very loud or very quiet, very euphoric or very depressed. Their conduct may seem strange in context and difficult to explain. Although edu-cators do not agree about what consti-tutes such a disability, behaviorally dis-ordered children often exhibit a number of behaviors that, although oc-casionally seen in most children, occur at a much greater frequency in children with behavior disorders. These include self-destructive behavior (such as head banging), temper tantrums, inability to tolerate frustration, moodiness and withdrawal, difficulty in making friends, and school phobia (unfounded fear of going to school). The child who occasionally has a temper tantrum when frustrated is seldom cause for concern; the child who tantrums over very minor frustrations several times a day may well be the cause of concern.

Psychological, environmental, and physiological causes have been associated with behavioral disorders. The psychological factors include, among others, frustration caused by delay of rewards or by conflict and childhood bereavement caused by separation from or death of a loved one. Environmental factors include family influences, parental characteristics, and methods of child management used by parents and teachers. Physiological factors, including genetic factors, are also suspected to be possible causes of severe behavior disorder.

The undesirable or inappropriate behaviors of behaviorally disordered children differ from those of normal children in three dimensions: (1) severity—the extremeness of the undesirable and inappropriate behavior, (2) chronicity—the length of time over which the undesirable and inappropriate behavior occurs, and (3) context—where and when undesirable and inappropriate behavior occurs. Teachers describe emotionally disturbed children as those who easily become lost in a tangle of irrelevancies, distortions, unpleasantness, disorganization, and nonproductive activity. Bower (1969) grouped emotionally disturbed behaviors into five categories:

(1) difficulty in achieving in school not due to ill health, (2) difficulty in establishing and keeping positive interpersonal relationships with peers and adults, (3) difficulty in demonstrating appropriate feelings under normal conditions, (4) difficulty in overcoming a pervasive mood or unhappiness or depression, and (5) difficulty in overcoming physical symptoms (such as pains) or fears associated with their problems. Peterson (1961) and Quay, Morse, and Cutler (1966) identified three types of emotionally disturbed behaviors that teachers find difficult to cope with: (1) aggressive, rude, attention-seeking, and hyperactive behavior; (2) anxious, hypersensitive, fearful, and withdrawn behavior; and (3) delinquent, truant, and antisocial behavior.

Children exhibiting mild to moderate behavior disorders can be educated in the regular classroom provided the regular teacher receives advice and consultation and possibly supplemental help from special education teachers who work with the child within the classroom or in resource rooms for part of the day, or they may be segregated in special classes. Severely disturbed children, such as those labeled psychotic, schizophrenic, or autistic, require special classes or special schools or institutions and may never enter the educational mainstream (Payne, Kauffman, Patton, Brown, & DeMott, 1979).

Treatments for behavior-disabled children include drug therapy, family counseling, psychotherapy for the children and/or their families, behavior modification techniques, and other forms of psychological or psychoeduca-

A BEHAVIORALLY DISORDERED CHILD

Jennifer King, 4, was described by her parents as highly distractable at home and by her teacher as extremely overactive. From her first day at the day care center, Jennifer refused to enter the classroom unless her mother was present. Her attachment to her mother was unusually prolonged, lasting throughout the year. After a half hour or so, Jenny's mother was usually able to slip out of the room unnoticed.

At times, Jenny appeared to be literally out of control in the classroom. She had an unusually short attention span, would often stare off into space, and would suddenly have outbursts of temper for no apparent reason. She would also frequently leave her activities and wander aimlessly around the center. Requests to return to what she was supposed to be doing were ignored and physical restraint by the teacher resulted in intense tantrums. Jenny rarely spoke to anyone, including peers, and spent most of her time playing alone. Her only interactions with peers were negative, involving fighting, kicking, and screaming.

Toward the end of the year, Mrs. Miller, Jenny's teacher, in an effort to prepare Jenny for kindergarten, asked Jenny's mother to wait in the hall rather than accompany Jenny into the classroom. Jenny reacted with a tantrum followed by whimpering that continued for the rest of the morning. After five days, Mrs. King and Mrs. Miller agreed that Mrs. King should again accompany Jenny into the classroom.

At the end of the year, noting Jenny's many problems, Mrs. Miller advised Mrs. King to seek special services for Jenny next year in kindergarten.

tional interventions, not all of which are appropriate for schools. When a local school is not equipped to provide treatment, teachers can suggest outside agencies. Since teachers have to respond to the children's behavior in the classroom, they need to know ways to help the children adjust to the school setting and to provide a responsive environment that meets their needs.
٭ Two major treatment strategies commonly used for behavior-disordered young children are the psychodynamic approach and the behavior analysis approach? The psychodynamic approach, derived from Freud's psychoanalytic theory, views behavioral disorders as the result of intrapsychic conflict. The emotional problems of adults are thought to result primarily from childhood events, thus placing extreme importance on early experience and intervention. Treatment is aimed primarily at removing the underlying cause of behavioral deviance. One of the psychodynamically based treatments for young children is play therapy. Axline (1974) provides an overview of this technique. These approaches are discussed in Chapter 6.

In contrast, behavior analysis theory argues that all behavior, including disordered behavior, is learned. The teacher's main task is to rearrange the environment so that disordered behavior is weakened and appropriate behavior is strengthened. To decrease negative behavior, children may be initially segregated into an environment that is easy to manage and then gradually integrated into the classroom. The teacher learns behavior management strategies to help these children maintain appropriate behaviors; otherwise such children might revert to their original condition. The chief technique in this procedure is reinforcement for appropriate behaviors.

Teachers who work with mildly or moderately behavior-disabled children must learn to understand them and discover ways to deal with their behav-iors. Teachers can analyze and alter the classroom milieu to promote more positive aspects of the children's behavior. A crisis-intervention teacher or resource-room teacher may serve as the classroom teacher's advisor, on call on a long-term basis.

All young children exhibit some inappropriate behavior at some time. This may be especially true when a child first enters a nursery school, day care center, or kindergarten class. In small amounts or for short periods of time, most of these behaviors are quite normal. It is only when a maladaptive behavior continues week after week with no sign of lessening, that the teacher should ask for consultation.

LEARNING-DISABLED AND DEVELOPMENTALLY DISABLED CHILDREN

Learning disability is a relatively new area of study, service, and research; thus definitions are still emergent. Some researchers suggest that learning disabilities are the result of neurological dysfunction or central processing deficits while others suggest the importance of behavioral antecedents. All agree that learning disabilities vary on a continuum from mild to severe (Hallahan & Kauffman, 1978).

In the preschool child, the term *learning disability* can refer to the imperfect ability of a child to listen, think, or speak. During the school years, the term may refer to a child's imperfect ability to read, write, spell, or do arithmetic. Many labels have been assigned to conditions that are thought to contribute to learning disabilities. Among the most commonly used are brain injury, perceptual-motor impairment, minimal brain dysfunction or damage, and dyslexia.

The National Advisory Committee on Handicapped Children of the United States Office of Education (1968) defines learning disabilities in this way:

Children with special (specific) learning disabilities exhibit a disorder in one or more of the basic psychological processes involved in understanding or in using spoken or written language. These may be manifested in disorders of listening, thinking, talking, reading, writing, spelling, or arithmetic. They include conditions which have been re-

---

A LEARNING-DISABLED CHILD

Since infancy, Steve, age 3, was a mystery to his parents and others who knew him. He looked normal with a healthy, robust body, sound ears, and what his aunt termed an intelligent look in his eyes. But something seemed wrong. Steve was often inattentive, was slow to develop language, appeared withdrawn and often acted in an impulsive manner. He was uncoordinated compared to other children his age and had considerable difficulty remembering things he heard.

Steve's mother decided to take Steve to a physician who tested and ruled out vision, hearing, and brain-injury problems. After extensive testing, the local school psychologist concluded that Steve suffered from a learning disability. Steve had an auditory processing dysfunction; he had difficulty understanding and interpreting things he heard.

The psychologist recommended placement in an integrated preschool program where a resource teacher worked with Steve approximately one hour a day, four days a week. Steve spent the rest of the time with his normally developing peers who, for the most part, noticed nothing different about Steve. After six months, Steve became noticeably more attentive and less impulsive. He also made gains in his motor coordination skills as a result of work with an occupational therapist.

---

ferred to as *perceptual handicaps, brain injury, minimal brain dysfunction, dyslexia, developmental aphasia, etc. They* do not *include learning problems which are due primarily to visual, hearing, or motor handicaps, to mental retardation, emotional disturbance, or to environmental disadvantage (p. 14).*

Behaviors or symptoms that may indicate learning disabilities in young children include hyperactivity, perceptual motor defects, general orientation defects, disorders of attention, impulsivity, disorders of memory and conceptual thinking, and specific learning defects, especially in language. The identification of a child's learning disability requires elimination of other causes of learning problems, such as mental retardation, cultural deprivation, poor teaching, or emotional disturbance.

Agreement is lacking as to what constitutes a developmentally disabled child. Federal legislation, however, specifies particular conditions including (1) mental retardation, cerebral palsy, epilepsy, or other adverse neurological conditions; (2) evidence of the disability before the child turns 18; and (3) the expectation that the disability is long-term and will continue, substantially handicapping the child. Because there is so much overlap, it may be useless to try to separate learning disabilities from developmental disabilities. Thus, developmental-learning-disabled may be a more appropriate description for these children.

The clinical model is one approach used to teach children with learning disabilities. This involves (1) diagnosing the specific learning problem, (2) establishing objectives to ameliorate the learning problem, (3) developing a program specifically aimed at the learning problem, and (4) assessing any changes in the original problem to evaluate the success of the program. This strategy requires simplifying the program and teaching directly to the child's areas of weakness. Task analysis is used to divide a complex skill into its simpler components, which can be learned separately and then reintegrated. This strategy is based on the assumption that children learn simpler tasks more easily than complex tasks, that learning difficulties are best attacked directly, and that learning is behaviorally based.

MENTALLY RETARDED CHILDREN

There is much controversy over the definition of mental retardation. Perhaps the most often quoted and widely accepted definition is that of the American Association on Mental Deficiency: "Mental retardation often refers to significantly subaverage general intellectual functioning existing concurrently with deficits in adaptive behavior and manifested during the developmental period" (Grossman, 1973, p. 5). Subaverage intellectual functioning is usually determined by an intelligence test score two or more standard deviations below the mean. Adaptive behavior includes sensory-motor communication, self-help, socialization, and academic and vocational skills. The developmental period is considered as being before an individual's nineteenth birthday. This definition is based on a description of present behavior without mention of potential intelligence. The IQ test is used in conjunction with other sources of information, such as class performance. The definition is also developmental, with diagnosis based on samples of behavior assessed according to a child's own age level.

There are two principle schools of thought on the causes of mental retardation. **Genetic theorists** argue that mental retardation is caused by specific genetic defects found in dominant or recessive genes or in some kind of chromosomal aberration. **Environmentalists** stress the critical role of experience in intellectual development and argue that, especially in the so-called mildly retarded child, the quality of the child's environment and experience in the early years accounts in many cases for children's slower mental development.

Mentally retarded young children are generally grouped into one of three categories: (1) educable mentally retarded (EMR), (2) trainable mentally retarded (TMR), and (3) severely or profoundly mentally retarded (SMR) (Smith & Neisworth, 1975). This classification system is rough and should be used with caution. EMR children, who make up the vast majority of the children labeled mentally retarded, generally score between 50 and 80 on

A MENTALLY RETARDED CHILD

Barbara, 7, has been diagnosed as educably mentally retarded. Her IQ, averaged over several testings, is 75, and she is said to have a short attention span and to work at a slow pace; she also exhibits poor language skills. In addition, she has limited ability to deal with abstractions and is often described by parents and teachers as having a low self-concept. She also appears more comfortable when playing with younger children.

Barbara's teachers note that she tends to require high levels of motivation and almost constant success. Learning activities are sequenced into small steps for Barbara with much repetition and careful teacher feedback.

School psychologists and counselors tell Barbara's parents that her education over time will emphasize basic literacy, math and human relations skills. Barbara, like other people with her disability, can become a skilled and highly valued worker.

IQ tests, indicating a rate of development around one-half to three-fourths that of the average child. These children, who are often candidates for mainstreaming, typically have interests that correspond closely to those of children of equal mental ages rather than to those of their chronological peers. It is generally believed that most mild forms of retardation are reversible, especially if intervention is initiated in the early years of life.

TMR children typically score between 25 and 50 on intelligence tests and are expected to develop at a rate one-third to one-half that of a normal child. These children, most of whom are unable to be mainstreamed, are generally incapable of learning ordinary academic subjects but can learn self-care tasks, common safety rules, and social adjustment in everyday situations, which can lead to productive lives in supervised environments.

SMR children, whose IQ scores are usually below 25, require considerable supervision, protection, and care. While some of these children learn to walk, feed themselves, and speak simple sentences, many are bedridden and often die before age 18. Obviously, the profoundly retarded child is not a candidate for mainstreaming.

Educational programs developed for the retarded child during the last few years share a number of goals, including the enhancement of potential skills, normalization (creating the greatest attainable degree of independence), and a variety of other curriculum objectives, among them basic readiness and academic development in communication and oral language, cognitive, and social skills.

There are currently a number of specific methods for teaching young mentally retarded children in use. One popular method, programmed instruction, involves carefully sequenced presentations of material organized into small steps to create a relatively errorless learning situation that prevents frustration (Blake, 1974). Teaching machines, programmed texts and computers using this procedure allow children to proceed at their own pace and can supplement the teacher's efforts. Behavior modification techniques that identify behavioral goals have been used successfully in social and academic learning with mentally retarded children.

Mentally retarded children's feelings of success can be built by pacing instruction to permit them to spend more time learning when it seems necessary. Slow learners may learn best through an active involvement in concrete discovery-oriented experiences that make learning meaningful to them.

Integrating mentally retarded children into the regular classroom requires a range of strategies to make learning accessible to them. They can learn from other children as well as from the teacher. An open classroom (which includes different goals and rates of learning for each individual and different degrees of structure) could provide an appropriate learning environment. It is more activity-based than the traditional class.

VISUALLY IMPAIRED CHILDREN

Visual impairment may be caused by a malfunction of some portion of the eye or optic nerve that prevents a person from seeing normally. Individuals with visual impairments can also have an anomalous development, disease, or injury that restricts proper functioning of the eyes. When the eyes of an individual do not function to allow normal sight in at least one of them, that person is considered visually impaired (Payne, Kauffman, Patton, Brown, & DeMott, 1979).

The term *blindness* refers to severe visual impairment and tends to imply sightlessness, although the term includes varying degrees of vision. Blind children may not be able to see at all or they may see objects dimly, blurred, or out of focus. When they do see an object, there may be occasional dark blotches appearing to float in front of the object, or they may see things clearly only directly ahead of them as if they were looking through a hole, or they may be able to see the periphery of a view, with the central part obscure or missing.

Standard definitions of visual problems generally cite three types of impairments: impairment of visual acuity, which results in seeing objects less clearly than does a normal person; impairment of field of vision, which affects the angle at which one can see; and impairment of color vision, which results in an inability to distinguish among certain colors. Of the three, impairment of visual acuity is most often encountered.

The legal approach and the educational approach are both used in defining visual impairment. In the legal definition—the most widely known and accepted—a person is considered blind if vision in the better eye after correction is 20/200 or worse, while a partially seeing person has a vision between 20/70 and 20/200 in the better eye after correction. (Using a standard measuring device, a person with 20/200 vision can see clearly at 20 feet what a normally seeing person can see clearly at 200 feet, and a person with 20/70 vision sees at 20 feet what the normal person can see at 70 feet.) Very few individuals cannot see at all, and according to most experts, the vast majority of legally blind persons have some useful vision (Smith & Neisworth, 1975). Legal definitions of visual impairment are stated in terms of vision in the better eye after correction. A person who loses one eye and with glasses has 20/20 vision in the other is not considered legally visually impaired.

The focus in educational definitions of blindness is not on any specific measure of visual acuity, but rather on the individual's ability to read print. Reynolds and Birch (1981) consider children to be educationally blind when they must be taught to read with the use of braille or other devices that do not involve sight. Partially sighted children can be taught to read regular or enlarged print with some special adjustment in instruction.

Thus two students with the same level of visual acuity from a legal viewpoint might be quite different in educational terms, with one reading braille and considered to be educationally blind, and the other reading large print and considered to be partially seeing.

At least three different types of visual acuity programs are of concern to regular classroom teachers: (1) myopia, or near-sightedness, (2) hyperopia, or far-sightedness, and (3) astigmatism. A student with myopia has sufficient nearpoint vision, but objects further away cannot be seen clearly. For this child, reading a book may not present a problem, but reading from a chalkboard might be difficult. In hyperopia, the child's near vision is weak and distant vision is better. For this child, extended periods of schoolwork demanding nearpoint vision can be fatiguing and difficult, and school learning problems can result. Astigmatism, the third type of vision problem, is an irregularity on the cornea or lens of the eye that distorts vision. Students with astigmatism often have deficiences in both near and distant vision. Within limits, each of these types of vision problems can be improved with corrective lenses. For the handicapped child, however, these corrections can still not bring vision to within normal limits.

There are several major causes of blindness and other visual impairments. Among the most common are the following:

1. Trachoma, the major cause of blindness in the world even though it is rare in the United States, is spread primarily by extremely poor hygienic conditions. Typically, a virus enters the eye and causes a chronic, contagious infection that scars the eyelid and cornea, thus distorting vision.

2. Diabetes, the third leading cause of blindness in the United States, is caused by failure of the pancreas to produce insulin. Diabetes can result in both damage to the retina and increased incidence of cataract and glaucoma.

3. Glaucoma, one of the leading causes of blindness in the United States, is caused by increased pressure within

A VISUALLY IMPAIRED CHILD

Alex, 8, is in second grade. His vision is 20/100 in his better eye after correction; his field of vision and color vision are normal. Alex's parents accept his impairment and do not unnecessarily restrict his activities. He enjoys the outdoors, participates on a limited basis in neighborhood games, and is expected to contribute to household chores.

Alex, working at approximately the same level as his school peers, is learning to type his assignments and reads with the aid of enlarged print. He also receives training in learning to listen carefully and in using a tape recorder. While Alex's teacher often allows him extra time to complete assignments, she demands high quality and expects him to follow the same classroom rules as the others. Alex's educational program, which includes a vigorous physical education program, is jointly planned with the resource teacher.

When Alex was younger he often engaged in blindism—stereotypic movements such as rocking or playing with fingers—which was a cause of some concern to his parents. These disappeared as he grew older. With some slight changes in the environment, Alex is expected to have a very successful educational, and ultimately vocational, career.

---

the eye. The onset of glaucoma is gradual and noticed only when it becomes significant. Glaucoma can be simple or acute; if simple, patients will gradually lose their peripheral field of vision. In the acute form, if left unattended, glaucoma can deteriorate into total blindness.

4. Rubella, or German measles, is a congenital cause of vision problems. If this viral infection occurs in the first trimester of pregnancy, it can result in abnormal growth in the developing embryo. Children who are victims of rubella are often multiply handicapped.

5. Macular degeneration is a disease that usually results in gradual loss of central vision but rarely total blindness. Caused by a malfunction of blood vessels feeding the retina, this disease generally manifests itself in poor central vision, poor color vision, and the loss of fine detail discrimination.

Students with moderate to severe visual impairments are usually identified at an early age (before entering preschool) and classroom teachers seldom play a dominant role in their initial referral and identification. Children with less serious problems, however, are often identified through the school as a result of periodic vision screening.

The regular teacher cannot, however, depend on early screening to reliably identify all children with defective vision. Teachers must be on the lookout for children with possible vision problems, referring them for intensive diagnostic testing. Indications of a visual problem include red-rimmed eyelids, swollen eyelids, frequent sties, eyes in constant motion, a contorted face when reading, body tension when trying to distinguish distant objects, constant blinking, rubbing eyes often, crossing eyes when reading, seemingly overly sensitive to light, and becoming irritable over work. In isolation, these behaviors would not lead one to suspect a vision problem since these same behaviors may indicate some other problem such as an emotional disturbance or a learning disability. If, however, these behaviors consistently occur in combination, referral for vision testing may be appropriate.

Moderate to severe visual impairment has three important educational implications for young children: (1) it limits their ability to acquire information, (2) it limits their mobility, and (3) it limits their ability to obtain feedback from the environment. Most visually impaired students can read normal print by bringing the print closer, by placing it in the range and position in which it can be viewed, by magnifying it, or by having the size of the print enlarged. Many visually impaired young children can be taught to use tape recorders and can learn to listen and comprehend at faster than normal rates.

For the young visually impaired child who is unable to read print, and for those with no useful vision, two primary options for reading print format are braille and the optacon. Braille is a touch print medium that uses embossed dots to represent specific letters, numbers, and contractions. The basic braille alphabet uses a cell 2 dots wide and 3 dots high and contains 63 possible dot combinations that stand for various letter, numbers, frequently used contractions or words, or punctuation marks. Braille books tend to be large due to the space required to print braille characters and the thickness of pages. Braille reading rates are substantially slower than print reading rates so that it takes more time to read a comparable quantity of material.

The optacon (optical to tactile converter) is an electronic device that translates print into tactile sensations that are imprinted on the reader's index finger. Thus, the reader feels the print as it appears on the page. The optacon is not a replacement for braille; it allows blind students to read newspapers, bank statements, and other printed materials not typically available in braille.

Visually impaired children encounter problems in moving around independently and in taking care of themselves. Most adults tend to be overprotective and to restrict the visually impaired child's movement-learning opportunities for fear of injury. Children can learn to become independent in self-care skills and to move around in their environment. Teachers should orient the visually impaired child to the physical environment and should not make any changes in the organization of the room without reorientation.

Teachers can assist visually impaired children to utilize the sensory channels they have so that they can acquire the maximum information possible from the environment. Sensory information can be gathered through hearing or touching, modalities that are less important to the fully sighted child because of their redundancy. Visually impaired children can learn shape concepts through touch and can determine distance and direction through sound. Visually impaired children must use existing senses to a larger degree than normal to compensate for their sensory impairment. Thinking abilities are practiced mentally using their available sense experiences. Many of the standard materials for young children (such as blocks, puzzles and other manipulatives) are appropriate for the visually impaired child. Teachers can assist them in using their materials and can also obtain and develop other similar materials.

HEARING-IMPAIRED CHILDREN

Individuals who are not able to hear sounds due to a malfunction of the ear or of the associated nerves have a hearing impairment that can be temporary or permanent, severe or mild. Myklebust (1964) has proposed four variables to define and classify hearing impairment: (1) degree of impairment, (2) age of onset, (3) cause, and (4) physical origin. The degree of the impairment and the age of onset have educational implications. As Streng, Fitch, Hedgecock, Phillips, and Carrell (1958) suggest:

The child who is born with little or no hearing, or who has suffered the loss early in infancy before speech and language patterns are acquired is said to be deaf. One who is born with normal hearing and reaches the age where he can produce and comprehend speech but subsequently loses his hearing is described as deafened. The hard of hearing are those with reduced hearing acuity either since birth or acquired at any time during life. (p. 9)

Defining and classifying hearing impairments, like visual impairments, is complicated. Hearing loss is generally defined along two dimensions: (1) the intensity or loudness and (2) the frequency or pitch of sounds that can be heard. Intensity of sounds is measured in decibels (db), usually measured in the 0 to 120 db range. Hearing losses are stated in db levels. Frequency is measured in number of cycles per second and is expressed as hertz (Hz). For example, 1000 Hz means that the sound wave vibrates 1000 times per second. The higher the Hz, the higher the pitch of the sound. When defining hearing loss it is important to take frequency into account because speech sounds vary in their frequency. While the human ear can hear sounds at frequencies between 20 Hz and 20,000 Hz, nearly all speech sounds occur between 500 Hz and 2000 Hz. This is the frequency within which hearing impairments are usually defined.

Hearing loss is measured using a pure-tone audiometric testing device. Typically, sounds are presented to each ear independently at varying decibel and frequency levels, and the minimum decibel level at which the person can hear the sound is recorded for each frequency. For young children, there are testing procedures available that measure automatic body changes in response to these sounds. Minute changes in heart rate, for example, can be assessed to determine whether a subject is hearing a sound.

There are two major types of hearing losses. A conductive hearing loss involves some kind of blockage or malformation that prevents sound waves from reaching the nerve fibers that transmit the impulses to the brain. Conductive losses are often amenable to correction by surgery or drug therapy and can often be compensated for by use of hearing aids.

A sensory-neural loss involves damage to the sensors or nerve fibers that connect the inner ear to the hearing center in the brain. Sensory-neural losses can be caused by a number of hereditary and medical causes and are generally irreversible. Children with sensory-neural losses generally cannot use hearing aids and must rely on other means of receiving auditory messages.

As with visual impairments, there are differences between legal and educational definitions of hearing loss. Hearing impairments are classified educationally in terms of language learning, since language development is the primary restriction associated with hearing loss. Reynolds and Birch (1981) provide the following educational classification of hearing impairment:

Children with little or no hearing in their first or second years do not learn language in the natural, informal way

most children do. They can be regarded as educationally deaf. The hard-of-hearing children are those who have significant hearing losses, but who learn language in the usual way, though in some instances imperfectly. (p. 532)

Implied in this definition is a distinction between prelingual deafness—which occurs at birth or at an early age, before language or speech has developed—and post-lingual deafness—which occurs following the development of speech and language. The age of onset of hearing impairments generally makes a difference in the language and conceptual framework from which a child will operate.

As with visual impairment, virtually all cases of moderate to severe hearing loss are discovered before a child reaches school age. A classroom teacher will be asked to accept a child who has been identified as having a hearing impairment and who is provided with some special education services. But some mild hearing losses are first noticed and reported by teachers. Behaviors that might be indicative of hearing problems include (1) difficulty in following directions, (2) turning the head to one side to listen, (3) inattention, (4) hesitancy to participate in large groups, especially where a lot of talking takes place, (5) discrepancy between the observed ability of a child and test scores, (6) persistent colds accompanied by earaches, (7) problems in understanding speech after a cold subsides, and (8) stubborn, withdrawn behavior used to project feelings of insecurity or isolation. A teacher observ-

---

A HEARING-IMPAIRED CHILD

Martha, 5, has been diagnosed as having a moderate hearing loss that falls within the 40 to 50 decibel range on a pure-tone audiometer. She has difficulty hearing normal conversation unless the person is quite close and even then background noise may render speech unintelligible. Martha wears a hearing aid and is learning speech reading. Her hearing loss is accompanied by mild speech defects that include inaccurate pronunciation and atypical speech rhythm as well as abnormal intonation. Her vocabulary is limited compared to her hearing peers and she is hesitant about speaking in class and participating in discussions.

Although Martha's hearing impairment was confirmed by an audiologist, it was first noticed by her regular first grade teacher. Among the telltale signs reported by Martha's teacher were: (1) an odd position of the head while listening, favoring the right ear, (2) inattention during discussion, (3) repeatedly saying "Huh?" and asking for repetitions, and (4) asking classmates for directions. When Martha's teacher suspected a hearing loss, she notified a school nurse who in turn contacted the audiologist.

Now, in class:

1. Martha is always seated in the front of the room.

2. The teacher and peers look directly at Martha while speaking.

3. The teacher and peers speak loudly and distinctly to Martha.

4. Martha has been assigned a buddy to help with directions and other verbal information.

5. Martha receives one-half hour of speech instruction twice weekly.

---

ing a combination of these factors in a child should refer that child for hearing testing.

The most pervasive effect of a hearing impairment in young children is in language and speech development (Northcott, 1978). Language is developed orally, and in the preschool years, practically all communication takes place in the oral mode. Language is a system that involves receiving and sending messages, and both these types of language activities are affected by hearing loss.

Infancy and early childhood are periods of phenomenal conceptual growth. The young child learns to identify many objects, actions, and feelings by learning that certain words stand for these things. Words are strung together into complex utterances according to a set of rules that are mastered by the time a child reaches school age. At an early age, young children learn the complexities of language and of speech production. For a hearing-impaired child, however, lack of normal aural reception mode serves as a major hindrance to language and concept development.

Somewhat related to the receptive language problems of hearing-impaired children are the difficulties they face in developing good expressive language or speech. The young child begins to learn to speak by a process of spontaneous babbling and vocal experimentation, hearing others, and gradually approximating speech sounds. Aural feedback on the child's own vocalizations and the ability to hear the speech of others are of primary importance in this process. Limitations in these abilities make speech development for young hearing-impaired children a difficult process.

The two primary alternatives to hearing the speech of others that have been developed for deaf individuals are speech reading and manual communication. In speech reading, a deaf person understands another person's speech by reading sounds from the movement of that person's lips, tongue, and face. The speaker needs to know no special code or communication system. Speech reading is not, however, an exact process since many sounds have the same visual appearance and a number of sounds cannot be seen at all. The efficient speech reader sees a portion of what would be heard and fills in many sounds and words through contextual cues. The level of conceptual development would appear to be an important factor in determining the success a child has in learning speech reading.

Manual communication, including sign language and finger spelling, is the second major communication alternative for the hearing-impaired. These methods allow deaf and hearing-impaired individuals to both receive and send verbal messages through a system that uses gestures along with hand and finger movements. Several signing systems are currently used in the United States, and not all deaf Americans use the same system. Some use American Sign Language, others use Manual English, and still others use Signing Exact English. There are definite and pronounced differences among these systems. The least ambiguous manual communication method is finger spelling, in which a unique position represents each letter and number. Most sign systems use finger spelling for unfamiliar words or for words for which signs are not available.

For a number of years debate has raged concerning which of these represents the best system of communication. Oralists have argued that manual communication separates the deaf person from the hearing world and that allowing deaf students to sign will dampen their enthusiasm for the difficult task of learning speech and speech reading. Advocates of manual systems, on the other hand, stress that conceptual development is critical for deaf children and that early use of manual communication methods allows the child to acquire more information about the world then can be acquired through oral methods. A third group of deaf educators advocates using a total communication approach combining oral methods with manual communication.

The speech and language problems of young hearing-impaired children have several important education implications. Research suggests that hearing-impaired children tend to lag behind their hearing-age peers in academic achievement, with the difference greater for deaf children than for the hard-of-hearing. Deficits in receptive and expressive language can also produce social isolation. In addition, as with the visually impaired, children with hearing losses can be restricted in the range and variety of their experiences, through neglect or overprotection. Although some young hearing-impaired children have trouble adjusting to and succeeding in regular class settings, many hearing-impaired students with well-developed speech reading and language skills are excellent candidates for mainstreaming.

The regular classroom needs to be modified to limit the problems such children must face. Unnecessary and confusing noises should be avoided. Speaking face-to-face with them and sitting them close to and facing the teacher during a discussion or other type of interaction can enhance the speech development of hearing-impaired children.

Hearing-impaired children need special help to develop their communication skills. Speechreading, sign language, and/or a combination of those two approaches are necessary to develop these skills. A resource or consultant teacher is essential in helping classroom teachers work with these children.

CHILDREN WITH COMMUNICATION DISORDERS

The two concepts *language* and *speech* are frequently confused and misused. Hallahan and Kauffman (1978) make the distinction as follows:

Language is the communication of ideas through symbols that are used according to semantic and grammatical rules. Thus defined, language includes the sign language of the deaf (e.g., American Sign Language), tactual symbol systems (e.g., braille), and conventional written language. . . . Speech is the behavior of forming and sequencing the sounds of oral language. (p. 224)

Language problems occur in oral, written, tactile, and gestural areas.

Speech is considered an integral component of oral language. Oral language disabilities occur when individuals do not understand ideas that have been discussed with them or when they do not express themselves meaningfully (Hull & Hull, 1973).

Oral language can be analyzed into receptive and expressive factors. The receptive factor involves the ability to discriminate what is being said or read and to understand the message. The expressive factor involves the ability to send a written or oral message. A deficiency in receptive or expressive factors can have multiple effects on an individual's oral language ability. According to Perkins (1977), a deficiency in speech is evident when an individual's speech is "ungrammatical, unintelligible, culturally or personally unsatisfactory, or abusive of the speech mechanism" (p. 4). Unintelligibility and unsatisfactory quality of speech are subjective judgments; thus defective speech depends on the listener.

Disorders in speech and language development are among the most common problems found in young handicapped children. Such disorders may occur as a primary handicapping condition or as part of another condition, such as cerebral palsy or mental retardation. *Articulation disorders*—the production of defective, inconsistent, or incorrect speech sounds—are among the most frequently found problems in young children's speech. They account for 60 to 80 percent of all diagnosed speech disorders in young children and generally involve misarticulation of sound such as *s, r, l, th,* and *sh*. Children with articulation disorders can exhibit several common types of errors. The first is omission, in which the child omits a sound, as in saying "at" for "cat." Another is substitution, in which the child recognizes appropriate sounds but uses the wrong one, as in saying "yeth" for "yes." A third is distortion, in which an attempt to approximate the correct sound is distorted. A fourth type of error is addition, in which the child improperly adds a sound to a word, as in saying "on-un the table."

Stuttering, in which the normal flow and rhythm of speech is disturbed by oscillations, fixations, repetitions, or prolongations of sounds, syllables, words, or phrases is another common speech disorder in young children. Stuttering generally occurs intermit-

tently in the child's flow of speech. The disfluency in the child's speech will vary with such factors as rhythm or rate or with linguistic factors such as initial sound, word length, grammatical function, and position in sentence.

Cluttering is a third speech disorder in young children. The characteristics of cluttering include excessively fast speech, disorganized sentence structure, garbled syllables and sounds, and excessive repetitions.

In addition to these speech problems, a number of voice or speech production disorders are also found in young children. They include hypernasality (in which excessive nasal emissions are made during speech), hyponasality (a failure to produce adequate nasal sounds), pitch levels that are too high or too low, speech that is too loud or too soft, and monotone (a lack of variation in vocal pitch or loudness). These voice or phonation disorders occur less frequently than the other speech problems described above.

Delayed verbal communication is also a common language disorder found in young children. In such a case the child does not acquire speech or oral langauge at the predicted normal time or with a standard degree of accuracy. Delayed verbal communication can be present even when the child's articulation and speech production are quite normal for a child's age.

Some therapeutic procedures used with young children who have language disorders include rewarding only gestures that are accompanied by utterance, encouraging verbal imitative behavior through appropriate reinforcement, and parallel talk by which children are helped to verbalize their

A CHILD WITH A COMMUNICATION DISORDER

Max, 6, exhibits poor articulation (producing inaccurate speech sounds) and nonfluency (stuttering and halting speech) that interfere somewhat with communication, attract unfavorable attention, and have resulted in a poor self-image. Max's articulation problems are thought to be the result of habitual baby talk from his parents and should be easily corrected. His nonfluency problem appears to be caused by emotional problems and may be harder to correct.

Max receives help with his articulation problems from a speech therapist for a half-hour three times weekly. Max's regular class teacher is trying to help him by developing a climate of tolerance and acceptance for his disability among his classmates. She has discussed Max's disability with them, encouraging them to show no reaction when Max stutters or misarticulates and to accept him as they would any other student.

thoughts. Regardless of the speech or language disorder found in young children, it is important that significant adults (e.g., teacher, parents, grandparents) not give undue attention to the problem, since that can increase anxiety and compound the child's difficulty.

Although speech therapists work with children who have speech and language disorders, regular classroom teachers play a vital role in promoting children's language development. They can provide a variety of rich and successful language experiences with a continuous interaction among handicapped and nonhandicapped children. Children need sufficient opportunities to produce speech communications and to receive rewards for their efforts, even though their achievements may seem small. Teachers should avoid making them too self-conscious or too defeatist as they try to communicate with others. The classroom teacher will probably not be able to assist severely impaired children, such as those with aphasia, a language disability, with their communications problems. These children should be referred to physicians and speech and language clinicians.

CHILDREN WITH PHYSICAL AND HEALTH IMPAIRMENTS

Physically and health impaired children have functional restrictions in relation to their physical ability (e.g., hand use, trunk control, mobility, strength and stamina). These conditions interfere with school attendance or learning to the degree that special services such as training, equipment, materials, or facilities are required (Hallahan & Kauffman, 1978). Both physical and health impairments can create obstacles to normal functioning in the classroom.

These deviations in physique or functioning can create behavioral inadequacies or restrictions within particular environments. A person in a wheelchair (a disability in most environments) can function appropriately in many situations where sitting for long periods of time is required. This individual is not disabled under these circumstances nor does the individual have a disabled mind. Among the more common conditions that teachers are apt to see in young children in integrated classrooms are (1) spina bifida, (2) cerebral palsy, (3) sickle cell anemia, (4) muscular dystrophy, and (5) epilepsy.

Spina bifida is a condition in which the spinal column is not fully developed and has an opening that prevents complete protection of the spinal cord. The child encounters few problems when there is no displacement or deformity of the spinal cord. If, however, part of the spinal cord or spinal nerve roots protrude through the opening, orthopedic impairment can result. Spina bifida can also produce motor impairment, as well as lack of bowel and bladder control. Some youngsters with spina bifida will miss considerable school because of operations, thus resulting in educational handicaps.

Cerebral palsy is a neuromuscular disability that results from injury to the brain before, during, or after birth. Young children with cerebral palsy will have difficulty with certain motor activities varying from mild involvement while walking, to self-help and com-

munication problems, to total incapacitation. In mild cases of cerebral palsy students have little or no difficulty succeeding in integrated classrooms. They may appear awkward or clumsy, or they may talk more slowly than other children, but when teachers and peers are sensitive to the condition, essentially normal activity is possible. Children with moderate cerebral palsy are also often placed in regular classrooms, since the medical condition itself usually has no direct effect on the learning capabilities of the student. The three types of cerebral palsy that teachers are most likely to encounter are (1) spasticity, which results in muscular tightness and difficulty in movement of limbs; (2) athetosis, which involves uncontrollable rhythmatic movement in the muscles; and (3) ataxia, which entails muscular incoordination and lack of balance.

Sickle-cell anemia is a genetic disorder, found predominately in Black Americans, that results in distortion and malfunction of the red blood cells, reducing the body's supply of oxygen and resulting in severe pain. During sickle-cell crises, the pain is often so severe it cannot be relieved, even when the child is in the hospital and given pain relieving drugs. The educational implications of sickle-cell anemia relate to the frequency of hospitalization and school absence as well as the occasional debilitating effects of the disease.

Muscular dystrophy is a progressive muscular disease that results in increasing muscular weakness and incoordination as children grow older. There are often temporary periods of remission, but students with muscular dystrophy gradually lose their ability to walk and perform other physical func-

ORTHOPEDIC IMPAIRMENT—A CEREBRAL PALSIED CHILD

Pam, 5, has a mild case of spastic cerebral palsy caused at birth by anoxia (lack of oxygen). It results in muscle tightness and difficulty in moving her limbs. Her disability is most evident in walking, self-help, and communication skills. She appears awkward or clumsy and talks more slowly than other children. Her medical condition does not, however, have any direct effect on her learning capabilities.

In school, Pam works on the same tasks as her peers with some slight modification and is considered one of the brighter students in the class. Pam is also popular, due in part to the teacher's preparation of her class peers through discussion. Pam's teacher often comments that there are several principles that guide her work with cerebral palsied children, including:

1. When students have unintelligible speech, it should be assumed that they know more than they are telling you.

2. The teacher should not hesitate to ask a student with poor speech to repeat a statement or to paraphrase a statement to see if it was heard correctly.

3. The student should be given ample time to answer questions.

4. Students should be encouraged to be as independent as possible in completing all self-help skills and activities.

5. The teacher should encourage peer relationships and support the cerebral palsied student in attempts to initiate peer interaction.

tions. Children who contract muscular dystrophy in the first few years of life have a limited life span, usually less than 20 years.

Epilepsy is a disorder of the brain that results in occasional periods of abnormal changes in electrical brain potentials that trigger subsequent seizures. There are two major types of seizures associated with epilepsy. The first, petit mal seizures, results in momentary loss of consciousness that is often either not noticed or mistaken for a lapse of attention. Grand mal seizures involve more extended loss of consciousness, accompanied by convulsive movements that can last several minutes. Seizure patterns vary greatly.

Some children will have a single seizure without a recurrence; others will have recurring seizures of varying frequency. Medication is usually helpful in controlling seizures, and except in extreme circumstances, epilepsy itself should not be sufficient cause for removing a child from the regular classroom.

The problems associated with orthopedic and health impairments that affect a child's educational opportunities are: communication, mobility, self-help skills, and social interactions. Many young children with orthopedic impairments also have associated speech problems. The combination of poor manual dexterity and unintelligible speech can often result in such children being able to share only a small part of their knowledge. For these children, receptive language is much better than expressive language, and teachers may assume that children know less than they actually do. When children cannot communicate verbally or in writing, alternative communication systems such as typewriters or communication boards are available. Communication boards are flat pieces of cardboard, wood, or plastic on which letters, words, numerals, and/or pictures are mounted. Children can send messages by pointing to letters and common words on the board. Communication is not impaired if alternative ways to communicate are found, and this is often successfully done with the only limitation being the form with which the message is sent.

Another common barrier for young, orthopedically impaired children is mobility—in the classroom, at school, and at home. Generally, such children's means of mobility are already determined by the time they get to school, and it is the task of the teacher to adapt the school situation so that locomotion is possible. Only experience can determine how a classroom should be arranged to accommodate a child in a wheelchair, and the teacher should expect that not all problems of mobility can be solved before an orthopedically impaired child arrives at school. Initial flexibility is probably the best strategy for successful adaptation of the school setting to the mobility patterns of the child.

Some physically impaired children do not have control over normal self-help activities such as toileting, dressing, and eating. These children must learn to let others know how to help them, and teachers must guard against overprotecting them. The goal should always be maximum independence in activities. Information from parents and/or school specialists can often be helpful in determining the child's level of self-help skills.

Other health impairments that regular class teachers may encounter, though with less frequency, include:

1. *Heart conditions*—Impairments resulting from malformations, mechanical problems, or injuries to heart muscles or vessels.

2. *Tuberculosis*—A bacterial infection, usually in the lungs, that can affect the organs, skin, heart, and bones.

3. *Leukemia*—A serious, often fatal disease of the blood marked by an increase in whole blood cells and resulting in progressive deterioration of the body.

4. *Bronchial asthma*—A condition in which bronchial tubes become constricted and excess mucus is produced that obstructs breathing and produces spasms in the bronchial musculature. An attack of bronchial asthma may occur because of an allergy, too much physical exertion, or an emotional reaction. Teachers must help such children with bronchial asthma avoid contact with known or suspected allergens (e.g., pollen, fabrics, animal hair), protect them from overexertion, monitor their medication, know what to do in case of attack, and communicate with parents and professionals about the child's medical management (Connor, 1975).

5. *Diabetes*—A metabolic disorder in which the body is unable to use carbohydrates because the pancreas fails to secrete adequate insulin. This leads to an abnormally high sugar concentration in the blood and urine. Teachers need to help the child follow the required medical regimen (e.g., diet, injections) and be aware of emergency procedures to use in case of severe insulin reaction or diabetic coma.

6. *Rheumatic fever*—A disease, caused by a streptococcal infection, that is characterized by acute inflammation of the joints, abdominal pain, nosebleeds, skin rash, and fever (Kelly & Verguson, 1978). Rheumatic fever can damage the heart by scarring its valves and tissues.

7. *Hemophilia*—A hereditary condition, found primarily in males, in which the blood fails to clot following an injury. This results in profuse internal or external bleeding. Even slight injuries can cause severe bleeding. Activities of hemophiliac children must be closely monitored.

8. *Lead poisoning*—A condition caused by large ingestions of lead primarily due to swallowing paint chips or chewing lead toys or other objects. Lead poisoning can result in impairment of the nervous system, muscle deterioration, and foot or wrist drop.

Readers interested in reading more about health impairments are encouraged to consult Bhorani and Hyde (1974), Chutorian and Myers (1974), Cobb (1973), and Connor (1975).

Because of the problems just described, as well as a tendency for normally-developing individuals to avoid those with physical limitations, many orthopedically impaired young children experience social isolation in school. Sometimes it takes longer to carry on a conversation with a child who has a speech problem, and many youngsters are not willing to take the time. Sometimes the presence of a physical handicap creates discomfort in another person, and students often express a frustration in not knowing what to say to a physically impaired peer. Without some teacher attention, an orthopedically impaired youngster can be an isolate in the classroom. On the other hand, with encouragement, solid friendships can be formed between physically impaired young children and their able bodied peers (Lee & Walker, 1980). An important factor in promoting the social acceptance of these children is to analyze the classroom and to make any modifications which are necessary for them to function as competently and independently as possible. Teachers also need to design learning experiences and movement activities which are within their capabilities.

SUMMARY

This chapter described various handicapping conditions that can be found in young children, including behavior disorders, learning and developmental disabilities, mental retardation, visual and hearing impairment, communication disorders, and physical and health impairments. Although each of the handicaps discussed in this chapter was presented separately, they do not always occur in isolation from one another. Teachers frequently encounter multiply handicapped children in the classroom. A combination of handicaps tends to complicate diagnosis and create problems in remediation.

Labeling children in the classroom is not as important as describing their educational strengths and needs. The disabling or strengthening aspects of their development should be considered in designing an individual pro-gram. The major disadvantage of labeling is that we can easily stereotype children and prevent them from being considered as individuals. Stigmas are often attached to handicapped children, and many educators are legitimately concerned that once children are labeled an expectation of low learning is created that becomes a self-fulfilling prophecy. Once children are placed in an educational track, no matter how informal, it becomes difficult to change them to a different track.

REFERENCES

Axline, V. *Play therapy.* New York: Ballentine Books, 1974.

Bhorani, S. N., and Hyde, J. S. Chronic asthma and the school. *Journal of School Health,* 1974, *46,* 24–36.

Blake, K. A. *Teaching the retarded.* Englewood Cliffs, N.J.: Prentice-Hall, 1974.

Bower, E. M. *Early identification of emotionally handicapped children in school.* Springfield, Ill.: Charles C. Thomas, 1969.

Chutorian, A. M., and Meyers, S. J. Diseases of the muscle. In J. A. Downey and N. L. Low (Eds.). *The child with disabling illness: Principles of rehabilitation.* Philadelphia: W. B. Saunders, 1974.

Cobb, R. B. *Medical and psychological aspects of disability.* Springfield, Ill.: Charles C. Thomas, 1973.

Connor, F. P., The education of children with crippling and chronic medical conditions. In W. M. Cruikshank and G. O. Johnson (Eds.). *Education of exceptional children and youth.* 3rd ed. Englewood Cliffs, N.J.: Prentice-Hall, 1975.

Grossman, H. J. (Ed.). *Manual on terminology and classification in mental retardation.* Washington, D.C.: American Association on Mental Deficiency, 1973.

Hallahan, D. P., and Kauffman, J. M. *Exceptional children: Introduction to special education.* Englewood Cliffs, N.J.: Prentice-Hall, 1978.

Hull, F. M., and Hull, M. E. Children with oral communication disabilities. In L. M. Dunn (Ed.) *Exceptional children in the schools.* New York: Holt, Rinehart, and Winston, 1973.

Lee, R. C., and Walker, J. Social interactions among physically handicapped preschoolers and their normally developing peers. Paper presented at the annual meeting of the American Educational Research Association, Boston, 1980.

Myklebust, H. R. *Psychology of deafness: Sensory deprivation, learning and adjustment.* New York: Grune and Stratton, 1964.

National Advisory Committee on Handicapped Children. *Annual Report.* Washington, D.C.: U.S. Office of Education, 1968.

Northcott, W. H. Integrating the preprimary child: An examination of the process, product and rationale. In M. J. Guralnick (Ed.). *Early intervention and the integration of handicapped and nonhandicapped children.* Baltimore: University Park Press, 1978.

Payne, J. S., Kauffman, J. M., Patton, J. R., Brown, G. B., and DeMott, R. M. *Exceptional children in focus.* 2nd. ed. Columbus, Ohio: Charles E. Merrill, 1979.

Perkins, W. P. *Speech pathology: An applied science.* 2nd ed. St. Louis, Mo.: The C. V. Mosby Company, 1977.

Peterson, D. R. Behavior problems of middle childhood. *Journal of Consulting Psychology,* 1961, *25,* 205–209.

Quay, H. C., Morse, W. C., and Cutler, R. L. Personality patterns of pupils in special classes for the emotionally disturbed. *Exceptional Children,* 1966, *32,* 297–301.

Reynolds, M. C., and Birch, J. W. *Teaching exceptional children in all America's schools: A first course for teachers and principals.* (rev. ed.) Reston, Va.: The Council for Exceptional Children, 1981.

Smith, R. M., and Neisworth, J. T. *The exceptional child: A functional approach.* New York: McGraw-Hill, 1975.

Streng, A., Fitch, W. T., Hedgecock, L. D., Phillips, J. W., and Carrell, J. A. *Hearing therapy for children.* (rev. ed.) New York: Grune and Stratton, 1958.

Part Two

PLANNING, ORGANIZING, AND COLLABORATING FOR MAINSTREAMING

Three

IDENTIFYING YOUNG HANDICAPPED CHILDREN

The identification of handicapped children enables the educator to discover children who are handicapped and to understand each child's specific abilities and weaknesses, in order to design appropriate programs. Because work with handicapped children is no longer limited to children already in school, the identification process begins with preschool children. Finding children not yet enrolled in school who may be handicapped is called *casefinding*. Casefinding is the process of identifying a population to be screened and usually involves recording the name of each child to be screened, the names of their parents, and their address and telephone number.

Handicapped children already in school may not have been identified either. Often children not previously identified as handicapped may, by their performance or behavior, suggest to the teacher that they have a handicapping condition. These children as well as those identified in the casefinding process need to be screened and, if a handicap is identified, should be put through a more elaborate diagnostic procedure. Screening usually involves limited testing or observation to identify those children who are not developing according to normal patterns. Diagnosis is a more complete educational evaluation of a child's skills and deficits for purposes of referring the child to an intervention program or, if necessary, designing an individual program for the child. Thus, a handicapped child is located, screened, and diagnosed before intervention is provided. This chapter is devoted to a discussion of these three areas as they apply to the regular early childhood teacher.

CASEFINDING

Casefinding, the first step in identification, includes procedures to locate preschool children for screening. Parents, schools, social agencies, and physicians are asked to refer children for screening.

39

Regardless of the method used to locate children it is important to institute a record-keeping process to ensure that the data on each child screened are maintained by the school system. The record system should be compatible with school records, whether maintained by computer or by hand.

Casefinding Methods

Locating young children who have handicaps or, because of delayed development, have potential handicaps can be difficult. Preschool children are scattered throughout the community and, unlike school-aged children, are not normally found in one setting. The procedures used in the casefinding process depend on the characteristics of the community, the types of resources available, and the nature of the target population. The process for locating children varies from state to state, but four principal methods are used: agency referral, media announcements, school records, and community survey.

Agency Referral. The most common means of referring handicapped children to preschool programs is through public agencies. Such agencies include public schools, health services, welfare and social services, day care centers, nursery schools, mental health facilities, speech and language clinics, diagnostic clinics, and various community agencies such as those supported by Easter Seals, United Cerebral Palsy, Crippled Children, and the Association for Retarded Children.

Agencies should be made aware of program activities, and their assistance requested in referring cases. Contact

with an agency or service can be made through personal visits, by phone, or by letter. An exact description of the population to be served as well as the range of services to be provided should be furnished to each agency contacted along with the name of a contact person, the telephone number of the school doing the screening, and a supply of referral forms.

Unfortunately, only a small percentage of handicapped children eligible for special programs are identified through agencies and services and these children are usually the obviously handicapped. Thus a broader approach must be used to identify and provide services for the mild to moderately handicapped child.

Media Announcements. A second means of locating children is through media announcements giving the time, place, and purpose of preschool screening and the name and telephone number of a contact person. It is important to recognize that public relations is a critical aspect of the process of identifying handicapped children. Announcements should be carefully worded and publicity campaigns carefully organized consistent with the nature of the target audience. Information can be disseminated by television, radio, newspapers, or mass mailings. Bulletin board notices posted in churches, synagogues, laundromats, supermarkets, beauty parlors, barber shops, and libraries are also helpful, as are announcements at PTA meetings and meetings of various civic organizations.

Media announcements educate the community, especially parents, about the purpose for and importance of early identification and intervention. Care should be taken not to alarm or confuse parents, but to provide them with reassurance and a clear explanation of the identification procedures and the range of services that will be available.

Media publicity can also be used to stress the importance of early intervention and to emphasize that, because handicapping conditions are sometimes subtle, it is a wise preventive measure for parents of apparently normal children to have their children screened. In general, announcements of screening sessions should be encouraging and positive in tone, but they should also be accurate. The publicity should not imply that all children who receive help at an early age will have no problems in school.

Publicity must also assure parents that their rights and those of their children will be carefully protected. Before any testing is done, for instance, parents must be given the opportunity to read and sign parent consent forms. Parents must also be assured that unless they consent, no test information will be shared with any other person or agency. These procedures are more than just courtesy measures. They represent the law, and the rights of all individuals involved must be carefully preserved.

School Records. Many schools ask parents to list the names of younger children in the family when they register their school-age children. A review of these records can reveal from 50 to 60 percent of the children eligible for screening (Feshbach, Adelman, & Williamson, 1974). Announcements of screening sessions sent home to parents of school-age children can also help locate the names of friends or neighbors who have preschool children.

Community Survey. A fourth method used to locate children for screening is to survey the community. In addition to locating children to be screened for handicapping conditions, survey information provides valuable data for school administrators to use in future educational planning. A survey can also help develop community interest in and support for the local school system by involving a large segment of the population in a common action.

Community surveys can be conducted in at least three ways. These include house-to-house canvassing, telephone campaigns, and canvassing through school children.

The most effective of the three approaches is a house-to-house campaign. A carefully organized survey can locate up to 95 percent of eligible children (Feshbach, Adelman, & Williamson, 1974). House-to-house canvassing provides the interviewer with an opportunity to acquire developmental data on children by questioning mothers about prenatal and birth history, the age at which the children first walked and talked, and so on. The interviewer, who may have the opportunity to observe and talk to the child in an informal setting, can provide parents with information on programs and services, answer questions and discuss their concerns. Finally, the interview may provide an opportune time to make an appointment for parents to take the child in for screening.

A telephone campaign can be useful in communities where at least 90 percent of the homes have telephones. Again the most economical method is to use volunteers. A community can also be canvassed by sending forms home with school-age children and with children in day care, nursery, and Head Start centers. Using these forms, parents can provide information on other young children in their families. These latter two methods, while less time-consuming and costly than a door-to-door campaign, are not as effective because they rely heavily on the initiative of parents.

Organizing the Location Team

When a method of finding children has been chosen, a staff must be selected and trained to locate them. The location team should be headed by someone who knows the community and who has contacts in public service agencies.

Locating children requires the involvement of many individuals in a coordinated effort. One individual should serve as the team leader, whose responsibilities include recruiting, training, and coordinating the activities of others. Other members of the team may include the staff of a cooperating school, paid professionals, and volunteers from the community. It is important to recruit volunteers, as casefinding methods such as house-to-house canvassing can be costly, diverting funds from the cost of providing services if volunteers are not used. Volunteers can be found through volunteer clearinghouses, senior citizen groups, or community service groups. And college students, especially those in education or child development, or parent groups in local schools can be tapped for volunteers.

In any plan for locating children, procedures must be developed to ensure that data are recorded completely, tactfully, and above all, accurately. As soon as location data are complete, screening may begin.

SCREENING

Screening is a procedure designed to identify those children who need further study because of suspected handicaps. A more intensive and complete assessment follows for children identified as possibly handicapped through the screening process.

There are generally two types of screening situations: (1) screening groups of children before they enter school, and (2) screening individual children in school. In the first instance, preschool children are taken to a center to be screened for possible handicapping conditions. This normally fol-

lows the location process described above. In the second case, children whom the teacher suspects may be handicapped are observed and tested.

Screening Children Before Entrance in School

This technique generally involves the screening of several preschool children at a central location to identify children with possible handicapping conditions. Teachers working in integrated preschools or in programs for young handicapped children may be called

upon to coordinate the screening process. The teacher's major responsibilities include selecting and arranging a screening site, a screening team, and screening devices.

The Screening Site.   A screening site must be large enough to accommodate the anticipated number of children. Screening devices have different space requirements and sites must provide adequate space for the use of specific instruments. For the process described here, minimum dimensions for a screening site are 25 feet by 50 feet. If possible, a list of potential screening sites should be developed. The following information should be collected for each: address of the site; name and telephone number of the administrator of the site; size and floor plan of the site; list of available furniture, including tables, chairs, and room dividers; list of

persons to contact for help in the community; and local media to contact for publicity.

The Screening Team.   Members of a screening team must be carefully selected and should understand that the major objectives of the screening procedure are to identify all children who may be potential candidates for special services, and to establish and maintain good public relations with parents of handicapped children and with the community at large. Typically, a screening team will be staffed with one greeter, two hearing and vision screeners, a speech and language clinician, a parent interviewer, and an early childhood professional (preferably one experienced in working with young handicapped children). If available, a social worker may be used to interview parents as well as to assess children's social-emotional development. A learning-disabilities specialist might also be included. Such a staff can screen 60 or more children a day.

The screening team leader, who may be a classroom teacher, should have organizational ability and good interpersonal skills. The leader's major responsibilities are to make local arrangements at the screening site and to be available during screening to answer questions that arise. Additionally, in advance of screening, the team leader must: (1) visit potential sites and select the most appropriate location, (2) estimate the number of children to be screened, (3) determine the size of the screening team, (4) complete publicity arrangements, (5) ensure that all necessary materials are available, and (6) make certain that team members have been trained.

The screening team should be trained well before the screening begins. During training sessions, each member's role should be explained, procedures to be followed during test day should be presented and discussed, and all assessment tools and materials should be reviewed. Members should be familiar enough with one another's responsibilities to be able to assume a different role on a moment's notice. A person well acquainted with the screening process and well known in the community can serve as the greeter—making parents feel welcome, introducing the child to the child interviewer and the parent to the parent interviewer, and making certain that the child is properly registered.

The parent interviewer develops rapport with the parents, helps them complete forms assessing their children's development and interviews

them to collect any pertinent information not included on the forms (e.g., the child's current state of health), recording all information accurately.

The child interviewer administers age-level tasks; observes and notes the child's social and emotional development, hearing and vision ability, and general physical development; and encourages the child's active participation in the interview and in other screening activities. The child interviewer must be able to observe and accurately record the many different responses and characteristics of young children and must be able to relate well to them. Paraprofessionals or nondegree child workers can be trained to administer most screening instruments efficiently and effectively (Lillie, 1977).

Speech and expressive-language screening is usually conducted by a speech clinician with the aid of the child interviewer. The role of the speech clinician is to conduct the actual screening, to train paraprofessionals, and to evaluate the data collected. Both the speech clinician and paraprofessionals should be able to (1) relate well to children; (2) elicit verbal output samples in a number of ways and record this information accurately; (3) assess children's ability to comprehend words, sentences, and concepts; (4) distinguish between correct and incorrect phoneme production; and (5) identify aberrant rhythm and vocal patterns. The speech clinician must also be available for follow-up evaluation of children.

One hearing and vision team consisting of two hearing and vision screeners, is needed for every three to five interviewers. In many states, trained hearing and vision teams, public health

nurses, or speech clinicians are available through federally or state funded programs or through public health agencies or other organizations. If professionals are not available, paraprofessionals must be trained by local personnel who meet appropriate state certification and other standards. Desirable characteristics of hearing and vision screeners include the ability to work as part of a team and to work well with young children.

In addition, it may be helpful to have one or two volunteers available to make parents comfortable, provide coffee, give children refreshments, and attend to siblings while parents are completing the initial forms.

Screening Devices. One of the most important decisions made by teachers is what instrument(s) to use in screening. Instruments should be able

to be given by trained volunteers or paraprofessionals with minimal supervision since few screening programs provide an all-professional team. A comprehensive screening instrument should assess all major developmental areas such as speech and language development, gross and fine motor development, social development, and the development of self-help skills. Instruments should reflect the language or dialect spoken by the children who are being screened and experiences with which the children are familiar. Instruments also need to be valid, providing information about the problems they are designed to screen; reliable, producing approximately the same results each time they are used; and practical so that they can be administered without too much difficulty or cost.

There are problems with most existing screening devices for young children. Reviewing the effectiveness of early childhood screening devices, Gallagher and Bradley (1972) concluded that the large number of *false positives* (children identified as having a handicap when in reality none exists) and *false negatives* (children identified as having no handicap when one really does exist) makes their widespread use problematic. Although false positives can be eliminated with diagnostic follow-up, false negatives are often undetected.

In addition to the problem of false positives and negatives, many children are misidentified, and many children identified as handicapped are labeled and are thus stigmatized. Despite these difficulties, the screening processes now in use are better than no screening effort at all. Without early screening, children may wait for months or years before assessment and intervention can begin and such delays may be harmful in terms of their augmenting effects on handicaps.

In recent years, a number of early screening devices have been developed. A description of some of the screening instruments used to identify mildly to moderately impaired young children is provided at the end of this chapter. Before selecting an instrument to use, the teacher should review it carefully to determine whether it is practical to administer, score, and interpret and whether it is suitable for the child and the situation.

Screening Individual Children in the Classroom

Many handicapping conditions can be identified through screening proce-

dures like those just described for preschool children. Other handicapping conditions, however, are subtle and are often not manifest until the child is in a classroom setting. Therefore, regular classroom teachers must also help identify potential handicaps in young children. Few adults are better qualified to help identify handicapping conditions than teachers of young children. Teachers have been trained to work with and observe young children. They see each child for long periods of time and in varied situations while other professionals only see the children in limited situations (e.g., an office or clinic) in which they may be ill at ease. Teachers also see each child in relation to a number of other children of similar age and interests, which allows them to judge the range of normalcy.

Throughout the school day, teachers have many opportunities to note strengths and to spot problems in children. The variety of structured and unstructured tasks found in the classroom provide multiple opportunities for social and verbal interactions as well as large and small motor activities and give teachers a chance to monitor children's development. When screening children, teachers must select an efficient and organized way to describe what behavior(s) each child engages in.

Anecdotal records, checklists, and rating scales are the most common approaches to educational screening in the classroom. These approaches are also used for assessment.

Anecdotal Records.   Keeping anecdotal records involves writing down everything the child does for certain

ANECDOTAL RECORD

Child's name: Tom Martin
Age: 3 yrs, 4 months
Date: 3/2/83
Setting: Outdoor free play
Time: 9:15–9:30 A.M.

Tommy is playing by himself in a sandbox in a play yard in which other children are playing. Tommy is far away from the other children and the teacher is standing roughly half way between him and the others. Tommy leaves the sandbox and walks over to climb the monkey bars. No other children are at the monkey bars. Tommy shouts to the teacher, saying, "Miss Garza, watch me." Tommy climbs to the top of the apparatus and shouts, "Look how high I am!" The teacher nods at him. Another child then begins to climb the apparatus. Tommy, seeing this, cries, "My monkey bars, you can't play!" He then climbs down and runs over to a tree, again demanding that the teacher watch him. This time the teacher ignores him, and Tommy runs to the sandbox where he sits down and quietly begins to cry.

periods of time or during certain activities. Its purpose is to produce as complete a description as possible of what the child does in specified settings. Wright (1960) suggests:

Begin reporting each observed sequence with a description of the scene, the actors, and the ongoing action. Report throughout in everyday language. Describe the situation as fully as the child's actions. This includes everything the child says and does, and also everything said and done to him.

Do not substitute interpretations that generalize about behavior for descriptions of behavior, but add such interpretations when they point to possibilities of fact that might otherwise be missed. Segregate every interpretation by some device as indentation or bracketing. Straight reporting must be left to stand out. (p. 84–85)

When making anecdotal recordings, notes taken on the scene of observation can be in improvised shorthand. These notes can be enlarged upon in writing after each observation period. A co-worker might read through the account and question the observer when the account is unclear. When long records are made, observers can work in rotation to minimize fatigue.

Regardless of the procedures employed, some common elements are found in anecdotal recording techniques. First, a time sequence, reported as large units of time (e.g., 10:00–10:50 A.M.) or multiple time samples (e.g., 9:00–9:03 A.M., 9:07–9:10 A.M.), should be given. Second, specific child actions should be noted. And third, anecdotal records should be narrative descriptions of behaviors that are plain and easy to read.

The following is an example of an anecdotal record completed by the teacher on a child suspected of having a behavioral disorder.

Teachers might employ this technique to observe a large range of child actions and to attempt to pinpoint specific problems. Anecdotal recording, however, may be difficult for some classroom teachers, since a teacher cannot concurrently give instruction and take such comprehensive notes. Thus this technique may be more appropriate for other observers such as a resource teacher, teacher aide, volunteer, or school psychologist.

Checklists.   Checklists provide teachers with the maximum of observer structuring and allow a quick and efficient examination of a wide range of behaviors. Behaviors to be noticed are established at the time the checklist is constructed, and the observer checks those items on the checklist that are descriptive of the particular child.

Checklists generally assess the child in the areas of language, preacademic, motor, social, visual, hearing, and general health development. Typically, a list of behaviors is provided for each developmental area and the teacher simply records whether (+) or not (−) the child engages in specific behaviors. For instance, a screening checklist for social development reported by Allen, Rieke, Smitriev, and Hayden (1972) contains the following items:

I. Child interactions with adults. Does the child characteristically, week after week:
  1. Resist separation from parents?   ____Yes   ____No   ____Sometimes
  2. Shy away from or act overly wary of new adults?   ____Yes   ____No   ____Sometimes
  3. Display an excessive number of attention-getting behaviors?   ____Yes   ____No   ____Sometimes
  4. Manipulate adults through such tactics as dawdling, lavish displays of affection, nearly inaudible voice level, tantrums?   ____Yes   ____No   ____Sometimes
  5. Refuse to accept adult help when obviously in need of it?   ____Yes   ____No   ____Sometimes

II. Interaction with other children. Does the child characteristically, week after week:
  1. Engage only in solitary or parallel play?   ____Yes   ____No   ____Sometimes
  2. Avoid certain children?   ____Yes   ____No   ____Sometimes
  3. Disrupt other children's play?   ____Yes   ____No   ____Sometimes

4. Flit from one play group to
   another, seldom settling in for any
   length of time?   _____Yes _____No _____Sometimes
5. Depend on grabbing, hitting,
   name calling, tantrums, or retreat
   to resolve conflict situations?   _____Yes _____No _____Sometimes
6. Engage in self-stimulatory behav-
   iors such as incessant thumb
   sucking, body rocking, head banging, self-directed monologues,
   unprovoked outbursts of shriek-
   ing, or hysterical laughing?   _____Yes _____No _____Sometimes

Similar behaviors are presented in other checklists for different developmental areas. For example:

Developmental Checklist

Visual and hearing development:
   Does the child appear to have eye
   movements that are jerky or un-
   cordinated?   _____Yes _____No _____Sometimes

   Have difficulty seeing objects?   _____Yes _____No _____Sometimes
   Consistently favor one ear? Seem
   to ignore, confuse, or not follow
   directions?   _____Yes _____No _____Sometimes
General health:
   Does the child seem to have an
   excessive number of colds?   _____Yes _____No _____Sometimes
   Have frequent absences because
   of illness?   _____Yes _____No _____Sometimes
   Have frequent discharge from
   eyes? ears? nose?   _____Yes _____No _____Sometimes
Language:
   Does the child use just two- and
   three-word phrases to ask for what
   he wants?   _____Yes _____No _____Sometimes
   Seem to have difficulty following
   directions?   _____Yes _____No _____Sometimes
   Respond to questions with
   inappropriate answers?   _____Yes _____No _____Sometimes

Seem to talk too softly or too loudly?	_____Yes	_____No	_____Sometimes
Seem to have difficulty articulating words?	_____Yes	_____No	_____Sometimes

Motor:

Does the child appear clumsy or shaky when using one or both hands?	_____Yes	_____No	_____Sometimes
When walking or running, does the child appear to move one side of the body differently from the other side?	_____Yes	_____No	_____Sometimes
Seem to fear or not be able to use stairs, climbing equipment, or tricycles?	_____Yes	_____No	_____Sometimes
Stumble often or appear awkward?	_____Yes	_____No	_____Sometimes

---

The warning signs appearing on any checklist are not, of course, exhaustive. Items on checklists should serve primarily to stimulate thinking about each child and lead to further planned observations. Checklists can provide an early warning sign that further assessment may be needed. Such measures can lead to better identification of potentially handicapping conditions in young children at a time when intervention is likely to be most effective.

Rating Scales. Rating scales call for observer interpretation of behavior. In completing a rating scale, the observer must make a judgment about the presence, absence, or extent of certain characteristics. The observer may be required either to assign a numerical value on a scale to a specific trait such as dependence, or simply to mark the appropriate word describing the frequency of a given behavior.

Rating scales have been most frequently used to screen young children with potential learning problems. Most scales have been found to be fairly accurate for predicting school success or failure. Haring and Ridgeway (1967), for instance, concluded that kindergarten teacher ratings were effective predictors of learning problems in children. Similarly, in an informal study, Rochford (1970) notes that 95 percent of the children who later developed learning problems were identified as early as kindergarten by teachers using rating scales. Keogh and Smith (1970) found teacher ratings to be consistently significant when correlated with achievement scores in the second grade.

Several classroom rating scales have been reported in the early education literature. Some of them are widely respected.

The Rhode Island Pupil Identification Scale (Novack et al., 1972) is used to identify young children with learning problems. The scale, comprised of 40 items reflecting behaviors associated with school failure, is in two parts. Part I consists of 21 items describing behaviors readily observable in the classroom; Part II consists of 19 items that evaluate a child's written work. Each item is rated on a 5-point scale.

The scale was standardized on a representative sample of 800 kindergarten through second grade children. Test-retest reliability scores were high (range 0.755 to 0.988) and most teachers described the scale as useful in helping to systematize classroom observations. Teachers also reported liking its conciseness, brevity, and relatively simple administration and interpretation.

The Pupil Rating Scale (Myklebust, 1971) helps identify young children with learning disabilities. Classroom teachers rate children in auditory comprehension, spoken language, orientation, motor coordination, and personal-social behavior. Each rating is based on a 5-point scale of behavioral description with a 3 being the average rating, 1 and 2 being below average, and 4 and 5 being above average. Scores are derived by adding the numbers circled by the teacher. The scale, standardized on over 2000 children, also provides for analysis of specific items or areas of behavior.

In addition to teacher rating scales, parents are sometimes asked to complete questionnaires regarding their children. The results are subsequently used as further indicators of the child's development. The *Parent Readiness Evaluation* (Ahr, 1968), for instance, is used to screen children, ages 3–9. This scale, which requires parents to administer several verbal and performance subtests, assesses general information, memory for words, reproduction of numbers, and knowledge of syntax and grammar. Similarly, the *School Readiness Survey* (Jordan & Massey, 1969) asks parents to screen child performance in seven areas including number concepts, discrimination of forms, color naming, symbol matching, speaking vocabulary, listening vocabulary, and general information.

Despite their general effectiveness, rating scales suffer from some inherent weaknesses. One is the ambiguity of the characteristics or traits being rated. What one person may judge to be dependent behavior another may not. Another possible problem is the "halo" effect: when raters feel positive toward an individual they tend to rate that person high on positive attributes and to play down negative traits. (To help reduce the halo effect teachers can rate all students on the same item before moving on to the next.) Finally, some teachers tend to avoid both extremes when rating children, giving every child an average rating. This tendency precludes identification of children who deviate from the group. In general, rating scales that include more precise definitions of the traits rated are preferable.

Whatever classroom screening procedure teachers use—anecdotal records, checklists, or rating scales—certain cautions must be observed in interpreting the results:

1. Screening data should not be used to make a diagnosis of any disorder. A premature diagnosis can be as damaging as failing to recognize a problem and can cause unnecessary hardship for both child and family.

2. Some behaviors are not what they appear to be. For example, a child who is constantly jumping out of his or her chair or pushing to the front of the group may be considered to have a behavior disorder. This, however, may be the child's attempt to bring things into closer eye or ear range because of a vision or hearing problem.

3. In deciding whether or not a child's behaviors are normal, the customs of the family or community in which that child lives must be considered. Since these may be different from those of the teacher, she must decide whether the behavior in question interferes with the child's ability to learn.

4. The degree, rather than the kind, of potentially disabling condition should be considered. Most inappropriate behaviors like crying, whining, sulking, or disobeying may be seen at some time in every child. Ordinarily, these actions are not cause for alarm unless they occur excessively; are used almost exclusively instead of other, more appropriate actions; and interfere with the child's healthy participation in various learning experiences.

Making Referrals

After screening data have been carefully considered, the teacher may wish to refer a child for further diagnostic testing. A referral represents a statement of concern about a student. In schools with special services, the referral is often the initial basis of communication between the classroom and special education teachers.

Most schools have standard referral forms for teachers to use. Typically, these form are clear, concise, and easy to complete. If necessary, the classroom teacher can seek help from special education teachers when filling out these forms.

The following four items are found on most referral forms:

1. *Statement of Child's Problem*
   The teacher is asked to write a specific statement about the child's problem. For example: "Bobby consistently refuses to join in group activities, seldom has positive interactions with others, and is often the subject of his classmates' ridicule, which makes him cry." In stating a child's problem, teachers should simply describe the behavior and avoid making inferences as to why the child behaves in a certain way.

2. *Specific Comments on Learning Strengths*
   These are descriptive comments that place an emphasis on the positive aspects of the learner's behavior; they can provide valuable ideas for programming.

3. *Documentary Evidence*
   Teachers should carefully present screening data gathered from various instruments to support the need for further diagnostic testing.

4. *Identifying Information*
   This includes the child's age, birth-date, date of referral, and any contacts the teacher has had with parents.

Screening is designed to gather initial information on learner characteristics. Such information should be re- corded carefully so it is available for later reference. In surveying students in the classroom, we are looking for those students whose behavior or performance appears to significantly deviate from that of the group. These are the students who need to be studied further in the next phase of the identification process—diagnosis.

DIAGNOSIS

Diagnosis, the final stage in the identification process, is an even more complete evaluation of a child's skills and deficits. It is conducted by a multidisciplinary team for purposes of choosing or developing an intervention program. There are two principal objectives in diagnosis: (1) to confirm or disconfirm the existence of a problem serious enough to require special programming, and (2) to gather enough information about a child's handicapping condition to make an intelligent decision on the least restrictive and most appropriate placement for the child.

Diagnosis typically involves gathering eight kinds of developmental information, depending on the individual child's handicapping condition. These include: (1) social history, (2) physical examination, (3) neurological examination, (4) psychological examination, (5) hearing examination, (6) vision examination, (7) speech and language examination, and (8) educational examination (Cross & Goin, 1977).

A social history is usually obtained through interviews conducted with the family by a social worker. In the interviews, information is gathered about the child's behavior in the home, ways in which parents deal with the child's problems, the parents' feeling and attitudes about the child, and the overall impact of the handicapped child on the family.

The physical examination, conducted by a pediatrician, is designed to provide a picture of the child's general health at present, a review of medical history, and any information about any physical defects that may be present.

Neurological examinations are most often administered by neurologists to children suspected of having learning disabilities. A neurological examination provides specific information about any central nervous system impairment. It also can reveal brain damage and detect the possibility of seizures or other malfunctioning.

Psychological examinations, conducted by school psychologists, involve administration of both standardized tests to assess general intellectual and academic achievement, general aptitude and specific academic achievement, and projective tests to determine the nature of a child's emotional responses. Such tests typically measure the child's performance against normative standards. The following standards for diagnostic tests have been suggested by Gallagher and Bradley (1972):

1. The test and its manual should be revised at appropriate intervals.

2. The test should state the purposes and applications for which it is recommended.

3. The test manual should indicate the qualifications required to administer and interpret the test.

4. The manual should report the validity of the test for each type of inference for which it is recommended.

5. The sample employed in standardizing the test and the conditions under which testing was done should be consistent with recommendations made in the manual.

6. Norms should be reported in the test manual in terms of standard scores based on an appropriate reference group or groups. (p. 104)

Speech and language examinations, generally administered by a speech pathologist, are designed to assess articulation, fluency, and voice problems as well as the child's ability to understand and/or use words and language.

Speech problems make up a large proportion of the handicapping conditions identified in the early years. Several different tests are used to identify speech and language handicapping conditions. They include hearing, visual, and educational examinations.

Hearing examinations consist of audiometric tests administered by audiologists or public health workers to determine if any type of hearing impairment exists. Visual examinations, which are conducted by an ophthalmologist or public health worker, are designed to detect visual impairment. An educational examination, conducted by the classroom teacher, involves a diagnostic assessment to determine the child's learning style and abilities, both in general academic achievement and in specific content areas.

When diagnostic testing has been completed, the results can be brought together to form an accurate picture of the child's condition. To prevent misinterpretation of the results, each piece of information must be carefully evaluated in light of other results—by people with expertise in the various areas and by people who know the child intimately. All findings must be explored in order to place the child in an appropriate program. This is done in the team or multidisciplinary conference. This conference and the teacher's responsibilities are discussed in Chapter 5.

SUMMARY

Identifying handicapping or potentially handicapping conditions in children is an important part of the teacher's job. This chapter presented methods for

casefinding, screening, and diagnosing young children. Some evidence suggests that careful early childhood evaluation procedures are effective in identifying even mildly handicapped children. The many alternatives for screening and diagnosing behavior presented in this chapter should be closely examined to match each child to the most appropriate technique.

Teachers must exercise special care in using screening data. They should not use this data to make a formal diagnosis or to label children. Screening data should not be used to raise parental anxiety by reporting that there is something wrong with a child; rather, screening data should be used to seek additional, more intensive assessment for the child.

SCREENING INSTRUMENTS

Title: The ABC Inventory
Authors: N. Adair and G. Blesett
Publisher: Research Concepts, Muskegon, Michigan. 1965.
Age range: 3.6 to 6.6 years

General Description

The ABC Inventory is designed to identify children who are likely to fail in preschool or kindergarten or who are not likely to be ready for first grade. The inventory, which can be administered to individuals or groups, usually by a trained diagnostician, takes about 9 minutes to administer and includes items related to drawing, copying, folding, counting, memory, general information, colors, size concepts, and time concepts. The manual reports extensive reliability studies and research on its effectiveness.

Title: The Comprehensive Identification Process (CIP)
Author: R. R. Zehrbach
Publisher: Scholastic Testing Service, Inc., Bensenville, Illinois. 1976.
Age range: 2.6 to 5.6 years

General Description

The CIP is designed to facilitate case-finding and screening of children. CIP, which can be administered to groups, is designed primarily for individuals and takes 30 to 40 minutes per child. CIP has been standardized on more than 1000 children and screens children using items from standardized instruments in 8 areas: cognitive-verbal, fine motor, gross motor, speech and expressive language, social/affective, hearing, vision, and medical history. The test can be administered either by a teacher or a specially trained non-professional.

Title: Cooperative Preschool Inventory (CPI)
Author: B. M. Caldwell
Publisher: Cooperative Tests and Services, Educational Testing Service, Princeton, New Jersey. 1970.
Age range: 3.0 to 6.0 years

General Description

The CPI provides a measure of achievement in areas regarded as necessary for success in school. The instrument, which can be administered in 10 to 15 minutes by a trained parent or teacher, consists of 64 items, scored as either right or wrong, grouped into the following areas: concept activation, sensory, personal-social responsiveness, and associated vocabulary. The number of correct responses is converted to a percentile rank for differing chronological ages.

The test was standardized on 1500 children from 150 Head Start classes nationwide. It is generally recognized by experts as a good screening tool, easy to administer and score and particulary relevant for disadvantaged preschool populations.

Title: Del Rio Language Screening Test
Authors: A. Toronto and D. Leourman
Publisher: National Educational Publishers, Inc., Austin, Texas. 1975.
Age range: 3.0 to 6.11 years

General Description

The Del Rio Language Screening Test is a language screening measure given in both Spanish and English. It is appropriate for English-speaking Anglo-Americans, predominantly Spanish-speaking Mexican-American children, and predominantly English-speaking Mexican-American children. The instrument, developed to fulfill the need for special education programs for Spanish-speaking children in the Southwest, consists of five separate subtests, each of which may be used alone or in combination with others. The Del Rio has been standardized on 384 children and adequate validity and reliability data have been established.

Title: Denver Developmental Screening Test (DDST)
Authors: W. K. Frankenburg, J. B. Dodds, and A. Fandal

Publisher: Ladoca Project and Publishing, Inc., Denver, Colorado. 1970.
Age range: 1 month to 6 years

General Description

The DDST is perhaps the most widely used screening device to aid in the early detection of delayed development in children. The test consists of 105 items grouped in four sections—personal-social, gross motor, fine motor, and language. The number of items administered varies according to the age of the child. Each test item is represented on the test form by a horizontal bar along the age continuum to indicate the ages at which 25, 50, 75, and 90 percent of the children in the standardization sample passed an item. Each section of the test is continued until the level of development is identified when the child fails any item that 90 percent of the children normally can pass at a younger age.

The DDST, which can be administered by a teacher or a specially trained nonprofessional, has been standardized on over 1000 children between 1 month and 6.4 years with separate norms by gender and for socioeconomic status. Reliability and validity data reported in the literature reveal generally favorable results, although the test was standardized on a limited regional sample with very few minority children. The DDST is considered to be an excellent screening device that is relatively simple to administer and interpret without special training in psychological testing. The accompanying manual provides very concise directions for scoring and interpreting responses.

Title: Developmental Indicators for the Assessment of Learning (DIAL)
Authors: C. Mardell and D. Goldenberg
Publisher: DIAL, Inc., Highland Park, Illinois. 1975.
Age range: 2.5 to 5.5 years

General Description

The DIAL is a prekindergarten screening test designed to identify children with potential learning problems in four developmental skill areas—gross motor, fine motor, concepts, and communication—that are assessed with 7 items each. DIAL takes approximately 20 to 30 minutes per child and is individually administered by a five-person team of professionals and/or paraprofessionals. The screening area is arranged into four stations plus a play and registration area. Cut-off points are provided at three-month intervals and results indicate whether children are "ok," need to be rescreened, or need a complete diagnostic evaluation. The manual reports extensive validity and reliability data standardized on a stratified sample of 4356 children.

Title: Eliot-Pearson Screening Profile (EPSP)
Authors: S. J. Meisels and M. S. Wiske
Publisher: Eliot-Pearson Department of Child Study, Medford, Massachusetts. 1976.
Age range: 4.0 to 6.0 years

General Description

The EPSP provides a brief and easy developmental survey of the perceptual, motor, and language domains. The survey, which can be given by teachers or trained nonprofessionals, takes approximately 15 minutes to administer. Several test items from the EPSP have been taken directly from standardized tests. While the EPSP has been trial tested on more than 2000 children, there is no evidence that this sample adequately represented cross-sections of society. Additionally, reliability and validity measures are still incomplete.

Title: Meeting Street School Screening Test (MSSST)
Authors: P. Hainsworth and E. M. Siqueland
Publisher: Meeting Street School, East Providence, Rhode Island. 1969.
Age range: 5 to 7.5 years

General Description

The MSSST is an individually administered screening test designed to detect problems in the motor, visual, perceptual, and language domains. The 20 minute test, which may be administered by trained teachers, psychologists, physicians, or nonprofessionals, was standardized on 500 kindergarten and first-grade children selected from a cross-section of the U.S. population. Norms are presented at half-year intervals, and extensive reliability and validity data are reported.

Title: Metropolitan Readiness Test
Authors: G. Hildreth, N. Griffiths and M. McGauvran
Publisher: The Psychological Corporation, Atlanta, Georgia. 1976.
Age range: 5 to 7 years

General Description

The *Metropolitan Readiness Test* is among the most popular batteries currently used in kindergartens and primary grades. It contains 7 subtests—word meaning, listening, comprehension, perceptual recognition of similarities, recognition of lowercase letters, number knowledge, and copying-assessing skills that contribute to first-grade readiness. The test, which is ordinarily given at the end of kindergarten or the beginning of the first grade, requires children to be able to write but requires little special training for administration and scoring. Norms are based upon a nationwide sample of beginning first graders, and reliability and predictive validity data are sound.

Title: Northwestern Syntax Screening Test (NSST)
Author: L. Lee
Publisher: Northwestern University Press, Evanston, Illinois. 1960.
Age range: 3 to 8 years

General Description

The NSST assesses initial deficits in both expressive and receptive use of syntax. The test, which takes approximately 20 minutes per individual to administer and is administered by a trained diagnostician, consists of a series of pictures designed to screen a child's comprehension and production abilities. Norms on the NSST are based upon 242 children between 3 and 8 years old. The NSST is widely used and respected by speech and language therapists.

Title: Preschool Screening System (PSS)
Authors: P. Hainsworth and R. Hainsworth
Publisher: First Step Publications, Pawtucket, Rhode Island. 1973.
Age range: 3.0 to 5.4 years

General Description

The PSS is an individual and group administered test that consists of a child test and a parent questionnaire. The PSS, which takes from 15 to 25 minutes to administer, screens information processing skills in language and visual-motor and gross motor skills. The parent questionnaire, also taking 15 to 25 minutes to administer, includes items regarding behavioral characteristics of the child's skills and behavior at home as well as a short medical and developmental history.

Normative data were collected on the PSS over 2 years on 600 children, and reliability and validity information are adequate. The PSS can be administered by any experienced examiner or trained technician or by a volunteer or paraprofessional supervised by an experienced technician.

Title: Slosson Intelligence Test (SIT)
Author: R. L. Slosson
Publisher: Western Psychological Services, Los Angeles, California. 1963.
Age range: 4 years to adulthood

General Description

The SIT is a simple individual screening instrument administered by either a teacher or a trained diagnostician. It consists of vocabulary, memory, reasoning, and motor items. Validity and reliability data for children under 4 are minimal; however, such data are adequate for individuals 4 through adulthood. The instrument consists of one or two items per age level (reported in six-month intervals) and items for the very young are given orally and require oral or simple motor responses. The SIT yields an IQ score that correlates well with the Stanford-Binet.

Title: The Vane Kindergarten Test (VKT)
Author: J. R. Vane
Publisher: Clinical Psychology Publishing Co., Inc., Brandon, Vermont. 1968.
Age range: 4 to 6.5 years

General Description

The VKT is a brief screening measure designed to detect problems in school readiness in vocabulary, perceptual motor, and draw-a-man tasks. It is individually adminstered by a trained psychologist taking from 25 to 40 minutes. The vocabulary and perceptual motor tasks were standardized on 1000 children and the draw-a-man tasks on 400 children representing a cross-section of the population in the northeastern United States. Thus, the VKT contains adequate reliability and validity data.

REFERENCES

Ahr, A. E. *Parent readiness evaluation of preschoolers*. Skokie, Ill.: Priority Innovations, 1968.

Allen, K. E., Rieke, J., Smitriev, V., and Hayden, A. H. Early warning: Observation as a tool for recognizing potential handicaps in young children. *Educational Horizons*, 1972, *50*(2), 43–55.

Cross, L., and Goin, K. (Eds.) *Identifying handicapped children: A guide to casefinding, screening, diagnosis, assessment and evaluation*. New York: Walker and Company, 1977.

Feshbach, S., Adelman, H., and Williamson, W. F. Early identification of children with high risk of reading failure. *Journal of Learning Disabilities*, 1974, 7, 639–644.

Gallagher, J. J., and Bradley, R. H. Early identification of developmental difficulties, in I. J. Gordon (Ed.), *Early childhood education: The seventy-first yearbook of the National Society for the Study of Education*. Chicago: University of Chicago Press, 1972.

Haring, N. G., and Ridgeway, R. Early identification of children with learning disabilities. *Exceptional Children*, 1967, *33*, 387–395.

Jordan, F. L., and Massey, J. *School Readiness Survey*. 2nd ed. Palo Alto, Calif.: Consulting Psychologists Press, 1969.

Keogh, B. K., and Smith, C. Early identification of educationally high potential and high-risk children. *Journal of School Psychology*, 1970, *8*, 285–290.

Lillie, D. L., Screening. In L. Cross and K. Goin (Eds.), *Identifying handicapped children: A guide to casefinding, screen-*

ing, diagnosis, assessment and evaluation. New York: Walker and Company, 1977.

Myklebust, L. R. *The pupil rating scale: Screening for learning disabilities*. New York: Grune and Stratton, 1971.

Novak, H. S., Bonaventura, E., and Merenda, P. F. *Manual to accompany Rhode Island pupil identification scale*. Providence, R.I.: Authors, 1972.

Rochford, T. Identification of preschool children with potential learning problems. In R. Reger (Ed.), *Preschool programming of children with disabilities*. Springfield, Ill.: Charles C. Thomas, 1970.

Wright, H. F. Observational Child Study. In P. H. Mussen (Ed.) *Handbook of research method in child development*. New York: Wiley, 1960.

Four

PLANNING AND ORGANIZING FOR AN INTEGRATED CLASS

Handicapped children are placed in regular classrooms because it is felt that they can learn best in these settings, with as little segregation and modification as is practical. Providing as normal a school experience as possible is the goal of this integration. Thus, handicapped children should have the opportunity to participate in many of the same activities and should be educated in the same manner as their nonhandicapped peers to the greatest extent possible. Teachers need to identify and adjust those factors in their classrooms that may be impeding the progress of handicapped children. Teachers also need to continuously evaluate the performance of the children in their classes so that instruction can be modified to focus on changing student needs.

There are no special techniques or magical formulas for teaching handicapped children in the regular class. No single method can be effective for all; each child and each classroom situation is truly unique.

PLANNING

The instructional strategies used with most normal children are effective with most handicapped children. However, there are times when programs need to be modified to accommodate to a child's disability. One approach to working with handicapped children is to plan prescriptively (Laycock, 1980; Haring & Schiefelbusch, 1976). While this is useful for children with some disabilities, it needs to be modified for use in regular classes. This approach has seven steps: (1) assessment, (2) setting objectives, (3) developing a plan, (4) selecting procedures, (5) implementing the program, (6) evaluating learner performance, and (7) revising the program.

Many of these steps are the same as those described for developing an *Individualized Educational Program* (IEP) in Chapter 5. The IEP is a written statement of the objectives, content, procedures, and evaluation of the handicapped child's educational program. IEPs are generally designed for long-range planning. The steps described here are applicable for short-term planning based upon the IEP and using much of the information already accumulated.

Assessment

Through an initial assessment of the child, information is gathered to help the teacher identify what skills and content the child has or has not mastered in different areas of the curriculum. Teachers should review teacher re-

ports; psychological reports; developmental, social, and educational histories; the reports of other educational specialists; and possibly medical reports. The teacher might also wish to confer with the child's previous teachers, the parents or guardians, the guidance counselor, the school director or principal, the psychologist, the parent liaison worker or social worker, and the school nurse. Each person may have information that could supplement the information to be found in the school record.

After reviewing this information, the teacher should then gather information about the child's current abilities by using the types of techniques described in Chapter 6. Since a single assessment can be unusually good or unusually bad, a number of different measures including formal tests and observation techniques, should be used to provide a more representative picture of the child.

Setting Objectives

Based on initial assessment the teacher can specify instructional objectives to serve as intended outcome(s). These objectives can relate to social skills or play behaviors as well as to academics. If written in behavioral terms, an instructional objective contains a statement of (1) the expected skills to be achieved, (2) the criterion for success in each skill, and (3) the conditions in which the student will be expected to perform each skill.

A simple instructional objective may be achieved in a single teaching step while a complex one may require a number of steps. Task analysis can be used to break down complex objectives into component parts and sequence instruction for them, moving from most simple to most complex. Teachers may develop a task analysis by watching a nonhandicapped child perform the task and then analyzing what is observed, by performing the task themselves and analyzing what they have done, by working backward from the final skills, or by brainstorming with colleagues as to the steps involved. Each step in the analysis should be described in specific terms and the teaching tasks should be of approximately equal difficulty. Teachers often find it helpful to work through a prescribed sequence of tasks themselves or to have the task analysis reviewed by a colleague in order to locate potential problems before working it through with a child.

Developing a Plan

The instructional (or lesson) plan should describe the arrangements to be used to teach specific children or groups of children in a class. Formats for writing lesson plans vary, but most plans contain common elements.

Instructional plans can be written on index cards, on charts, or in a teacher's plan book. They can be posted in the room where instructional activities will take place if more than one adult will be involved.

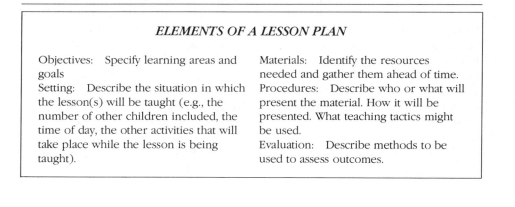

ELEMENTS OF A LESSON PLAN

Objectives: Specify learning areas and goals
Setting: Describe the situation in which the lesson(s) will be taught (e.g., the number of other children included, the time of day, the other activities that will take place while the lesson is being taught).

Materials: Identify the resources needed and gather them ahead of time.
Procedures: Describe who or what will present the material. How it will be presented. What teaching tactics might be used.
Evaluation: Describe methods to be used to assess outcomes.

Selecting Instructional Procedures

Instructional procedures include use of both teaching techniques and instructional materials. Some of the techniques used to encourage learning among handicapped children are: verbal instructions, modeling, manual guidance, prompting, fading, shaping, practicing, and generalizing.

Verbal instructions such as "Place the pictures in the right order," "Begin each sentence with a capital letter," or "Match the object with the appropriate picture," tell the children how to perform a task. These instructions should contain the information necessary to perform the required skill and should be given when the learner is attentive. There are times when verbal instructions alone are inadequate. Demonstrating a skill, perhaps while providing a verbal explanation, can be used along with other techniques.

The teacher may demonstrate a skill and then ask the child to imitate the performance of that skill. This is called *modeling*. Skills can also be modeled by other children, or a more permanent model can be provided through illustrations (e.g., copying the teacher's arrangement of colored blocks or copying a name from a printed name card). Modeling can occur directly as when the teacher demonstrates a self-help skill, or less directly as when the teacher shows a film, reads a story, or gives a puppet show. The child should be expected to pay attention while the skill is being modeled; the demonstration should be short and simple; and the model should be a valued individual.

In providing *manual guidance* the teacher physically guides the learner through performance of a skill. Manual guidance is effective when children have difficulty in understanding directions or have motor deficits, as do orthopedically impaired or cerebral palsied children. It helps if children experience how it actually feels to accomplish the skill to be learned. For example, the teacher may stand behind a child, take the back of his hands, move his fingers to grasp the top of his trousers and apply an upward pull to complete pulling up his trousers.

When using manual guidance, teachers should apply gentle, continuous pressure in guiding the child. If the child resists, stop for a moment to help her relax, or try some simple movement like raising and lowering her arms. It is also important to give the child a verbal cue before beginning the guidance procedure, combining verbal instructions with manual guidance and encouraging the child to associate the two together. After a while, manual guidance can be gradually removed or limited to only a small part of the entire skill.

Prompts, or *cues* signal the child to perform a certain skill in a particular situation. Verbal prompts are short statements, usually an abbreviated form of instruction, that tell children what to do. For instance, a teacher can prompt a child to move scissors correctly by saying "open—shut," or to build high block buildings by saying "steady it." Indirect verbal prompts are verbal statements or questions that imply a specific action. For instance, if a child is in a warm classroom wearing a heavy coat, the teacher might say, "Isn't it warm here?" or "Aren't heavy jackets for outside?" Gestural prompts are nonverbal signals such as pointing to, touching, or tapping the correct answer; waving hi or goodbye; or shaking one's head to indicate yes or no. Visual prompts, which are pictoral or symbolic cues, include such techniques as using books of exaggerated size to draw attention to the book area, or placing the correct choice in a discrimination task closest to the child.

Prompts or cues should be gradually removed so that students can perform skills under natural conditions. This is sometimes called *fading*. For example, beginning handwriting programs commonly require students to trace letters, then to write letters following a dotted line, then to write letters when only the beginning points are provided, and finally to write letters when no extra cues are provided.

Shaping is a procedure that builds on successive approximation to some skill, for example, reinforcing a student for sitting in place for progressively longer periods of time. In shaping block building a teacher might first encourage a child to place one block upon the other. Later the child might be encouraged to build enclosures; then more complex building could be encouraged. To shape legible writing, a teacher might begin by expecting a child to produce letters that approximate the correct form. Gradually, the teacher adjusts the criteria so that eventually only letters of the correct size, form, and slant are accepted.

Practice or *drill* involves the opportunity to perform a task repeatedly in order to increase the quality and fluency of a skill. Students, for example, can practice to increase their accuracy and speed in reading sight words or math facts.

Children should be helped to generalize, that is to use or transfer the skills taught in one situation to other situations. Without such *generalization*, gains made in the classroom or treatment setting are of limited value. Many skills generalize naturally for most individuals without any emphasis placed on the process. A number of basic techniques to enhance transfer of training can be used. If children learn behaviors that will be rewarded by others, these will probably transfer. Teachers can also create behavior traps: situations that allow elements in the natural environment to support learning. Teaching in different settings and with different people involved is also effective. Another method is to support incompatible behavior, that is, any behavior that is physically impossible to emit at the same time as an undesirable behavior.

Implementing a Plan

Just as no two teachers will plan the same way, so no two teachers will implement a plan in the same way. There are, however, some common elements in all teaching. The suggestions that follow for teaching young handicapped children should prove useful.

Several current textbooks on early education for the handicapped provide additional guidelines for working with handicapped children, including those by Allen (1980), Fallen and McGovern (1978), Lerner, Mardell-Czudnowski, and Goldenberg (1981), and Neisworth, Herb, Bagnato, Cartwright, and Laub (1980).

*SUGGESTIONS FOR TEACHING YOUNG HANDICAPPED CHILDREN

1. *Implement the plan as developed as much as possible.* Teachers often function spontaneously in a classroom. Nevertheless, they should use the plans they have developed even though modifications may be needed. If a plan has been well designed, it should allow for flexibility when translated into action.

2. *Be certain that the learner is attentive.* Some handicapped children have difficulty concentrating on learning tasks for extended periods of time. Teachers must help such children stay on task. Having a variety of activities available by which to achieve the same goal often helps.

3. *Encourage constructive divergent thinking.* Constructive imagination is a worthwhile educational goal and may provide the foundation for adult creativity. Most young children are naturally creative. All children, handicapped or otherwise, should be encouraged to develop productive divergent thinking skills.

4. *Offer opportunities for the child to make choices.* Children might be able to choose what is to be done, when it should be done, where it should be done, and sometimes, whether or not it should be done. Teachers must, of course, monitor children's choices to be certain they are neither overwhelmed or underchallenged.

5. *Be consistent.* Children generally learn better when they know what to expect. Clearly specifying the rules or standards for classroom behavior and the consequences for noncompliance with those standards helps avoid problems.

6. *Actively involve the child in learning tasks.* Young children, especially the handicapped, need to be actively involved in learning. Give children opportunities to manipulate materials, ask questions, and engage in discussions, dramatic play, group investigations, and learning games.

7. *Observe the child closely.* The teacher must be observant of the child's approach to a task, watching for wavering of attention or any blocks to progress.

8. *Give specific feedback.* Provide information about the child's performance. The sooner feedback is provided and the more specific it is, the more learning will be facilitated.

9. *Support the child.* Support and reinforcement can increase desirable social skills in children as well as increase preacademic and academic performance.

Evaluating the Program

Information should be collected on a regular basis to determine whether the instruction that was planned has been successful. If the information gathered at the end is similar to the initial assessment data, then conclusions concerning student learning can be easily made. Continuous observation and assessment of a child's performance helps the teacher determine the effectiveness of an instructional program and facilitates adapting the program to meet the child's changing needs.

Revising the Program

Any planned program, once implemented, requires some modification. In some cases, only minor refinements are needed; in others, the teacher must redesign the program. Adjustments are made based on evaluation of the program as it has been implemented.

ORGANIZING FOR INSTRUCTION

Although a good part of planning involves design of teaching-learning strategies, planning also deals with providing the resources needed to implement those strategies. The teacher must look at the basic resources in the classroom—time and space—and determine how best to use them since they are available only in limited quantity. Other materials must be gathered and arranged. Furniture and basic equipment is generally provided from the start of the school year and is seldom augmented. These may need to be deployed in different ways at different times to serve different purposes. Adequate supplies and human resources must also be found. School resources can be supplemented; parents can be asked to contribute materials, some of which they might otherwise discard, and volunteers and even the pupils themselves can supplement the teacher by helping to provide instruction. Provision of resources must often be planned well ahead of time and teachers must think about how best to use them.

Room Arrangement

The way teachers arrange the physical elements of a classroom can either support or interfere with their plans. Most classrooms have certain basic attributes that establish the limits of what can be done. The size of a room, its lighting, placement of windows, availability of water, and accessibility of bathroom facilities are things a teacher cannot change. Rooms may also have permanent built-in storage areas, bulletin boards, and other such things that also cannot be changed but that might be worked around.

Generally, schools provide basic classroom furniture including tables, chairs, desks, shelves, cabinets, and whatever else is considered essential. Painting easels, a phonograph, and a tape recorder may also be provided along with books, paper, art supplies, and physical education or climbing equipment. Preprimary classrooms generally have a good deal of play material and manipulatives as well. Teachers can augment these basic supplies during the school year by ordering additional materials and by soliciting contributions from parents, businesses, and community groups. Unfortunately, teachers themselves are often forced to provide some resources not supplied by the school; those might include pictures, small rugs, pillows, soft furniture, plants, and even small animals.

Teachers of young children may not know ahead of time that they will have a handicapped child enrolled in class

or what that child will be like. Teachers must be ready to modify their teaching when a handicapped child is enrolled or identified.

When a handicapped child is enrolled in a class, the teacher needs to check the classroom to make sure it is adequate to serve that child's needs and that no unnecessary obstacles are present. Often traffic patterns need to be assessed so that free movement throughout the classroom is possible without some children interfering with the work of others. Access to stored supplies, water, cleanup supplies, and toilet facilities should also be checked. The teacher should also assess the room to see that there is no unnecessary clutter. Although clutter is often of minimal significance to normal children, it can be distracting to many handicapped children: visual clutter makes it difficult to focus on important

visual elements; auditory clutter may make it hard to hear significant sounds; and physical clutter may interfere with children's movements around the room.

Care should be taken to ensure that the environment is safe for all and meets all children's needs. The room arrangement should be kept simple, especially at the beginning of the year. As the children get used to the room and learn to handle a more complex environment, the teacher can gradually increase the amount and range of materials provided and the number of activities available.

It is important that teachers and children establish and enforce safety rules. For example, crutches should be kept close to the child and wheelchairs, crutches, canes, or other equipment must be kept out of traffic areas. In addition, handicapped children, whether orthopedically or visually impaired, may accidentally bump into things or people. A wheelchair can easily swing or roll to the wrong place. Running in the classroom should be prohibited; this will protect not only the visually impaired but all other children as well.

The availability of adequate light, the color of walls and equipment and the sound absorbing qualities of elements in the room need to be carefully considered along with variety and flexibility. Storage space and locker facilities for personal belongings and classroom materials and equipment should be accessible to all children.

Placement of furniture and equipment that seemed good may prove to have certain disadvantages once a handicapped child becomes part of the class. Such children may, for example, need periods of isolation if social or sensory distractions keep them from successfully dealing with school work. A change in furniture arrangement—using bookshelves to partially screen an area, for example—might provide a degree of isolation while allowing the teacher to easily supervise activities.

Sometimes furniture needs minor modification such as placing crutch tips on table legs so they will not slip. Sometimes furniture needs to be rearranged, for example, placing a desk for a visually handicapped child in a spot where there will be adequate light from a window or fixture without undue glare. Sometimes new furniture or equipment will need to be procured: perhaps a table high enough for a child in a wheelchair to use or a tape recorder to be used primarily by a handicapped child.

Outdoor spaces for large-muscle activity must be provided to meet the needs of all children. Equipment and activities should be adapted for handicapped children to allow them to participate in as many outdoor activities as possible. Health and safety considerations are particularly important for blind, deaf, physically disabled, and mildly retarded children, and care should be taken to identify hazards and avoid possible accidents within and around the school.

Some orthopedically handicapped children, especially those with poor sitting balance, need special seating arrangements. A chair with arms or with sides high enough to protect the child from falling to either side might need to be used. A high-backed chair will support the child's trunk and keep the head upright. Some children may be unable to sit on the floor without support. A minimal amount of support can be provided by sitting them against a wall or removing the legs of a chair and using its seat and back on the floor.

Once a room has been set up, it is often advisable to make as few basic changes as possible in the arrangement. Visually handicapped children need to become oriented to a classroom when school starts and must be reoriented whenever changes are made; changing the room too often can be confusing. Continual rearrangement of space can also be distracting to other handicapped children and may especially upset behaviorally disordered children who depend on the regularity of life to provide the necessary structure for their behavior.

Learning Centers

Many primary classes are organized with desks or tables set in rows or semicircles. This allows all the children to focus on the teacher and allows the teacher to supervise all of the children at the same time. Such an arrangement makes good sense when everyone in the classroom is doing the same thing at the same time under the teacher's direct supervision. In many prekindergartens, kindergartens, and primary classes in which programs are more individualized, teachers arrange their rooms into learning centers.

A learning center is a section of a room set aside for a particular kind of learning activity. It is at least partially segregated from other sections of the room so that children can work within a center with some degree of isolation. Establishing learning centers supports individualization. Different activities can take place in different centers with children working individually or in small groups on individual projects, functioning in their own styles and operating at their own paces. Learning centers are often helpful in mainstreaming children in a classroom since the handicapped child can work alongside other children without necessarily engaging in the same activity. Thus, learning centers allow classrooms to be child centered rather than teacher centered, they help individualize learning and allow for independent, active participation of the children (Blake, 1977).

In nursery-kindergarten classes, there may be a dramatic play center, a construction center, an arts and crafts center, a manipulative material center, a library center, a music center, and a display center. In primary classes, with their more academic orientation, centers may be organized around subject matter areas: a math center, a reading and writing center, a science center, an arts center, and a social studies center. Learning centers can also focus on topics that cut across subject matter areas: an environmental studies center, for example, or a school newspaper center or a center for studying the community.

Each center should be provided with the materials and resources necessary to support active learning. Adequate space should be provided as well. A block building center will contain wooden building blocks of varying sizes and shapes, along with toy cars, miniature people, and other accessories that enable children to construct multifaceted buildings. A sociodramatic play center can contain dress up clothes and props to support play around a specific theme. Providing food containers, a toy cash register, paper bags, and a few baskets will encourage supermarket play, while white aprons or jackets, wooden tongue depressors, a stethoscope, and the like could encourage hospital play.

Many centers are designed for open-ended activities, but they can also be designed with greater structure so that more prescribed activities develop. A library center might have a variety of books in it to encourage children to read. It could also have a tape recorder or paper and pencils available for children to use to record their descriptions and comments about what they have read and to write short reports. A math center might have manipulative material for counting and measuring as well as sets of task cards upon which are written directions for specific activities in which children should engage. If children cannot read, the directions on the cards can consist of pictures or rhebus writing, in which words and

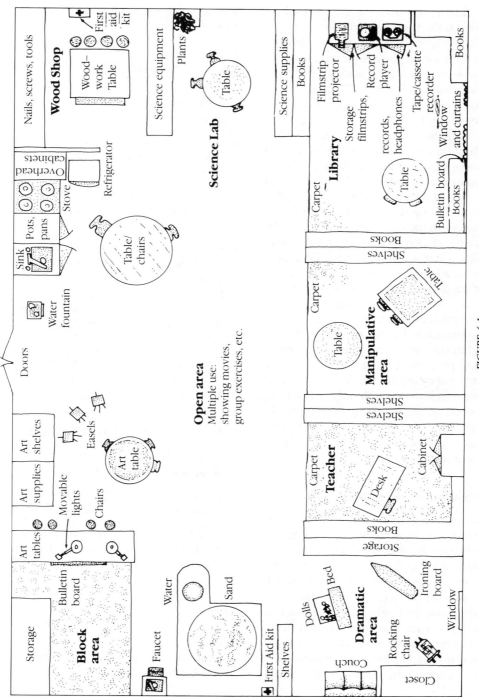

FIGURE 4-1

pictures are combined. No matter how directions are provided, the centers should be designed so that the learning activities engage children and so that some record can be made of children's activities and learning. Checklists such as those described in Chapter 3 are useful for that.

Activities should also be designed so that children can function with limited input from the teacher. When not otherwise engaged, the teacher can circulate among the various centers or focus on a group of children while others in the class are busy with their own independent activities. This means that materials should be readily accessible and each center should be designed for easy cleanup. Keeping materials in tote trays or plastic shoe boxes is useful, as is marking shelves to show where each set of materials belongs. Children have to be given directions and practice in using learning centers when they are started. Teachers might want to start out with only one learning center at the beginning of the school year, then expand when children indicate they are capable of their independent use.

Instructional Materials

Instructional materials include manipulative materials, worksheets, reading or math textbooks, and workbooks. Since most early childhood programs do not have an abundance of funds, materials must be purchased wisely. When choosing materials, teachers must consider learner characteristics, teachers concerns, and cost-effectiveness. The following questions can be useful in determining the extent to which materials correspond with instructional needs.

Learner Characteristics

1. Is the material compatible with program objectives?

2. Is the material appropriate for the learner's interest, age, and grade level?

3. Does the material require prerequisite skills that the intended learner has?

4. Is the material compatible with the child's strengths and needs? For example, if the child learns best through auditory stimuli and responds best through verbal answers, does the material play to these strengths?

5. Is the specific medium of the material (e.g., activity cards, games, filmstrips) appropriate for the student?

6. Is the material well made and safe?

7. Is the material flexible, permitting self-pacing by the learner?

8. Is the material appropriate for learners at different skill levels?

9. Is the material attractive and relevant to the learner's interests and background?

Teacher Concerns

1. Does the material require specialized training and skills for the teacher to use it effectively?

2. Does the material fit within the existing classroom structure?

3. Are accompanying manuals or other support resources helpful?

4. Does the material include a suitable evaluation component?

5. Does the material demand too much teacher time for preparation, supervision, and evaluation?

6. Does the material portray any race, sex, or handicapping condition in a negative or stereotypic manner?

Cost Effectiveness

1. Is there hidden cost in the material? Does the cost compare favorably to costs of similar materials on the market?

2. Is the material durable and likely to give reasonable service over time?

3. Can enough students benefit from the material to justify the expense involved?

If no appropriate materials are available, the teacher might be able to adapt materials used in the past or construct his or her own materials.

Special Curriculum Materials

Regular and resource room special education teachers often use one or more of a variety of curriculum materials, often produced commercially, to supplement the regular instructional material available in the classroom. Among the more widely used programs

for handicapped children in integrated, early education settings are the *Portage Guide to Early Education,* LAP (Learning Accomplishment Profile), DISTAR (Direct Instructional System in Arithmetic and Reading), and GOAL (Game-Oriented Activities for Learning) programs.

The *Portage Guide to Early Education* (Bluma et al., 1976) is a product of the Portage Project, a First Chance program begun in 1969 to train parents to teach their handicapped children in the home. The original target population was handicapped preschoolers, ages 0–6, in rural areas of Wisconsin, who would be educated at home. In 1976 the *Portage Guide* was expanded to accommodate handicapped children in Head Start, kindergarten, and primary classes.

The *Portage Guide* consists of a developmental checklist of 450 skills in social, cognitive, language, self-help, and motor domains; and a set of curriculum cards (color-coded by domain) that match each skill. Each curriculum card describes the skill to be taught and suggests materials and activities to assist in teaching it. When a child has successfully learned a skill, the teacher presents the next skill on the developmental checklist. Activity charts describe the goals to be achieved, how often skills are to be practiced, and the types of rewards to be used.

LAP (Sanford, 1974), according to its developer, is suitable for both normal and developmentally delayed children. The curriculum was developed by the Chapel Hill Training Project at the University of North Carolina and consists of six skill domains—gross and fine motor, social, self-help, cognitive, and language skills.

LAP materials include two paperback books, *The Learning Accomplishment Profile* and *The Manual for Use of the Learning Accomplishment Profile,* that list a series of developmental behaviors, instructions for assessing and recording these behaviors, and lesson plans for 44 weeks of instruction. Also available is a *Planning Guide for Preschool Children,* an early LAP for children birth through 31 months, a book of learning activities for children 12–72 months, and a planning guide, based on Bloom's (1956) taxonomy of educational objectives, for gifted preschoolers. Both the *Portage Guide* and the LAP materials contain checklists that can be used for criterion-referenced evaluation.

DISTAR (Englemann et al., 1974) is a curriculum for teaching arithmetic, reading, and language skills. While originally developed for disadvantaged preschoolers, it is used today primarily for kindergarten and primary aged children with academic and learning problems who receive instruction in resource rooms. DISTAR provides a sequenced curriculum with intensive oral drill in verbal and logical patterns. The general instructional strategy is that of teaching a rule followed by application of that rule. A verbal formula is learned by rote and then applied to a series of analogous examples of increasing difficulty. The main characteristics of the DISTAR method are: (1) fast-paced instruction; (2) reduced off-task behavior; (3) a strong emphasis on verbal responses; (4) carefully planned, small-step instructional units; and (5) heavy work demands requiring children to concentrate for up to 20 minutes per lesson.

GOAL (Karnes, 1972, 1973) uses a psycholinguistic model (derived from the Illinois Test of Psycholinguistic Abilities) to guide language instruction. Since inadequate language skills represent one of the greatest problems for the young handicapped child, verbalizations in conjunction with manipulation of concrete materials are considered to be the most effective means of establishing new language responses. A game format (card packs, lotto games, models and miniatures, and sorting, matching and classifying games) is used to create situations in which verbal responses can be made in a productive, meaningful context without resorting to rote learning. If a child is unable to make a verbal response, the teacher supplies an appropriate model. When the child begins to initiate personal responses the teacher has an opportunity to correct, modify, and expand the verbalization. GOAL is designed to be used in three, 20 minute structured periods throughout the school day.

Other special instructional programs include the following:

The RADEA Program (Walling, 1976) is designed to increase the adaptive behaviors of children between the developmental ages of 0 to 7 years. The program concentrates on developing specific information processing skills including auditory and visual perception, perceptual motor, oral language, and functional living skills. Each area of the curriculum is analyzed into sequenced component tasks. Materials include a teacher's manual, task-activity cards, daily progress charts, individual progress profiles, test scoring sheets, picture cards, and recorded cassettes to use in auditory training.

Project PAR Sequential Curriculum for Early Learning (Cole & Stevenson, 1976) is designed primarily for children 4 to 6 years of age with minimal learning difficulties. The intent is to help prevent academic failure and to prepare the slow learner for successful placement in a regular mainstreamed classroom. PAR contains a card file of classroom activities and color-coded pages of activities designed to promote developmental skills in cognitive, physical, social, and emotional areas. The curriculum also comes with a comprehensive planning guide and an evaluation form that help facilitate record-keeping.

School Before Six: A Diagnostic Approach (Hodgen, Koetter, LaForie, McCord, & Schramm, 1974) focuses on the needs and strengths of children 3 to 5 years of age in the language, socioemotional, gross, fine, and perceptual motor domains. A discussion is presented on problems typically shown by children in each domain along with a normal developmental sequence of skills. Diagnostic procedures, detailed directions for instructional tasks, simple recording forms, and suggestions for teaching are also provided.

The *COMP Curriculum and Activity Manual* (Willoughby-Hulb, Neisworth, Laub, Hunt, & Llewellyn, 1980) is a behaviorally based curriculum providing sequenced objectives for children from birth through 5 years of age in communication, self-care, motor, and problem-solving areas. Activities and teaching strategies for each objective are suggested, along with evaluation

methods and forms for recording children's progess.

Curricular Programming for Young Handicapped Children—Project First Chance (Bos, 1980) covers five skill areas—body management, self-care, communication, preacademics, and socialization—for handicapped children between 2-1/2 and 6-1/2 years of age who do not have severe visual or hearing impairments. Individual and group oriented activities are presented by skill area. Each activity specifies a behavioral objective, prerequisite skills, and a description of teaching materials and recording procedures.

Learning Abilities: Diagnostic and Instructional Procedures for Specific Learning Disabilities (Adams et al, 1972) is designed for mainstreamed preschool and kindergarten children with learning disabilities, emotional disturbance, mental retardation, physical handicaps, hearing impairments, or language delays. The curriculum is designed to aid classroom teachers in identifying a child's strengths and in planning individualized instructional programs. Each program contains specific objectives, suggested classroom materials, suggested evaluation procedures, and progress-record sheets.

The Cognitively Oriented Curriculum (Weikart, Rogers, Adcock, & McClelland, 1971) is a Piaget-based program for disadvantaged and educably mentally retarded children 3 and 4 years of age. Activities are presented for each of four content areas—classification, seriation, temporal relations, and spatial relations. An introduction to Piagetian theory and an outline of developmental stages is included along with instructions for using the curriculum. An activity guide gives examples of activities organized according to levels of symbolization (i.e., concrete object level, index level, symbol level, and sign level) and levels of operation (i.e., motoric level and verbal level).

An Experimental Curriculum for Young Mentally Retarded Children (Connor & Talbot, 1970) provides programming in seven areas of development for preschool educably mentally retarded children—self-help, social, intellectual, manipulative, imaginative creative expression, and motor skill areas. The curriculum guide presents objectives, teaching procedures, and activity ideas for each developmental area, all organized according to developmentally sequenced levels. Suggestions are also provided for programming in different settings.

The Wabash Guide to Early Developmental Training (Tilton, Liske, & Bousland, 1977) covers the motor, cognitive, language, self-care, and number concepts skill areas for infants to school-age children. This curriculum contains sequenced objectives, record forms, equipment lists, and detailed descriptions of teaching strategies and activities.

Learning Language at Home (Karnes, 1977) is a parent-oriented curriculum for normal children 3 to 5 years of age or for handicapped children at this developmental level. The intent is to train parents to use game-like activities to interact with their children and support their language development. The activities, based on the Illinois Test of Psycholinguistic Abilities, are sequenced according to difficulty. Each activity contains an ob-

jective, a list of materials needed, a step-by-step procedure, and related criterion activities. Additional suggestions for stimulating language development and assessing child progress are described in an accompanying manual.

A range of other organized teacher materials is also available. Lerner, Mardell-Czudnowski, and Goldenberg (1981) provide an extensive listing of many of these, including brief descriptions of each. They are classified into the areas of perceptual-motor, concepts, communications, social-affective, and comprehensive learning materials.

Scheduling

The way activities are organized throughout the day may need to be modified when handicapped children are integrated into a regular classroom. Since some handicapped children require more time to get set for learning tasks and to complete them than do their nonhandicapped peers, the daily schedule needs to be flexible. If learning centers are established, as suggested above, then the day can be organized into large blocks of time during which children alternate among a number of different learning tasks. This avoids the problem of some children having to wait for others to complete a task before moving on to new work. It also allows children to get started at learning tasks at varying times during the day, which allows the teacher to use time more freely, working with children when they need help rather than ushering all the children

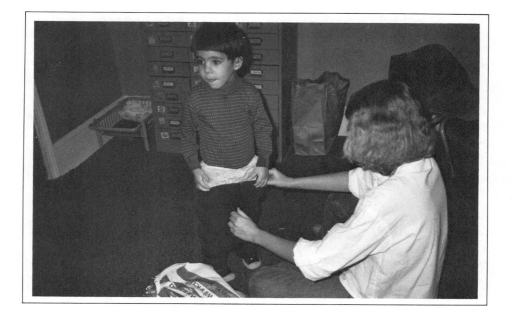

through activities together. The more flexible the teacher is with use of time, the more individualized the instruction can be, providing for the learning needs of all children in the class.

Transitions may present particular problems in an integrated classroom. Some handicapped children need more specific instructions on what to do while others have difficulty getting the necessary material together. To facilitate getting started, teachers can plan learning units for each child, putting materials into learning packets for the children before the school day begins. It is also helpful to provide children with adequate initial instructions in how to perform the learning tasks, possibly utilizing the same strategies over again to the extent that they serve the children's needs.

Cleanup may also present problems in an integrated classroom with some children needing special help or extra time. Handicapped children may find it difficult to put materials away properly. Instruction and demonstrations in cleanup procedures are often helpful. Pairing a handicapped child with a nonhandicapped child at cleanup is also useful.

Classroom schedules have to take into account the fact that some handicapped children are removed from class for special instruction or therapy during the school day. It is often possible to arrange schedules so that these children are not removed from their regular class during those times deemed most important by the classroom teacher because the child is doing particularly well in learning activities, because particularly important classroom instruction occurs then, or because those times allow for greatest social integration of handicapped and nonhandicapped children. Both the classroom teacher and the specialist have to be flexible in scheduling to provide the most appropriate educational programs.

Coordinate a Team Effort

When teachers become involved in educating handicapped children they must begin to become more a part of a team than was ever expected of them as members of the school staff. This is because preschool and primary classrooms are predominantly self-contained, and unless there are children mainstreamed in a class, the individual teacher generally assumes responsibility for the total education of the children in the class, possibly with a teacher aide or an assistant acting as an extension of the teacher. These additional personnel assume responsibility for teaching acts based on the decisions that the classroom teacher has made.

From the beginning of the identification process, however, the classroom teacher must team up with others on behalf of the handicapped child. Identification and assessment strategies require competencies far beyond those of the typical teacher. In fact, no one person can provide all services necessary for working with the handicapped. Only by pooling knowledge and skills can the quest for the most appropriate education for handicapped children come to fruition. In addition, the due

process requirements of such programs require that parents as well as children be involved in decision-making and in implementing the educational program.

The team to be assembled includes many people. The actual membership of a team may vary from school to school. The school administrator—whether principal or director—may serve as captain of the team, identifying appropriate team members, coordinating the efforts of all, and providing the backup to facilitate the team effort; or she or he may serve in a less active role. In addition, a range of specialists might be involved: psychologists, social workers, speech and language specialists, health professionals, special educators, social workers, parent-liaison workers, and others who might have a contribution to make.

Each person on the team will see the child's problem from his or her own perspective. The specialized knowledge that allows each person to contribute to the team also provides the perspective from which the child is seen and the diagnosis is made. Early childhood education has always been an interdisciplinary field with a commitment to the education of the whole child; an understanding of the child as a complete human being is basic to the development of a program concerned with each area of development and learning. Classroom teachers should not be intimidated by the specialized knowledge that other team members may bring to the school setting. While each specialist has knowledge-in-depth in a limited field, each lacks the perspective that the generalist teacher can bring. It is the teacher who has a sense

of the whole child, sees the way the child functions in a variety of situations, under different challenges, and in different social and physical settings. The understanding that comes from this total knowledge must temper any judgment that arises from knowledge of any one single attribute of the child. The classroom teacher has a major contribution to make in any decisions that the team arrives at concerning the most appropriate educational program for any handicapped child.

The team continues to work on behalf of the handicapped child well beyond the point when an Individualized Educational Plan (IEP) is developed, although not every member of the team will maintain the same level of involvement. Although the classroom teacher may have responsibility for the handicapped child's education most of the time, it is important that communication continue between teacher and specialist so that the efforts of all can be well coordinated. A special educator may also serve as a resource person to the teacher, making suggestions regarding instructional strategies, helping the teacher collect information on learning and behavior, providing supplementary material, and responding to requests the teacher might make. The resource teacher might also help with referrals for services beyond those available in the school.

As members of the team work with one another, they should develop new perspectives and be able to see the educational enterprise from one another's viewpoints. Each member of the team will be undergoing an educational experience through this team effort, learning right along with the handicapped child who is the focus of the process.

Along with the positive benefits of working as a team, there are costs. Teachers who work within a team can feel they lose some of their autonomy and flexibility of action. Decisions are not made by them alone: they must consult with others, justify their positions, and possibly make compromises. In addition, the process of communication requires time for team members to speak with one another, to plan together, and to record their actions. Conflicts can arise and will require attention if they are to be resolved. The leadership qualities of the school administrator may be tested in these situations, as she or he responds to a need to provide additional resources, to use interpersonal skills to clear up differences, and generally to facilitate the work of all involved while protecting the integrity of each team member.

Even with the involvement of many people, classroom teachers may feel that the burden and responsibility for the handicapped child is primarily theirs. In a way this is true, because in the long run, what happens between handicapped children, their peers, and their teachers in the regular classroom during the day will have the greatest impact on that child's education. Teaching continues to be a lonely profession, but there are things that can be done to make it less lonely. Teachers can look for others to assume some of the teaching tasks in the classroom: when teacher aides or assistants are available, they can share some of the burden, volunteers can also help, and many teachers have found that other children in the class can assume some of the responsibilities for instructing handicapped children.

Serving Handicapped Children

In public schools, handicapped children are usually served in either resource rooms or special classes. Special classes are designed primarily for children whose handicaps preclude mainstreaming as a placement. They are a type of special education service in which the child spends most or all of the school day in a self-contained classroom, apart from the regular education program and apart from nonhandicapped peers.

Resource rooms provide mainstreamed handicapped children with individual or small-group instruction in a special room outfitted for that purpose (Jenkins & Mayhall, 1973; Reger, 1973; Lilly, 1979). The emphasis is on teaching specific skills, either academic or behavioral, that the student needs. Thus, children are based in the regular class with their age-mates and leave only for certain periods of the school day for specific lessons.

Schools generally use one of three variations on the resource room model: the noncategorical, the categorical, and the itinerant.

In *noncategorical resource rooms,* which are the most widely used, children are provided with programs based on individual need. In this approach, a single instructional group could include cerebral palsied, emotionally disturbed, mentally retarded, and learning-disabled children who have the same instructional needs. This model, according to Hammill and

Wiederhold (1973), has at least three advantages: (1) handicapped children do not have to be transported to a school that has an appropriate categorical class; (2) a greater number of children can be served daily than can be served in a self-contained class; and (3) close communication is promoted between resource teachers and regular class teachers. The *categorical resource room* operates in the same way as the noncategorical resource room except that to qualify for placement, the child must fit into a specific group and be identified for example, as, mentally retarded, emotionally disturbed, or learning disabled.

In the *itinerant resource program* variation, the resource teacher is not based in any one school but travels among a number of schools. Such a teacher may visit from 20 to 50 children in as many as seven or eight different schools on a regular basis. The major advantage to this approach lies in the mobility of the teacher, which makes it effective in rural areas and with preschools that have small enrollments. It does have its problems, however. Since itinerant resource teachers are not based in any school, they may have difficulty being fully accepted by the staff in the schools they visit. In addition, much time is spent in transit, and transporting of materials from school to school may be a problem (McCarthy & Ray, 1971).

Resource consultant teachers may function in resource rooms, categorical or noncategorical, or as itinerant teachers. They are usually certified special education teachers who perform a variety of administrative, consultative, and direct-instructional functions.

Within the resource room, the resource teacher typically tests children to identify needs and then develops appropriate objectives, strategies, and methods for meeting those needs. With the assistance of an instructional aide, this teacher also provides direct teaching to children, usually in basic skill areas.

Outside the resource room, resource teachers act as advisors to regular classroom teachers, assisting in planning and implementing the children's programs. They may help teachers adapt or develop materials, or they may suggest commercially available materials. They also work jointly with classroom teachers to determine instructional objectives, teaching-learning procedures, and standards of acceptable performance by the handicapped in the mainstreamed classroom. With this type of help, most regular class teachers can provide successful learning opportunities for handicapped children.

Scheduling is a major problem for both resource and regular class teachers. It is not always possible to schedule students into a resource room for academic instruction when their classmates are receiving similar instruction. As a result, both the resource and regular class teacher must address these important questions:

1. When during the day can children be scheduled for instruction in the resource room?

2. Which regular class activities will students miss while attending the resource room?

3. What are the consequences of attending the resource room for instruction in academics?

Such scheduling issues are best resolved when classroom and resource teachers plan collaboratively. Any method for rendering service will be greatly enhanced by a spirit of coordination, cooperation, and communication among professionals.

Peer Tutoring

When a teacher is alone with a class of children, there is a limit to the number of interactions that are possible with individuals and small groups. Using peer tutors can provide the handicapped child with more instructional time than a teacher could provide alone, thus increasing the individualization in a classroom.

Young children can effectively teach tasks involving simple skills or activities that can be learned through modeling or imitation. Academic learnings that are simple to understand and that contain a sequence of objectives as well as many nonacademic learnings can be taught by peer tutors. Having a child read to another or to a group or having a child help another child count objects might help provide a young handicapped child with an understanding of the process of grouping and counting or of what is involved in gaining meanings from the printed page. Some of the areas in which peer tutoring is useful are listed in Figure 4-2.

Tutors should be selected because they wish to act as tutors; they should volunteer rather than be assigned. In part, wanting to be a tutor grows out of the relationship the teacher has with the children in the class. Children will want to tutor for a teacher who is warm and supportive. A good way to solicit

---

○ Teaching appropriate social behavior.

○ Teaching initiation of positive social interactions.

○ Teaching appropriate use of classroom materials.

○ Teaching play behaviors.

○ Teaching identification, discrimination, and labeling of colors, shapes, and simple quantities.

○ Teaching speech patterns.

○ Teaching basic letter-sound associations.

○ Teaching a simple sight vocabulary.

○ Teaching appropriate responses to oral reading.

○ Teaching spelling of simple words.

○ Teaching basic computational facts.

FIGURE 4-2
Areas in which young peers can function as tutors

volunteers for tutoring is to hold a short meeting with the class describing the tutoring program and providing examples of the kinds of activities involved in tutoring. Then the children could be invited to volunteer. Their decisions will thus be based on some understanding of what is expected of them. Even then, some children who volunteer may wish to withdraw along the way. This should be allowed.

Training tutors before they begin work with handicapped children anticipates difficulties and saves much time later. The training will vary depending upon the ability level of the tutors and the tasks expected of them. In informal tutoring, training is less extensive, perhaps only requiring brief instructions as to what is expected. In primary classrooms, for example, children may be paired off and given flash cards with addition or multiplication facts written on them. These children may only be told to teach each other

the facts on the cards. Other tasks require more elaborate training.

Tutors may be trained in small group sessions initially with individual training sessions provided later. Figure 4-3 is an example of a program for training peer tutors.

In supervising tutors, the teacher circulates around the classroom, observing interactions that take place, providing encouragement and praise, giving tutors instructional tips, and tutoring occasionally to provide a positive model. Praising tutors for good work is important. The teacher maintains responsibility for the teaching situation and should be available to deal immediately with problems and requests for help.

The tutors' skills also need to be continually improved. Teachers should check on learning problems that may go unnoticed, occasionally asking a student to read a page, respond to a set of flash cards, or perform some other

Objective: To train a nonhandicapped child to initiate positive social contacts with handicapped isolate peers.

Setting: Small training room near the child's classroom.

Procedures:

1. The teacher tells the nonhandicapped child that she is going to learn how to help the teacher by getting a certain child to play with her. The teacher indicates that asking children to play a game is what they will practice first.

2. The teacher models and explains how to play the game.

3. The tutor role plays and explains how to play the game.

4. During the role-playing activity, the teacher corrects the child's behavior and praises her for her efforts.

5. The teacher instructs the tutor that it is also important to give children toys to play with.

6. The teacher models how to approach a child and give her a toy.

7. The tutor role plays this procedure.

8. During the role playing the teacher corrects the child's behavior and praises her efforts.

9. The teacher models steps 2 and 6 with the isolate child while the tutor observes.

10. The tutor conducts steps 2 and 6 with the isolate child as the teacher observes and provides corrective feedback and praise.

11. The tutor conducts training while the teacher occasionally watches.

FIGURE 4-3

Program for training nonhandicapped children to initiate social contacts with isolate peers

task related to the tutorial. With this information the teacher can plan alternative procedures that could correct observed problems. A teacher can pick up problems before they become too distracting and can deal with them as necessary.

As tutors become more proficient, the teacher can supervise less directly, circulating through the room less frequently and paying less attention to specifics. But teachers should resist the temptation to decrease the amount of supervision prematurely. Direct supervision should be withdrawn tentatively, with the teacher increasing involve-

ment if children appear to be having difficulty. Telling tutors how to behave is never enough. The teacher must continually model those behaviors the tutors are to emulate and constantly offer praise as the tutor engages in instructional activities with children. The teacher must be concerned with being the kind of teacher she or he wishes the tutor to become.

Teachers can confer briefly with the tutor after each tutoring session, or at the end of the day. Such conferences allow the teacher both to gain information from the tutor and to discuss the child's progress and provide additional feedback for the tutor. Conferences are also a good time to discuss and plan new strategies with the tutor. Readers interested in learning more about peer tutoring are encouraged to consult Guralnick (1978); Gartner, Kohler, and Riesman (1972); and Devin-Sheehan, Feldman, and Allen (1976).

SUMMARY

Integrating a handicapped child into a regular classroom requires a great deal of thought and effort. Planning an individual program for that child may have to be done more systematically than is customary, with modifications made in the physical and temporal arrangements of the class as well as in the activities planned. The teacher will become a member of a multidisciplinary team concerned with the total education of that handicapped child. A resource room might be used to augment regular classroom instruction. Teachers must learn to use all resources available to them, including those that other children in the classroom provide. It is only through optimal use of all resources that the most appropriate educational experience can be provided for a handicapped child in an integrated setting. In the process of planning and implementing the plan, not only will the learning of the handicapped child be enhanced, but the learning of all those involved, adults as well as children.

In planning activities for handicapped children, it is important that we do not overdo the need to focus on specific needs and disabilities. While a handicapping condition may require teaching very specific skills and concepts in isolation, only by embedding these skills in the ongoing activities of the class and integrating learning will handicapped children become capable of living as normal a life as possible. Thus, teachers need to conceive of the school experience as a totality and focus on integrated experiences for all children.

REFERENCES

Adams, A. H. et al. *Learning abilities: Diagnostic and instructional procedures for specific learning disabilities*. New York: The Macmillian Publishing Co., 1972.

Allen, K. E. *Mainstreaming in early childhood education*. Albany, N.Y.: Delmar, 1980.

Blake, H. E. *Creating a learning-centered classroom*. New York: Hart, 1977.

Bloom, B. S. (Ed.). *Taxonomy of educational objectives. Handbook I: The cognitive domain*. New York: McKay, 1956.

Bluma, S. et al. *Portage guide to early education*. rev. ed. Portage, Wis.: Cooperative Educational Service Agency, No. 12, 1976.

Bos, C. *Curricular programming for young handicapped children: Project First Chance*. Tempe: Arizona State University, 1980.

Cole, K. J. and Stevenson, A. H. *Project PAR sequential curriculum for early learning*. Saginaw, Mich.: Saginaw County Child Development Centers, Inc., 1976.

Connor, F. P., and Talbot, M. E. *An experimental curriculum for young mentally retarded children*. New York: Teachers College Press, 1970.

Englemann, S. et al. *DISTAR*, Chicago: Science Research Associates, 1974.

Fallen, N. and McGovern, J. (Eds.). *Young children with special needs*. Columbus, Ohio: Merrill, 1978.

Gartner, A., Kohler, M. M., and Riesman, F. *Children teach children*. New York: Harper and Row, 1972.

Guralnick, M. J. (Ed.). *Early intervention and the integration of handicapped and nonhandicapped children*. Baltimore, Md.: University Park Press, 1978.

Hammill, D. D. and Wiederhold, J. L. *The resource room: Rationale and implementation*. Philadelphia: Journal of Special Education Press, 1973.

Haring, N. G. and Schiefelbusch, R. L. *Teaching special children*. New York: McGraw-Hill, 1976.

Hodgen, L., Koetter, J., LaForie, B., McCord, S., and Schramm, D. *School before six: A diagnostic approach*. St. Louis, Mo.: CEMREL, 1974.

Jenkins, J. and Mayhall, W. Describing resource teacher programs. *Exceptional Children*, 1973, *40*, 35–36.

Karnes, M. B. *Game oriented activities for learning* (GOAL). New York: Milton Bradley, 1972, 1973.

Karnes, M. B. *Learning language at home*. Reston, Va.: The Council For Exceptional Children, 1977.

Laycock, V. K. Prescriptive programming in the mainstream. In J. W. Schifani, R. M. Anderson, and S. J. Odle (Eds.). *Implementing learning in the least restrictive environment: Handicapped children in the mainstream*. Baltimore, Md.: University Park, 1980.

Lerner, J., Mardell-Czudnowski, C. M., and Goldenberg, D. *Special education for the early years*. Englewood Cliffs, N.J.: Prentice-Hall, 1981.

Lilly, M. S. (Ed.). *Children with exceptional needs: A survey of special education*. New York: Holt, Rinehart and Winston, 1979.

McCarthy, J., and Ray, M. C. Providing services in the public schools for children with learning disabilities. In D. Hammill and W. Bartel (Eds.). *Educational perspectives in learning disabilities*. New York: John Wiley and Sons, 1971.

Neisworth, J. T., Herb, S. J., Bagnato, S. J., Cartwright, C. A., and Laub, K. W. *Individualized education for preschool exceptional children*. Germantown, Md.: Aspen Systems, 1980.

Reger, R. What is a resource room? *Journal of Learning Disabilities*, 1973, *10*, 609–614.

Sanford, A. *Learning Accomplishments Profile*. Winston-Salem, N.C.: Kaplan School Supply, 1974.

Tilton, J. T., Liske, L. M., and Bousland, S. R. *Wabash guide to early developmental training*. Boston: Allyn & Bacon, 1977.

Walling, J. *The RADEA program*. Dallas, Tex.: Melton Book Company, 1976.

Weikart, D. P., Rogers, L., Adcock, C., and McClelland, D. *The cognitively oriented curriculum*. Urbana: University of Illinois, 1971.

Willoughby-Hulb, S. H., Neisworth, J. T., Laub, K. W., Hunt, F. and Llewellyn, E. *COMP curriculum and activity manual*. University Park: The Pennsylvania State University, 1980.

Five

DEVELOPING INDIVIDUALIZED EDUCATIONAL PROGRAMS

Until recently, regular classroom teachers played a minor role in designing the educational programs of handicapped children. Administrators, psychologists, and special educators often excluded them from decisions regarding placement and programming of these children (Turnbull, Strickland, and Brantley, 1978). Public Law 94-142, however, requires classroom teachers to assume an active role in developing Individualized Educational Programs (IEPs) for handicapped children who will be mainstreamed. For this reason, early childhood educators who work in integrated classrooms must become familiar with all aspects of the development of these required programs.

An IEP is a written statement about the objectives, content, implementation, and evaluation of a child's educational program (White & Haring, 1980). IEPs are required by law in order to determine that handicapped children are provided with a meaningful education appropriate to their needs and abilities. The IEP is a jointly-arrived-at formulation of the educational objectives proposed for the child, how they are to be attained, and how the results will be evaluated.

This chapter provides an overview of Individualized Educational Programs, what they are, who develops them, how they are developed, and what information they contain. The reader interested in more information on IEPs might consult Morgan, 1981; Tymitz-Wolf, 1981; and Siders and Whorton, 1982.

THE IEP TEAM

An IEP is developed by a multidisciplinary team that consists of individuals from different professional disciplines, including the child's teacher, the special education teacher, an evaluation specialist and other ancillary personnel.

Each brings a different set of professional competencies and perspectives to bear on the assessment of and planning for the child's needs. It also includes the child's parent(s) or guardian(s) and the child (when appropriate). Each member of this team, known as the child study or IEP team, plays a unique role in the process of formulating the IEP.

The IEP team may be chaired by the building principal, a special educator, the classroom teacher, or another member of the team. The chair schedules and presides over the IEP conference, advises parents of their rights, calls upon individual staff members to present and discuss assessment data, and presents the school's recommendations for programming. The chair also sees that the basic components of the IEP are stated in writing

and that the completed IEP is signed by all members, including the parents.

The child's teacher(s) is anyone who has or will be providing direct instruction to the child. Normally, this includes both the child's regular and special class teachers. Their responsibilities include describing the child's classroom performance, explaining to parents the various techniques that will be used, and answering any questions about what will occur in the classroom.

The teacher can also help to prepare the parents for the IEP meeting by explaining the purposes of the IEP and the IEP conference, reviewing the events that will occur, discussing with parents their rights and responsibilities, and mentioning questions parents might be asked so they can think about them before the conference. Such questions might include:

o What are the most important skills for your child to learn?

o Are there problems for your child at home that might be addressed at school?

o What methods have you found effective in rewarding and punishing your child?

By providing questions ahead of time, parents will have an opportunity to think about the kind of comments they would like to make at the IEP conference.

Parents must be informed of and should agree to all actions concerning their child, including referral of the child to the child study team. If parents do disagree with the IEP, an appeals procedure must be followed. The team must also try to find a time and place to meet that is convenient for the parents and, if neither parent can attend, the team is expected to involve parents in other ways. Telephone calls, including conference calls, can be used. Additionally, the team is required to keep a record of its attempts to arrange meetings and to see that the parents are informed of the outcomes of any meetings they do not attend.

At the IEP conference, parents should be encouraged to take an active role in designing their child's program. They should be made to feel comfortable and should be asked to express their views about the child's curriculum and educational services. Parents should also be prepared to describe their child's out-of-school behavior, to participate in making placement decisions and to specify what type of responsibility they are willing to assume in implementing the IEP.

The child, when appropriate, should be included in the team meetings. Although this is not a widely practiced option, especially with younger children, children in junior or senior high school do occasionally participate.

The evaluation specialist, often the school psychologist, is generally called upon to report on and interpret psychological evaluations (including standardized tests) of individual children and to make recommendations to the team based on these evaluations.

Ancillary staff are auxiliary personnel who are included on the team when the child has a disability that requires the services of a particular specialist. If a child has difficulties in speech or language, for example, a communications disorders specialist should be included in the team. If the child is blind, a mobility instructor might be included. If the child has a physical disability, a physical or occupational therapist, or both, should be on the team to help assess the child and assist in writing the IEP. Other staff members who may be involved in developing the IEP include curriculum specialists, audiologists, ophthalmologists, social workers, guidance counselors, medical and health personnel, and representatives of community agencies, such as Easter Seals, that serve the handicapped. Table 5-1 summarizes the responsibilities of each member of the ancillary staff in helping to formulate an IEP.

The IEP is considered the product of a team effort with individuals with different specific concerns and different perspectives jointly working in the interests of the child. While in most cases all team members will agree as to the nature of the child's problem and

TABLE 5-1 Ancillary personnel and their responsibilities on the IEP team	
Personnel	**Responsibilities**
Evaluation Specialist/ School Psychologist	Administers and interprets developmental and diagnostic tests; makes observations of child in the classroom.
Speech and Language Therapist	Evaluates and treats language disorders as well as disorders of articulation, voice or fluency; serves as resource consultant to teacher.
Physical Therapist	Evaluates and treats physical handicaps involving gross motor movements; frequently designs programs for gross motor development or to provide exercise fitting the child's needs.
Occupational Therapist	Evaluates and treats disorders involving fine motor movements, especially those associated with the self-help skills (buttoning, zipping, and tying) as well as skills related to writing.
Audiologist	Identifies hearing impairments; tests, quantifies loss of air and bone conduction, and determines whether referral to an otologist (physician who treats the ear) is indicated for a hearing aid or for medical treatment.
School Nurse	Evaluates a variety of minor health problems; refers more serious problems to appropriate medical specialists.
Social Worker	Investigates homes and neighborhoods; prepares summaries of cases served by other social agencies; assists in acquiring social and personal data.
Physician	Diagnoses, treats, and refers organic-based problems, including vision and hearing problems, nutritional deficiencies, and organic brain damage, as well as health problems.
Special Class Teachers	Remediate areas of exceptionality such as mental retardation or learning disabilities; consult with regular class teachers on educational methods and materials.

the most appropriate education program for the child, this is not always the case. When disagreements arise, a team member has the option of writing a dissenting opinion to be appended to the IEP.

STAGES IN DEVELOPING THE IEP

In most cases, the team develops the IEP in the following stages.

Referral.   The first stage, referral, occurs when the parents, teachers, principal, physician, or other ancillary personnel request that a child they suspect is handicapped be assessed. The referral process must be initiated by a representative of the local educational agency, who informs the parents and then helps select and organize the IEP team. The team then meets to review the referral and, when appropriate, interviews the referral agent about the nature of the child's problem, when it occurs, and what, if any, strategies have been tried to remediate it.

Preliminary Diagnostic Screening.
The next stage, preliminary diagnostic screening, provides data on the history of the referred student. This informa-

tion may come from the child's cumulative school record and from interviews with parents, teachers, and other personnel who are knowledgable about the child's educational, psychological, emotional, social, and physical status. After reviewing the student's history, the IEP team decides to either accept or reject the referral. If the referral is accepted, written parent permission is obtained for the third stage-assessment.

Assessment Plan.   An assessment plan must be designed and administered based on the information as to the child's needs obtained in the preliminary screening. The plan may involve administering standardized tests or more informal inventories in such areas as self-help skills; general readiness; perceptual capabilities; or reading, language, and social skills. It may

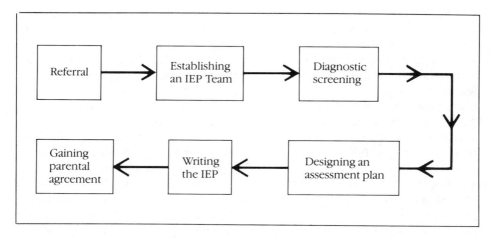

FIGURE 5-1
Stages in developing an IEP

TABLE 5-2
Sources and uses of information for developing the IEP

Source*	Use
1. Referral forms	Helps form hypotheses on cause of child's problem and determine other kinds of information needed.
2. School records	Provide information on student's education history and whether or not there are recurring problems in student's background.
3. Standardized tests (norm-referenced tests)	Tell how child compares with other children in such areas as development and achievement.
4. Criterion-referenced tests	Assess child's level of accomplishment in relation to a set of goals, without reference to accomplishments of other children.
5. Observation	Provides a picture of child characteristics and behaviors (e.g., social interactional) in the classroom or other environments.
6. Interviews with parents/guardians	Provide information on child's behavior in settings other than the school.
7. Work samples	Provide samples of child's performance.

*Chapter 6 on assessment, presents each source in detail.

---

also involve classroom observations. At some point prior to the IEP meeting a representative of the school must meet with the parents to present, interpret, and discuss the assessment data collected. If, based on all available information (see Table 5-2), the team decides that special education services are advisable, they proceed to the final stage—writing the IEP.

Writing the IEP.   The IEP may be written in two steps. In the first step, a preplanning session, staff members who work with the child meet to exchange information and to write a preliminary draft of the IEP. This draft is then presented to the parents for discussion, revision, and, hopefully, their approval in the IEP meeting.

Responsibility for actually writing the IEP customarily falls upon the IEP committee chair with help from other team members, although this can vary from school to school. Teachers and specialists usually identify specific long- and short-term goals and related treatment plans. Although there are variations by state and by school district in the forms used for recording them, the IEP must contain written statements of the child's present levels of performance and of annual goals and short-term objectives; the special education and related services to be provided; the extent to which the child will participate in regular education programs; the objective criteria by which progress on the IEP will be measured; a justification for the child's educational placement; and written parent approval.

CONTENTS OF THE IEP

The **statements of present levels of performance** describe the child's current educational achievement in such areas as academic achievement and social, vocational, psychomotor, and self-help skills. These statements should relate actual school performance as observed by teachers and others as well as test results. The IEP team typically reviews current assessment data, identifies areas in which instruction is needed, and summarizes the child's present functioning level.

SAMPLE STATEMENTS OF PRESENT LEVEL OF PERFORMANCE

Tom, a third grade student, is experiencing mild learning problems and, based on a case evaluation and referral, is considered eligible for special education and related services. At the IEP conference, Tom's evaluators and teachers bring samples of his classwork and test scores. The team, including Tom's parents, generate the following statements describing his present levels of performance:

1. Tom reads at beginning first grade level as measured by the Metropolitan Achievement Test and the Dolch Sight Word List. Results of an informal reading inventory administered by his teacher showed that Tom read a first grade reader at less than 10 words per minute and comprehended approximately 30 percent of what he read.

2. An arithmetic test showed that Tom's computational skills were average for a third grader but that, because of reading problems, he had considerable difficulty in completing story problems.

3. Tom's daily school work indicates that his penmanship is almost illegible.

4. Teacher observation records show that Tom is often out of his seat, talks out a great deal, and is generally off-task during work periods.

Tom's planners at the IEP conference identified the following general educational needs: (a) to improve reading fluency and comprehension, (b) to increase accuracy in solving story problems in math, (c) to increase legibility of his penmanship, (d) to decrease the number of talkouts and out-of-seat behaviors, and (e) to increase the amount of time spent working on school-related tasks.

In the example provided, the description of present educational performance was written in clear, concise language. The instruments or processes used in evaluation were identified. Other examples of statements describing a young handicapped child's present levels of performance are:

○ Bob reads 85 percent of the Dolch Sight Word List at the first grade level.

○ Ellen can read silently at a 1.1 grade level, demonstrating good comprehension when answering oral questions concerning facts, the main idea, and sequencing of events, but has poor comprehension when answering questions requiring her to draw inferences.

○ Teacher observations show that Marie seldom interacts positively with other children during free play in the classroom or outdoors.

○ Based on the Peabody Individual Achievement Test (PIAT), Edward is functioning approximately one year below grade placement in listening comprehension, word recognition and analysis, hearing sounds in words, and phonic spelling of words.

○ Samuel's cursive handwriting is often illegible. He has problems with letter formation and spacing and reveals habitual reversals of *b* and *d* and inversions of *m* amd *w*.

Once team members are satisfied with the statements of present levels of performance they proceed to write the annual goals.

An **annual goal** describes what the individual is expected to learn by the end of a school year. These goals, written for each area of disability, should be based on the child's present performance levels and should represent a reasonable estimate of how well the child might be expected to progress in the new program. Priorities for annual goals should also be established according to the student's most immediate needs. The number of goals developed depends upon such variables as the student's chronological and mental age, the amount of instructional time devoted to each area, and the priority needs of the student.

In the hypothetical case of Tom, cited earlier, it was decided, based on present levels of performance, that he needed to improve his reading fluency and comprehension, increase the legibility of his penmanship, decrease the number of talk outs and out-of-seat behavior, and increase the time spent on school-related tasks. His IEP team might translate these needs into the following annual goals, ordered in terms of importance:

By year's end, Tom should:

1. be reading on at least a beginning second grade level at a rate of 30 words per minute with less than 2 words per minute incorrect and at an 80 percent comprehension level

2. be able to compute at least three different types of story problems

3. be able to write legibly all upper and lower case cursive letters in isolation and, if possible, connected writing

4. stay in his seat for at least 60 percent of assigned work periods

TABLE 5-3
Combining related skills into annual goals

Skill area	Related skills	Goal
Academics	Write lowercase cursive letters Write upper case cursive letters Form whole words	Child will write all lower and upper case letters in cursive and use them in connected writing.
Motor	Draw triangles with pencil Draw circles with crayon Draw squares with pen Color pictures Cut out pictures Paste pictures	Child will be able to draw common geometric shapes (e.g., triangle, circle, square) with pencil, crayon, and pen; use crayon to color pictures; cut them out; and paste them up.
Social	Interact appropriately with boys Interact appropriately with girls Interact appropriately with regular class teacher Interact appropriately with special class teacher Interact appropriately with parents	Child will interact appropriately with peers, all teachers, and parents.

5. raise his hand 80 percent of the time before speaking during assigned work periods

6. spend at least 80 percent of assigned work periods working on school-related tasks

Goal statements do not define exact instructional tasks that students need to learn. Instead, they furnish long-range direction for an individual's program development. One problem in writing an annual goal is in deciding how narrow or global the goal should be. The aim, according to many school district guidelines, should be to identify and group related skills into clusters. For example, a kindergartener working on self-help skills, would have an annual goal stating that she or he will be able to put on inner and outer clothing instead of three separate goals such as the ability to put on a (1) coat, (2) hat, and (3) shoes. Table 5-3 provides several other examples illustrating how to combine related skills into a single annual goal.

In writing annual goals, the team should recognize that, especially with handicapped children, goal-setting is a complex process. It involves making predictions about children who do not progress in the normal manner and about whose progress we have little knowledge to guide us. For these reasons, annual goals are viewed by educators as only an estimate of where a child will be at the end of one year. Local educational agencies are seldom held accountable if the child does not achieve the projected growth.

Short-term instructional objectives describe the program steps that will move the child from his or her present levels of performance to the performance level required by the annual goal. These are usually established by the classroom teacher. Separate objectives are usually written and sequenced, from simple to complex, for each goal. Generally, short-term objectives describe what a child might be expected to achieve in one or two months; but shorter or longer intervals are acceptable so long as there is a direct relationship between progress on the objectives and attainment of the goal.

For Tom, who had an annual goal of computing three types of story problems, the IEP team might recommend the following short-term objectives:

Goal: to compute 3 types of story problems.
Short-Term Objectives:

1) Given a worksheet with story problems yielding equations such as $2 + 3 = N, 9 - 6 = N, 4 + 7 = N$, Tom will compute 20 problems with 90% accuracy for 3 consecutive days.

2) Given a worksheet with story problems yielding equations such as $2 + N = 5, 2 - N = 1, 7 + N = 100$, Tom will compute 25 problems with 90% accuracy for 3 consecutive days.

3) Given a worksheet with story problems yielding equations such as $N + 6 = 9, N - 7 = 10, N + 1 = 16$, Tom will compute 30 problems with 90% accuracy for 3 consecutive days.

4) Given a worksheet with all three types of story problems— $2 + 3 = N, 2 + N = 5, N + 3 = 7$ —Tom will compute 20 problems with 90% accuracy for 3 consecutive days.

Short-term objectives, should be written in clear, concise, and observable terms. Verbs such as *list, solve, point, write, say,* or *compute* are preferred because they are explicit as to what the learner will do to demonstrate having reached a goal. In addition, many state regulations require that short-term objectives include at least four components—(1) a learner, (2) an observable, measurable skill, (3) conditions under which the skill will be performed, and (4) a standard or criterion—as in these examples:

○ Given 5 typed paragraphs, each containing 5 declarative sentences with no punctuation marks (*condition*), Tom (*the learner*) will correctly place a period at the end of each sentence (*skill*) with 90% accuracy (*criterion*).

○ Given a worksheet containing 20 two-digit subtraction problems with renaming (*condition*), Jenny (*student*) will compute all problems (*skill*) with at least 90% accuracy (*criterion*).

○ Craig (*the learner*) will correctly put on and tie his shoes (*skill*) with 90% accuracy (*criterion*) when they are placed before him by his teacher (*condition*).

TABLE 5-4
Sample form for writing short-term objectives

Child's Name: Bob Smith

Goal: To compute 3 types of story problems

Condition	**Behavior**	**Criterion**
Given worksheet containing:		
1. 20 story problems yielding equations such as $2 + 3 = N$, $4 + 1 = N$	compute	90% accuracy for 3 consecutive days
2. 25 story problems with equations such as $2 + N = 3$, $1 + N = 7$	compute	90% accuracy for 3 consecutive days
3. 30 story problems with equations such as $N + 6 = 7$, $N + 4 = 11$	compute	90% accuracy for 3 consecutive days
4. 30 story problems with all three types of equations: $N + 6 = 7, 2 + N = 5$, $2 + 3 = N$	compute	90% accuracy for 3 consecutive days

---

It is often unnecessary to write out the entire objective in the form shown above. A more efficient way to write short-term objectives is shown in Table 5-4. The arrangement implies that the short-term instructional objectives contribute directly to the annual goal and that both the goal and objectives were written for a particular child.

In writing short-term objectives, team members can draw on a variety of sources including commercial materials, school district curriculum guides, and textbook skill charts. Generally, these sources contain large numbers of objectives in specific skill areas—math, reading, or language—that are arranged in levels of increasing complexity. Assessment instruments for determining entry and progress on the curriculum can also be included. The IEP team can adapt these sequences and objectives to meet the needs of the individual.

If commercial materials or curriculum guides are not available or are inadequate to assist the team in writing and sequencing objectives, the team can develop their own. The aim here is to break goals into smaller steps, arrange the steps in logical order, and then write each step as a short-term objective.

A statement of special education and related services needed to achieve each short-term objective must be listed in the IEP. Specifically, the planners should note the type of special education service, the extent to which it is needed, the setting that will best pro-

---

DEVELOPING SHORT-TERM OBJECTIVES

Barbara, a motorically handicapped preschooler, has an annual goal of developing the pincer grasp. Her IEP team identifies the following short-term objectives:

1. Barbara will hold a rocker stacker ring in her hands for one minute.

2. Barbara will pick up three objects placed 1 inch away from her in one minute using a palmar grasp.

3. Barbara will pick up six 1-inch cubes using a pincer grasp in one minute.

The team would probably decide that an occupational therapist would be best to evaluate Barbara's progress. They would then note on the IEP the special service of occupational therapy, the name of the therapist, when these services would begin and end, and how the services would be evaluated.

---

vide the needed support, how much time will be provided, and who will provide the service.

Special media and materials not routinely used in regular classrooms must be listed on the IEP next to the short-term instructional objectives for which they will be used. Examples include hearing aids, low vision aids, prosthetic devices or adaptive equipment, special transportation, or special instructional materials such as Language Masters or audiotapes. It is helpful to list these materials by name, author, publisher, and level and to indicate the dates on which the materials will be used. A brief comment on the potential effectiveness of the materials may also be included.

The projected date for initiation and termination of special education services are also included. This helps to prevent handicapped children from having to wait to receive services. In addition, by recording the anticipated duration of services, the team is better

able to assess individual progress and to set realistic aims for students in future years. The school system will also benefit by being better able to determine when openings will occur in existing programs and when services will be available. Because students may progress faster or slower than anticipated, statements of duration of services, like annual goals, are viewed as estimates.

The nature of the student's participation in regular education must be spelled out in the IEP. This statement, reported as the percentage of time (or number of hours) to be spent in the regular classroom, serves to emphasize the importance of placement in the least restrictive environment and the importance of helping the child maintain as much contact with nonhandicapped peers as possible. Activities such as recess and lunch, as well as academic instruction, should be included. The team should be careful, however, to list only those activities in which planned, meaningful interaction will occur. The following is a sample statement:

"Joan, age 7, will attend social studies, art, and physical education classes with regular class peers for three hours daily."

Appropriate objective criteria and a schedule for evaluating progress must, by law, be included to ensure that progress is being made and to ascertain whether revisions of the IEP are necessary. The exact method and criteria to be used to evaluate progress must also be specified in the IEP. Procedures for reviewing progress on annual goals and short-term objectives should be conducted at least annually (but preferably at shorter intervals), and should address the following questions:

1. Is the educational placement still appropriate?

2. Are the same ancillary staff still necessary?

3. Are the deficits being remediated?

4. Are the recommended goals and procedures still appropriate?

5. Are assigned responsibilities of team members being carried out?

6. If the plan is not appropriate, are adjustments necessary in the goal statements, timeliness, instructional objectives, instructional strategies, materials, resources, personnel involved, or monitoring system?

If the team decides that major program revisions are required, they must obtain written parent permission for a new program.

Besides specifying evaluation criteria, the team must also recommend and justify an educational placement for the child. This statement describes the child's placement and why it was selected, and states that the entire team (including the parents) agrees with the placement.

Upon completion of the IEP, regulations require that parents agree in writing to the decisions made by the IEP team. Thus, IEP forms include a signature line on which parents or guardians indicate their approval. If parents disagree about any matter concerning the child's evaluation or program, including the IEP itself, the local school must provide mechanisms for appeal, including impartial due process hearings. In any due process hearing, which is chaired by an impartial hearing officer who is not an employee of the school, the parent has a right to: (1) be accompanied by a lawyer or other counselor, (2) present evidence, (3) confront and cross examine witnesses, and (4) obtain a transcript of the hearing or a written decision by the hearing officer. If dissatisfied with the decision of the hearing officer, parents have a right to appeal to their state educational agency and, if still dissatisfied, to federal or state court.

In addition to the specific items reviewed above, the IEP should also include basic biographical information (e.g., date of birth, sex, home address), the names and positions of each person on the IEP team, meeting dates, and individual recommendations of team members who may disagree with the final IEP. Sample forms on which IEPs can be written follow.

SUMMARY

This chapter has described *Individualized Educational Programs* or IEPs. The IEP should be written by a child study team that includes the teacher, the parents or guardians, other personnel, and in some instances, the child. It must spell out specific long- and short-range goals and objectives for the child and how these will be accomplished and under what circumstances. It must also state specifically how the effectiveness of the program will be evaluated.

Once the IEP is developed and approved, placement of the child has been made, and services have been initiated, instructional intervention in the mainstream can begin.

REFERENCES

Morgan, D. Characteristics of a quality IEP. *Education Unlimited*, 1981, *3*, 12–17.

Siders, J. A., and Whorton, J. E. The relationship of individual ability and IEP goal statements. *Elementary School Guidance and Counseling*, 1982, *16*, 187–193.

Turnbull, A., Strickland, B., and Brantley, J. *Developing and implementing individ-ualized educational programs*. Columbus, Ohio: Merrill, 1978.

Tymitz-Wolf, B. Guidelines for assessing IEP goals and objectives. *Teaching Exceptional Children*, 1981, *14*, 198–201.

White, O., and Haring, W. G. *Exceptional teaching*. Columbus, Ohio: Merrill, 1980.

SAMPLE IEPs

IEP forms differ from state to state, and within states, from school district to school district. The following sample IEPs are included to give the teacher an idea of what such forms might be like, the kinds of information they might include, and the type of space constraints the teacher will have to deal with. The two IEPs included are copies of actual IEPs developed for two children of different ages, with different problems, and from different communities. They have been modified to eliminate any identifying information. They are representative of what teachers actually do in regard to IEPs, rather than of what an ideal IEP might look like.

DIVISION FOR EXCEPTIONAL CHILDREN
INDIVIDUALIZED EDUCATIONAL PROGRAM

(Attach assessment data)

Student's name: Aaron Anderson

Date of Birth: 6/25/78   Age: 4 yrs. 4 mos.

School: Adams   Grade: preschool   Class: Recommend integrated class

Current Services: Currently in nonintegrated ECH class

Program Level(s) Recommended: Integrated preschool class

Related Services: Speech therapy 2 times weekly; Orthopedic therapy one
day a week for a month to learn how to maneuver in corrective shoes.

I give consent for my child (named above) to receive program(s) and service(s)
as described

_____

Signature

_____

Relationship to child

_____

Date

Date(s) of IEP Meeting(s): 10/18/82

Dates of IEP implementation From: 10/18/82

To: 5/18/83

IEP Development Team

Signatures	*Position*
_____	Chair
_____	D.E.C. Representative
_____	Referring Teacher
_____	Parent

Formal testing and evaluation information

Test used	Pre-test date	Post-test date	Tester	Comments
Alpern-Boll	8/18/82		Maxine Saul	
Chronological Age	4 yrs. 2 mos.			
Physical Age	3 yrs. 9 mos.			
Self-Help Age	5 yrs. 1 mo.			
Social Age	3 yrs. 4 mos.			
Academic Age	3 yrs. 0 mos.			
Communication Age	3 yrs. 11 mos.			

Present level of performance	Annual goals	Short-term objectives	Evaluation criteria	Projected date of mastery	Special materials, strategies, and/or techniques
I) Cognitive A) Aaron is able to imitate a *t* and *u*. B) He is able to draw a diagonal line from corner to corner on a 4" square paper. C) He counts 10 objects in imitation and builds a bridge with 3 blocks in imitation.	I) Cognitive A) S will develop basic concepts of color, size, shape, and number.	I) Cognitive A) Given a choice of 5 colors, S will point to color named by teacher. B) When asked, S will rote count to 5. C) When asked, S will correctly identify big and little objects. D) Given a choice of 4 shapes, S will identify and name triangle, circle, and square.	80% accuracy 100% accuracy 100% accuracy 90% accuracy	5/83 3/83 2/83 4/83	

Present level of performance	Annual goals	Short-term objectives	Evaluation criteria	Projected date of mastery	Special materials, strategies, and/or techniques

II) Self-help
    Aaron dresses himself, with some difficulty fastening. He buttons and unbuttons and zips and unzips when not requested to work the catch. He has good feeding skills and uses utensils well. He can prepare some of his own food (e.g., sandwich) and can go to the bathroom unaided, with some accidents at night.
 	
III) Motor
    A) In gross motor skills, S is able to jump from 8″ height, pedal a tricycle and turn corners, and bounce and catch a large ball.
    B) In fine motor skills, he cuts a 4″ line, grasps pencil and crayons in the proper way, and can screw together a threaded object.					

Present level of performance	Annual goals	Short-term objectives	Evaluation criteria	Projected date of mastery	Special materials, strategies, and/or techniques
IV) Socialization. S has just completed two months in an ECH* program and has thus had few opportunities for interaction with peers. He follows short, simple rules in adult directed games and will repeat rhymes, songs, or dances. S is also able to describe feelings about self such as mad, happy, and love.	A) S will develop associative and cooperative play skills. B) S will increase attending skills.	A) S will play at a cooperative level with at least 1 other child for 15 minutes. B) S will learn to take turns. C) S will ask permission to use a toy that a peer is playing with. D) S will sit and attend to a task for 15 minutes.	Teacher Observation Teacher Observation Teacher Observation Teacher Observation	5/83 1/83 1/83 5/83	
V) Communication When requested, S can tell his full name, explain how common objects are used, and carry out a series of 3 directions. He also imitates much of the adult speech he hears.					

*Early Childhood Education for the Handicapped

INDIVIDUALIZED EDUCATIONAL PROGRAM

Date: 6/11/83

Name: Charlene Martin

Date of Birth: 12/10/74

School: Southview El.   Grade: 2

Parents Name: Mr. & Mrs. Henry Martin

Address: 2275 S. Washington Street

Phone: 555-8376

Personnel Attending Conferences (names)

Classroom Teacher: Ian Dower

Special Education Teacher:

Psychologist:

Speech & Language Specialist: Rose Wheeler

Social Worker:

Parent: Mr. & Mrs. Martin

Other: George Wall, OTR; Sandy Decker, PT

Present Levels of Performance

Reading: Second grade reader

Language Arts: Generally first
    grade

Math: First grade

Other: Charlene has Downs Syndrome

Annual Goals:

1. Improve articulation of sounds.
2. Improve auditory processing.
3. Improve expressive language skills.
4. Continue strengthening knees,
   hips, and ankles.
5. Continue improving balance.
6. Continue improving visual-motor
   skills.
7. Continue improving proximal joint
   stability.

Child's Strengths:

Reading skills

Socialization skills

Child's Deficits:

Body tone

Visual motor development

Articulation production in
    conversational speech

Auditory processing; expressive
    language

Participation in Regular Program

Areas of study: *Percentage of time:*

regular multi-age   all day

primary class

Assessment used:

Annual goal	Specific objectives	Methods	Comments
Expressive language	Encourage conversational interchange in spontaneous speech. Expand use of adjectives in phrases and sentences. Establish appropriate use of *is* and *are*. Increase expressive vocabulary. Reinforce appropriate use of pronouns (*be*, *she*, *they*) in sentences. Expand length of utterances in sentences to an average of 5 and 6 words. Establish the use of *who*, *what*, and *where* questions. Establish appropriate reversals of words in questions.		
Articulation	Reinforce correct production of /p/ /b/ /w/ /h/ in conjunction with clinician at Community Language Clinic.		
Auditory processing	Recall a four-stage command. Listen to questions and respond appropriately. Verbally relay incidents of the previous day and week. Comprehend categorization of items (food, clothing, animals, etc.).		
Improve balance	Balance on L or R foot, eyes open for 5 sec.	Ball Gymnastics Seated bounce Roll hips forward/back; Roll hips L & R hop on 1 foot walk straight line; various patterns	
Increase muscle strength Hip extension & abduction	Do 10 hip extensions and 10 hip abductions L and R	Ball gymnastics: prone—airplanes	

Annual goal	Specific objectives	Methods	Comments
Knee extension	Use 2# weight on ankle; do 10 extensions L and R seated, feet unsupported	Side-lying leg lifts. Floor exercises—prone and seated, feet unsupported—leg extensions.	
Gross motor		Trike riding Jumping Jacks Angels in the snow Run & kick ball Jump down from height	
Eye/hand coordination	Catch ball independently in various situations	Ball handling (bounce, catch). Catch ball bounced 1' to either side. Catch ball thrown 2-3' above head. Imitate clapping—regular and irregular rhythms.	

Six

ASSESSING YOUNG HANDICAPPED CHILDREN

Educational assessment is an important part of the design of an individualized education program for the young handicapped child. It enables the teacher to become familiar with a child's abilities and deficiencies early and in a way that can be used to improve educational programming. Assessment generally involves systematic observation and analysis of a child's abilities and deficits. Initial assessment provides teachers with diagnostic information and determines a starting point for educational programming. Ongoing assessment helps evaluate the effectiveness of current instruction and suggests new directions for educational plans. Assessment is usually conducted by the teacher with the help of others —paraprofessionals and parents and frequently ancillary personnel such as speech and language therapists or school psychologists. The attributes measured may include language, motor, perceptual, social, self-help and cognitive skills, and in some instances, math and reading skills or readiness.

Program development for handicapped children involves five general steps: (1) determining the educational goals for the program, (2) determining the child's functional level in relation to each of these goals, (3) designing and implementing an educational program, (4) periodically reassessing the child's progress, and (5) continuing the present plan or devising new strategies to achieve the goals.

To carry out these tasks, classroom teachers must be familiar with various information gathering and evaluation techniques. These include observation techniques, assessment inventories, and formal and informal tests, as well as techniques for recording the information and making judgements.

All assessment involves some type of observation. It may involve observing a written response on an assignment, observing behavior in a specially designed, highly controlled test situation, or observing reactions and behavior that occur naturally during routine classroom activities. Each kind of observation has its own advantages and disadvantages and provides different information.

Teachers need to be concerned with the validity, reliability, and practicality of the assessment techniques available to them. **Validity** concerns the extent to which a technique assesses what it is supposed to assess. To be valid, a reading readiness test should be related to children's abilities to benefit from reading instruction and should predict the child's success in learning to read. A test of intelligence that requires a child to read or to follow extensive verbal directions may actually be testing language ability and not be a valid indicator of intelligence.

Reliability indicates the consistency that characterizes a means of measuring behavior. Sometimes chance will so influence a child's score on a test, for example, that repeated testing yields very different results. Such a test is un-

reliable. Sometimes young children's characteristics are so changeable that it is difficult to find a reliable measure. A test that is only valid would not be useful to a teacher.

Practicality relates to the ability of the teacher to use the assessment technique with ease. Some techniques, such as direct observation, may be too time consuming to be practical for a teacher in a self contained classroom. Other techniques may require skills beyond those expected of a teacher. Thus, giving a Wechsler Intelligence Test to a child is impractical unless there is a psychologist available to administer it.

There are four principal techniques used by teachers to assess child behavior in the classroom: (1) direct observation, (2) assessment inventories, (3) standardized tests, and (4) informal tests.

DIRECT OBSERVATION

Direct observation involves systematically watching and recording child behavior as it occurs. Many behaviors of young children are easily assessed by observation; these include showing respect, cooperation, levels of dramatic play, or increases in sentence speaking. Such observation also allows teachers to assess such variables as group participation and responsiveness, individual performance in group situations, attitudes toward school work, student-teacher interactions, and the effectiveness of different teaching methods and materials. Direct observation provides

teachers with an immediate view of performance in natural settings.

Because observations leave intact the natural scheme of things, they are seen as an appropriate measurement technique by most in early childhood educators (Goodwin & Driscoll, 1980).

Observations help focus teacher attention on what actually happens rather than allowing them to rely on impressions or subjective judgments. Young children are open and relatively unchanged or little bothered by being observed. They are less likely to camouflage or alter their behavior when observed than are older children or adults. By comparison, a formal test instrument elicits unusual or new behaviors from young children and often signals them to alter their behavior in accordance with the new situation (Lowenbraun & Affleck, 1976).

Guidelines to Observation

Teachers and others who work with young children are in a unique position to collect observational data on their students. Because of their daily association with children in familiar settings, teachers are able to observe children's performance for extended periods of time. With a little training and practice, teachers can learn to observe children's behavior objectively and precisely.

Types of Observation

A number of different types of observation techniques can be used by teachers. These include both direct and indirect forms of observation. Direct forms are specimen records, event records, duration records, time sampling, event sampling, placheck (planned activity check), student participation charts, media, and work samples (Cooper, 1974). Indirect forms include anecdotal records, checklists, and rating scales. These forms can be used in combination. Indirect forms of observation, which don't require the observer to record all behaviors, often include teacher impressions and require teachers to make judgements. This is less the case with the more direct forms. Indirect forms of observation are discussed in Chapter 3. Direct forms are discussed here.

Direct Observation

Direct observations should be systematically recorded to note the child's strengths and weaknesses in specific skill areas and should be used as a continuous measure of student progress. A brief overview of observational techniques is provided below. The reader wishing more detailed information is encouraged to read more extensive works by Almy and Genishi (1979), Boehm and Weinberg (1977), Irwin and Bushnell (1980), Goodwin and Driscoll (1980), Salvia and Ysseldyke (1981), and Sattler (1981).

Specimen Records.   Specimen records, which are the fullest accounts of children's behavior, are obtained when a teacher follows a single child for a period of time and records everything that happens to that child or that is done. Such a record provides a complete picture of a child, and the manner and context in which the child functions. The teacher can read over these records a number of times, each time abstracting the information that is most useful for a particular purpose. Patterns of behavior will stand out and a sense of the child will be projected.

Although such complete observations are rich in information, teachers seldom collect them. They require the teacher's total attention for relatively long periods of time, and most teachers find the demands of classroom teaching too great to allow them to withdraw from interactions with children for the required periods of time. Sometimes teacher aides, student teachers, volunteers, or other personnel might be available to relieve the teacher to observe or to collect such records themselves.

GUIDELINES FOR COLLECTING OBSERVATIONAL DATA

1. *Be specific in the language you use.* Describe specifically what you see in ways that others will be able to visualize. Be precise and descriptive in your language, using adverbs and adjectives that characterize what you see. Try to leave out judgements and inferences. If you are using a category system, define your categories ahead of time. Try to label your categories in ways that others will understand them. Try to establish categories that are mutually exclusive so you do not have to make a judgement as to which category to check during an observation.

2. *Describe the setting in which the child is observed.* The setting includes date, time of day, classroom activity, work assignment, and people and materials involved during the observation. Awareness of any or all of these items may help the teacher understand what sets off certain children's behaviors that are under study.

3. *Understand the purpose underlying the observation.* If you are observing to identify the antecedents of a problem, focus on times that will highlight the problem. If a child is having academic problems, observe when academics are being taught. Observing a child during free play periods might not help you understand the way that child approaches academics.

4. *Obtain as much information as is practical and necessary.* How many observations you make, how long they are, when you make them, and how you make them depend on your purposes, as well as what is possible for you. If a child manifests behavioral problems, sample that child's behavior in a number of physical and social settings at different times of the day. This will help determine if this is a general problem, a problem with a single child or a single activity, or a problem that occurs only at a certain time. This sort of information can help in coming up with solutions that might work for you.

5. *Experiment with different procedures and forms.* It is a good idea to practice various observational techniques serveral times before actually collecting data.

6. *Check reliability.* If at all possible, have another person observe the same student at the same time and compare records. The degree to which two observers agree can serve as an index of reliability.

7. *Be as unobtrusive as possible.* Try to be matter-of-fact in your observations. Be as inconspicuous as possible in watching a child and recording behavior.

Duration Recording. Duration recordings help the teacher determine how much time a child spends engaging in a particular activity or behavior.

The amount of time a child spends doing her or his work or the length of time a preschooler engages in isolate, parallel, or cooperative play are exam-

---

DURATION RECORDING

Day (observe 15 minutes each day)	*Total minutes spent in isolate play*
1	7
2	14
3	11
4	8
5	12
	Total = 52 minutes

---

ples of types of activities best assessed by duration recording. To record these child behaviors, a watch or clock can be used. During a given observation period the teacher simple notes the time a behavior or activity starts and when it stops, and then records the length of time between these two points. A teacher might, for instance, observe a child during free play for 5 days for 15 minutes each day (a total of 75 minutes), recording the duration of isolate play and totaling the amount each day. The data might appear as above.

The teacher interested in translating the total time spent in isolate play into a percentage of total observation time would use the following formula:

$$\frac{\text{duration of isolate play}}{\text{total observation time}}$$

$$= \frac{52 \text{ min.}}{75 \text{ min.}} \times 100 = 69\%$$

Duration recording can be time consuming for the observer, but can be used efficiently when the teacher is assisted by a special class teacher or an aide.

Time Sampling.   Time sampling is concerned with determining the degree to which a behavior occurs by observing and recording the incidence of that behavior at specific time intervals. The assumption is that the behavior occurs when the child is not observed in approximately the same degree as during the times observed. To sample behavior this way, a period of time is set for observation and is broken down into equal intervals with observations made at the end of each interval. A thirty-minute period may be sampled by dividing it into 10 three-minute segments, with the teacher observing very briefly at the end of each segment. The 10 observations would then represent a sample of behavior for the entire thirty-minute period.

Time sampling is useful to teachers, especially for frequent behaviors, because it does not require constant attention. Teachers can engage in other instructional activities observing only at the end of each interval.

Event Sampling.   A teacher might wish to note how often during an ex-

---

TIME SAMPLE

Ms. Bell wishes to determine the degree to which a child interacts socially with others during the play period. The thirty-minute play period would be divided into 10 three-minute segments with observations made at three-minute intervals. If the child is observed interacting with another child, Ms. Bell enters a plus (+). If the child is not interacting she enters a minus (−). The record might look like this:

		−	+	+	−	+	+	−	−	+	+
minutes	3	6	9	12	15	18	21	24	27	30

These data reveal that the child was observed interacting 60 percent of the time the observer sampled the behavior.

---

tended period a particular behavior occurs for a child. Rather than sample over time, the teacher might note each time that behavior occurs. This is called event sampling. For example, a teacher who wants to know the extent of independent reading that occurs in class might set up a chart that lists the names of each child in the class. Columns are then assigned for each type of reading behavior such as going to the reading area, reading alone, and reading with a group of children. The teacher can then put a tally mark in the appropriate column next to a particular child's name whenever a reading behavior is observed. Such a chart might look like this:

Child	Goes to reading area	Reads alone	Reads with others

Wrist golf counters, hand tally digital counters, or simple tally marks written on a piece of paper can also be used to keep track of how often a child performs a skill. Event recording is most often used with behaviors that occur quite frequently. When used regularly, this form of recording helps teachers

---

EVENT SAMPLE

Mr. West has two boys in his second grade class who often talk to one another. Mr. West is interested in recording the talk between the boys before he intervenes to reduce it. During several 15-minute work sessions, the number of verbal interactions between the boys is tallied. Mr. West defines talking as any time either boy speaks to the other. Thus, if one boy speaks to the other and the other replies, two interactions are recorded. Using this definition, Mr. West can now count the number of times these boys talk to one another.

---

notice small improvements in child behavior. The advantages to using event recording are its simplicity and its minimal interference with ongoing teaching.

Placheck.　Placheck (planned activity check) is a recording technique for teachers interested in observing groups of young children (Risley, 1971; Hall, 1971). In using placheck:

1. The teacher selects and defines the child behavior(s) to be recorded in a group of children in a specific area.

2. At given intervals (e.g., every 8 minutes) the teacher counts, as quickly as possible, the number of children engaged in the behavior(s) and then records the total(s).

3. Next, the teacher counts and records how many individuals are in the area.

4. The number of children present in the area is then divided by the number of children engaged in the behavior and this quotient is multiplied by 100 to find the percent of those engaged in the behavior. This is illustrated in the following formula.

$$\frac{\text{number of children engaged in an activity}}{\text{number of children engaged in the area}} \times 100 = \frac{\text{\% of children engaged}}{\text{in that activity}}$$

PLACHECK

Ms. Beck, the first grade teacher, wants to check on what portion of her students are working on a math assignment during a 30-minute period.

　Every 10 minutes, she quickly counts how many are working on the assignment. She then counts the number of pupils present (20). During the first 10-minute period she finds that 10 of the 20 are working; during the second, 15 of the 20 are working, and during the third, 8 of the 20. These findings translate into 50 percent, 75 percent and 40 percent respectively.

Sample participation chart		
Observer: Mr. Garcia *Activity:* Working in the block building area *Time:* Activity time for one week		
Children	**Tally**	**Total number of times observed in area**
Carol	⫻⫻ ⫻⫻ ⫻⫻ ⫻⫻/	21
Bob	⫻⫻ ⫻⫻ ⫻⫻ ⫻⫻	20
Ted		0
Alice	////	4
Mickey		0
Betty	////	4

Sample Participation Chart. In this procedure for observing several students simultaneously, the names of the pupils are listed in a column with a space beside each name in which to record the sequence and frequency of each child's participation in group activities or discussions. Each child's participations are then totaled and compared with the number of participations of the others in the group. A teacher who is concerned that a small number of students dominate a certain activity area in the room might use the participation chart to test that hypothesis. Cartwright and Cartwright (1974) provide additional discussion and illustrations of the use of participation charts.

Media. Audio-visual media can be used to augment the paper-and-pencil techniques teachers use in their classrooms. A child or group of children can be videotaped or audiotaped while engaging in different activities. The teacher can use the tapes to capture ongoing behavior for analysis at a later date. When tapes are saved, comparisons can be made between those taken at different times. This technique, while often costly and time-consuming, can be valuable for studying child behavior if the equipment is available and if there are people available to tape the class. The teacher can then take time to review the tapes and abstract material from them when children are not present.

Children's photographs may be taken by teachers or classroom aides during different activities over a period of time. The teacher can collect these and analyze the children's expressions, activities, and interactions with others. But there are dangers in making inferences when the context of a photo may not be recalled. Expressions are difficult to interpret and the same expression in a child's face may be judged differently in different contexts. Photographs are best used in combination with other procedures such as anecdotal reports.

Work Samples. Worksheets, penmanship samples, or art products may be used to assess a child's progress when teachers periodically select samples of the child's work, store them, and then look back over the work to determine whether or not the child is making progress. Work samples are generally best used in combination with other techniques.

ASSESSMENT INVENTORIES

Assessment inventories consist of statements of developmentally sequenced behaviors in areas of gross motor, fine motor, cognitive, communication, preacademic, and self-help skills that have been developed for use with specific preschool populations such as Downs Syndrome, emotionally disturbed, and learning-disabled children. The items included in the inventories are derived from one or more of three principal sources: (1) standardized tests such as the Stanford-Binet Test of Intelligence or the Illinois Test of Psycholinguistic Abilities (ITPA), (2) observations of young children in classroom settings by practicing teachers and educational experts, and (3) developmental guidelines such as those compiled by Gesell and Ilg (1949). The process typically involves teachers watching and then checking those items most descriptive of the child's present performance level. Figure 6-1 contains a sample inventory.

In spite of their widespread use, assessment inventories tend to have a number of problems. Often the test maker fails to provide data to back claims that items are developmentally sequenced. In addition, the instrument may not have been tested with large and representative samples of children. Teachers and administrators must be aware that unless the authors of an assessment inventory explicitly report data on standardization, the developmental nature of the assessment tool is in question.

Another problem related to use of these inventories is that their authors sometimes fail to report reliability data. For example, the inventory may be constructed in such a way that two observers cannot be certain that they are viewing the same behavior. Or accompanying instructions may be too vague to convey exactly what is to be observed. Thus, instructional decisions made by two professionals observing the same behaviors may differ because of lack of clarity as to what is to be observed.

Another shortcoming concerns inappropriate use of screening devices. Many program developers use screening devices for assessment purposes. However, screening devices are gross measures designed to detect the possibility of a handicap; they are not specific enough to be used in assessment. The purpose for which a test was designed must govern its use.

Finally, many assessment inventories are not detailed enough for use with young handicapped children. This would cause the child's initial level of functioning to be recorded inaccurately, and small but significant levels of progress would not be detected.

FIGURE 6-1

A sample preschool assessment inventory*
(Check item that best reflects child's skills.)

	Gross motor skills	Fine motor skills	Preacademic skills	Self-help skills
36–48 months	Walks on a line. Balances on 1 foot for 5 seconds. Uses slides without assistance. Rides trike.	Traces diamond. Imitates cross. Copies circle. Places small pegs in pegboard.	Points to 6 base colors. Rote counts to 3. Counts 2 objects and tells how many. Does 7-piece puzzle.	Pours well from pitcher. Spreads with knife. Buttons and unbuttons clothing. Uses toilet independently.
48–60 months	Walks backward heel-toe. Bends from waist with knees extended to pick things up. Walks up and down steps alone.	Traces triangle. Copies cross. Copies square. Prints a few capital letters.	Names 6 basic colors. Names circles, squares, triangles. Rote counts to 10. Matches and sorts objects by texture.	Cuts food with knife. Laces shoes. Knows own name/city/street.
60–72 months	Walks a balance beam. Can cover 2–3 yards hopping. Turns somersault. Jumps from 12 inches landing on toes.	Copies triangle. Copies first name. Prints some numbers. Cuts out simple shapes.	Names some letters. Names some numerals. Counts 6 objects and tells how many. Copies block design.	

*Adapted from the Preschool Profile, University of Washington

In spite of these problems, assessment inventories are popular and teachers should be familiar with the most commonly used inventories. An annotated list of such inventories is provided at the end of this chapter.

SOCIOMETRICS

Sociometrics uses a rating scale to assess the degree to which individuals are accepted within a group. Most sociometric scales are simple to construct and administer. The most common sociometric technique used with young children is peer nomination (Wallace & Larsen, 1978). Typically, children are presented with a hypothetical situation (e.g., birthday party) and asked to choose one or more classmates they would like to play with, sit next to, eat lunch with, or carry out any other prescribed activity with. Children may be asked to nominate one child, a group of children, or an ordered set of children. Teachers may also ask children to identify persons they least like.

Among the questions children are likely to be asked are:

1. Which classmate(s) do you most like (or least like) to play with?

2. Which children get you into trouble?

3. Which child would you most like (or least like) to sit next to at our birthday party?

4. Which children do you think are bossy?

Sociometrics has most often been used in early childhood classes to test a child's popularity within a group (Asher, Oden, & Gottman, 1978).

STANDARDIZED TESTS

Standardized tests, also known as norm-referenced tests, have limited educational value for use with young children, especially the handicapped, because they are designed to be administered following standard procedures (Salvia & Ysseldyke, 1981).

Standardized tests do serve two useful purposes, however. Their test scores are helpful in obtaining services or funds, which frequently require evidence of the child's performance or status on some scale. In addition, a good standardized test administered by a well-trained or experienced examiner can provide information on the child in comparison to same-aged peers. For instructional purposes, however, informal tests, naturalistic observation, or assessment inventories may be more valuable to the teacher.

Standardized tests currently in use in the field of early education are designed to measure a number of traits including intelligence, achievement, affective development, personality, and language development. These tests are widely used with young children. Over the past decade, however, there has been growing disillusionment with traditional standardized test procedures and increasing documentation of their shortcomings, particularly with young children. A detailed review of standardized instruments for young children can be found in Goodwin and Driscoll's *Handbook for Measurement and Evaluation in Early Childhood Education* (1980).

INFORMAL TESTS

Informal tests involve observation of children's performance on day-to-day instructional tasks. These techniques are used most frequently for assessing academic skills. For instance, a teacher who administers and scores a spelling, math, or reading test is engaging in informal assessment. Informal assessment tools include teacher-made skill tests and teacher-made placement tests.

Skill Tests

Skill tests are designed to measure academic skills such as writing numbers, spelling words, stating multiplication facts to three, or using punctuation in sentences. Typically, the teacher presents an activity or structures a situation that requires the child to perform the desired skill and then informally assesses the child's ability to perform it. For example, a teacher who gives a student a worksheet with a series of 20 sentences, each requiring a period, question mark, or exclamation point can tell how competent the student is in using punctuation skills. Skill tests can be administered throughout the school year prior to initiating instruction in a certain area or upon its completion. Figures 6-2 and 6-3 present two examples of skill tests.

FIGURE 6-2
Specific skill test

Decording words with short vowels:
    Ask the child to read the words and sentences orally. Record the child's exact pronunciations.

CVC* words	dip	hip	kit	mix
CCVC words	brim	flip	skid	thin
CVCC words	dish	fist	hint	lick
Words in sentences	Dick and Pip will go on the ship.			

*C = consonant, V = vowel

FIGURE 6-3
Specific skill test

Dividing one-digit divisors into two-digit dividends, without remainders.

Row 1

$4\,\overline{)24}$ $\qquad$ $5\,\overline{)35}$ $\qquad$ $7\,\overline{)49}$

Row 2

$5\,\overline{)25}$ $\qquad$ $10\,\overline{)50}$ $\qquad$ $8\,\overline{)32}$

Row 3

$8\,\overline{)72}$ $\qquad$ $8\,\overline{)64}$ $\qquad$ $7\,\overline{)56}$

Placement Tests

Commercially or teacher-made placement tests determine where a child should begin instruction by sampling skills and tasks from a curriculum that is graduated in difficulty. These tests typically present samples of items in the order in which they are presented in the curriculum itself. If the curriculum has been sequenced from least to most complex, the sampling of tasks should indicate where the child is having difficulty, thus indicating where the child should begin work.

To create a placement test, the teacher may go through a set of graduated curriculum materials selecting a sample of tasks for each different step presented in those materials. To increase the usefulness of the test, some teachers present items in the same manner as they are shown in the curriculum. For example, a teacher interested in designing a placement test for a spelling book might select every fifth word from each list found in the three spelling levels at which the child is performing. The child is then asked to spell these words until she or he experiences failure. The teacher examines the words spelled, determines the point at which the child began missing words, and determines a placement point for spelling.

The same technique can be used for placement in a mathematics book. The teacher selects the mathematics texts for grades one, two, or three and then systematically extracts items that sample the skills presented in the material. However, since many commercial materials focus on more than one skill area for a specific academic subject, a mathematics book might include work in the areas of computation, problem solving, money, time, and geometry. Skills may vary widely across these different strands; thus, separate placement points in a time-telling sequence, a subtraction sequence, a money sequence, and a problem-solving sequence might be necessary.

Informal assessment devices such as those described above can be used to evaluate a child's performance in any instructional area. In addition to teacher-made skill and placement tests, situations or tasks can be structured to determine how a child deals with problem-solving situations. Piagetian conservation tasks or an obstacle course set up to observe how the child handles his or her body, crosses his or her midline, or balances on a walking beam are other examples of this type of assessment.

RECORDING ASSESSMENT DATA

There are a number of ways to record assessment data. It may be recorded in the form collected, the percentages computed may be recorded, or graphs may be developed from the data. Whatever method of recording is selected, it should be easy to maintain and appropriate to the type of data collected and the skill measured. It should also communicate effectively to those using the information.

Raw Data

For some skills only the raw data, that is, the information as it is collected, need be recorded. The teacher may, for instance, keep a simple daily record of the number of occurrences of a skill or behavior such as talking out in class, sharing appropriately with others, hitting other children, and so on. A simple tally sheet might be appropriate for counting the number of occurrences of a skill or behavior (see Figure 6-4).

Raw data might also record the number of correct and incorrect responses for a specific skill. For instance, a teacher might give a child 10 story problems to solve each day. By keeping the number of problems con-

FIGURE 6-4 Tally sheet		
Date		**Number of instances of sharing**
9/5	////	4
9/6	///	3
9/7	///	5
9/8	///	3
9/11	/	1
9/12	//	2

FIGURE 6-5

Record of correct and incorrect responses on spelling test

Date	Spelling list #	Correct responses	Incorrect responses
9/6	1	7	8
9/8	2	9	6
9/8	3	12	3
9/11	4	4	11
9/2	5	5	10

stant, the teacher could record daily the correct and incorrect responses. A possible format for recording this raw data is illustrated in Figure 6-5.

Computed Data

To make raw data collected in assessment easier to compare over time, the teacher might wish to compute percentages correct from the data. This may involve calculating percentages of correct and incorrect responses or the rate of their occurrence within a specified time period. The teacher might note, for example, that when given 30 sentences, Susan correctly used punctuation in 24 of them. This represents 80 percent of the items. Figure 6-6 provides an example of a data-recording device using computed data.

Graphs

The use of graphs is often the most efficient and effective way to display assessment information. The graph illustrates in a visual manner the changes in

FIGURE 6-6

Example of data-recording device using percentage scores

Name: *Bob J* Step on sequence	Date	Skill area: *Multiplication* Percentage
1 digit × 2 digits	1/3	82
1 digit × 3 digits	1/24	88
1 digit × 4 digits	2/7	84
2 digits × 2 digits	2/21	90

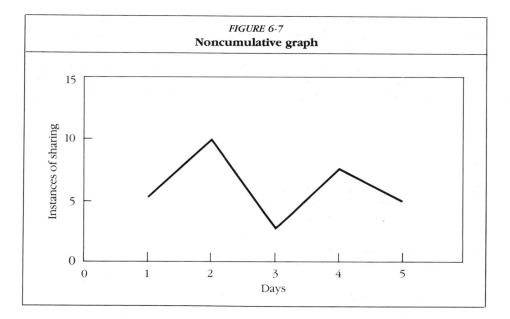

FIGURE 6-7
Noncumulative graph

a child's performance over time. Graphs can be used to help teachers make instructional decisions and communicate effectively to parents and other professionals.

Graphs are particularly useful because of the number of dimensions that can be recorded and the many ways the devices can be used. These include:

1. The number of correct or incorrect responses

2. The frequency of a skill

3. The number of responses per specified time interval

4. The percentage of accuracy of the behavior

5. The amount of time or duration in which a behavior occurred

Standard graphic arrangements employ two axes drawn at right angles—a horizontal axis (X axis) and a vertical axis (Y axis). Usually the units of measurement are amount of the skill or behavior (frequency, rate, percent, proportion, duration) for the Y axis and units of time (minutes, sessions, days, weeks) for the X axis.

Noncumulative graphs are constructed by plotting the amount of the skill (Y axis) at the intersection of the time section (X axis) and then, after the points have been placed, connecting them by a line.

For example a teacher may be concerned with a student who fails to share with others during 29 play periods. For 5 consecutive days, the teacher records the number of sharing instances and finds that there were 7, 9, 3, 6, and 5 occurrences respectively. Figure 6-7 is a graphic presentation of the sharing.

Frequently, teachers will want to present multiple classes of assessment data on the same graph. This is usually accomplished by using different symbols to represent different skills, persons, or settings. For instance, a teacher may be interested in representing the sharing, smiling, and positive talking behaviors of the same student on the same graph over a 5-day period. The same strategy might be used to graph assessment data for different settings.

SUMMARY

This chapter has examined assessment of young handicapped children in integrated settings, specifying various techniques of classroom assessment and systems for recording assessment data. The purpose of assessment is to determine a child's skills and deficits in order to select a starting point for instruction and to evaluate the effectiveness of ongoing instruction. Effective assessment should occur regularly over time.

Assessment information should feed into instructional programming. The results of that assessment should be used to develop individualized educational programs (IEPs) and to evaluate their effectiveness. Instruments that are used by teachers to assess children, their capabilities, and their achievement need to be carefully matched to the goals and values of the classroom program. An annotated list of assessment instruments is in this chapter. Some of these are designed for general use, while others were created in relation to a specific program. Teachers should be aware of the purposes of any assessment instruments they select to find those that match their particular program.

ASSESSMENT INSTRUMENTS

Title: Assessment—Programming Guide for Infants and Preschoolers
Author: W. Umansky
Publisher: Developmental Services, Inc., Columbus, Ohio. 1974.
Age range: 0–72 months

General Description

This instrument is designed to aid teachers in determining the needs of a child through systematic observation and to provide guidelines for planning a program to fit the child's specific needs. A child is assessed in five areas—motor, perceptual-motor, language, self-help, and social-personal—with items often listed under several different areas. The test, which is well standardized on both handicapped and nonhandicapped children, is comprised primarily of developmental guidelines and requires observing children in natural settings only. A complete evaluation of the child may take several weeks.

Title: Basic Concept Inventory
Author: S. Engelmann
Publisher: Follett Publishing Company, Chicago, Illinois. 1967.
Age range: 3–10 years

General Description

This test provides a comprehensive checklist of basic concepts (e.g., sentence comprehension, pattern awareness) that are needed to succeed in a regular first grade. It is a criterion-referenced, individually administered test intended primarily for culturally disadvantaged preschool and kindergarten children, slow learners, emotionally disturbed, and mentally retarded children. The instrument may be used as a basis for either remedial instruction or diagnostic evaluation. Extensive reliability and validity data have been reported.

Title: Behavioral-Developmental Profile
Authors: M. Donahue, A. Keiser, L. Smith, J. D. Montgomery, U. L. Roecker, and M. F. Walden
Publisher: The Marshalltown Project, Marshalltown, Iowa. 1975.
Age range: 0–6 years (for handicapped and culturally disadvantaged children)

General Description

This profile assesses skills in the language, cognitive, fine and gross motor,
personal-social, self-help, and cognitive areas. These developmental areas are collapsed into communication, motor, and social abilities. A total of 327 items are grouped into age categories with one-month segments for the first 12 months, three-month segments for 12 to 24 months, six-month segments for 24 to 36 months, and twelve-month segments for 36 to 72 months.

Each item is briefly stated in behavioral terms, and an individually administered direct test is used. Test items are based on patterns of "normal" child development. The profile is used with a score sheet that identifies a success level, an emergent level, and a level indicating that the child is unable to perform. The test can be administered by a teacher or other trained professional, and it is useful to educators employing a diagnostic-prescriptive approach.

Title: Bender Motor Gestalt Test
Author: L. Bender
Publisher: American Orthopsychiatric Association, Albany, New York. 1938.
Age range: 4 years and up

General Description

The Bender Motor Gestalt Test is used to detect visual perceptual difficulties as well as the possible presence of brain damage. Designed for individuals ages 4 and up, it consists of 8 designs that are copied by the child under standard conditions and scored according to errors in reproduction. This test, although widely used among educators, lacks substantial population norms.

Title: Boehm Test of Basic Concepts (BTBC)
Author: A. E. Boehm
Publisher: Psychological Corporation, Atlanta, Georgia. 1971.
Age range: Approximately 4.5–7 years

General Description

The BTBC measures mastery of concepts in the areas of quantity, number, space, time, and other areas considered important for achievement in the first years of school (K–2). This test is individually administered and takes 15 to 20 minutes to administer each of two test booklets. The test may be given in one or two sessions. No special training is required to administer the test and percentile norms by grade and socioeconomic level are provided. Limited reliability and validity data are available.

Title: Bunks' Behavior Rating Scale (BBRS) (Preschool and Kindergarten Edition)
Author: L. Bunks
Publisher: Western Psychological Services, Los Angeles, California. 1977.
Age range: 3–6 years

General Description

The BBRS is designed to record behavioral or learning disorders indicative of organic brain dysfunction. There are 105 items, clustered into 18 groupings, that are rated by the teacher on a 5-point scale indicating the degree to which each identified behavior is present in the child. Among the behaviors assessed are: self-blame, anxiety, impulse control, anger control, sense of identity, aggressiveness, and social conformity. The scores for each subscale are recorded on a profile sheet and then plotted on a horizontal number line. The number line is divided into three sections—not significant, significant, very significant—indicating the degree of the problem. Having each child rated by several observers in several situations increases the validity of the instrument. The examiner may be anyone who knows the child well (e.g., parents, teachers, or aides).

The instrument has been standardized on a large number of children. Extensive reliability and validity data are reported.

Title: California Preschool Social Competency Scale (CPSCS)
Authors: S. Levine, M. Freeman, and M. Lewis
Publisher: Consulting Psychologists Press, Inc., Palo Alto, California. 1969.
Age range: 2.5–5.5 years

General Description

This scale, designed for observing in the preschool classroom, measures the adequacy of preschoolers' interpersonal behavior and the extent to which they assume social responsibility and independence. It consists of 30 items representative of critical behaviors in the young child's social functioning. The child is observed over time in a variety of situations and ratings are based on that child's typical performance.

The statements within each item are ordered by level of competence and numbered cumulatively from 1 through 4. The rater, after determining the appropriate level, circles the number representing the rating for that item. A child rated 4 is presumed to be able to perform at all prelevels on that item. Total raw scores are converted to a percentile score by reference to the appropriate table of norms, and can be graphed on the back of the scale booklet.

The scale has been standardized on a representative sample of children, and acceptable validity and reliability are reported. The CPSCS is easy to administer and, because it directly measures performance on a task in a natural setting, is useful as a criterion measure of the effectiveness of social interventions.

Title: Carolina Developmental Profile
Authors: D. L. Lillie and G. L. Harbin
Publisher: Kaplan School Supply Corporation, Winston-Salem, North Carolina. 1975.
Age range: 2–5 years

General Description

This profile is a criterion-referenced behavior checklist designed for use with the *Developmental Task Instructional System* developed by the same authors. The goal of the combined system is to prepare children for formal academic instruction in the early elementary school years. It focuses on 6 areas: gross motor, fine motor, visual perception, reasoning, receptive language, and expressive language. Items are sequenced within the devel-

opmental area, and a task number, task description, and developmental age are assigned to each item. If the child completes the task, the teacher checks "can do," if not "cannot do" is checked.

The test, which is easy to administer and score, should be given in a large room over several different sessions. All visual materials are included in the profile, but additional materials such as blocks, balls, and scissors must be gathered before administering. Performance criteria for each item are easily interpreted but there are only 5 items for each age in each area, providing somewhat limited information.

Title: CIRCUS
Authors: A. Scarvia, G. Bogatz, A. Draper, G. Tangeblut, W. Sedwell, N. Ward, and A. Yates
Publisher: Educational Testing Service, Princeton, New Jersey. 1974.
Age range: 4–6 years

General Description

CIRCUS measures the instructional needs of children in order to plan individualized educational programs. CIRCUS consists of 17 instruments, 5 of which are devoted to language. There are also measures of qualitative understanding, visual discrimination, perceptual-motor coordination, letter and numeral recognition, sound discrimination, visual and associative memory, and problem solving. Three instruments, which must be completed by the teacher, are also included: one for classroom activities, one for test-taking behavior, and one that surveys the child's educational environment.

CIRCUS may be administered by a teacher to groups of children, and users may select those instruments that fit their needs. A teacher's manual is provided for each instrument along with a pupil's booklet in which children mark responses.

Title: Criterion-Referenced Placement Test
Author: G. Cast
Publisher: MAPPS project, Exceptional Child Center, Logan, Utah. 1975.
Age range: 0–5 years

General Description

This test assesses children's entry level skills in receptive and expressive language and motor development. The instrument is designed for use with the Curriculum and Monitoring System (CAMS). The test items were developed from the sequenced objectives in CAMS and may be administered by anyone who works with young children. It takes 20 to 25 minutes to administer.

Title: The Development Profile II
Authors: G. D. Alpern and
M. S. Shearer
Publisher: Psychological Development Publications, Aspen, Colorado. 1981.
Age range: 0–12 years

General Description

The Development Profile II is designed to help teachers construct individual curriculum prescriptions for children. It contains 217 items arranged into 5 scales and ordered into 4 age levels. The profile is administered in an inter-view by an adult rater who knows the child well.

The test can be administered in 20 to 40 minutes by a trained examiner, and explicit and easily understood directions are included in the manual. The standardization sample consisted of 3008 subjects randomly selected to represent all socioeconomic and cultural sections of the population. Extensive reliability and validity data are reported, and the test manual provides detailed discussion regarding test construction, item analysis, and standardization procedures. The instrument generally involves parent input, which can be very valuable.

Title: Developmental Therapy Objective Rating Form (DTORF)
Author: M. Wood
Publisher: University Park Press, Baltimore, Maryland. 1972.
Age range: Approximately 3–8 years

General Description

The DTORF contains 144 carefully sequenced objectives in 4 areas—behavior, communication, socialization, and academics—used to indicate both developmental milestones already achieved and criteria for grouping as well as to provide a basis for planning. The rating form takes 36 minutes to administer and is generally completed by a team of professionals who know the child well. The DTORF was originally designed for emotionally disturbed children at the Rutland Center Model in Athens, Georgia.

Title: Frostig Developmental Test of Visual Perception

Author: M. Frostig
Publisher: Consulting Psychologists Press, Palo Alto, California. 1961.
Age range: 4 years and up

General Description

The Frostig test measures 5 perceptual skills—eye-motor coordination, figure-ground perception, constancy of shape, position in space and spatial relationship—via a paper-and-pencil test for young children. Norms starting at age 4 are used to compute a perceptual quotient. Remedial activities and programs related to test results are also provided.

Title: Goldman-Fristoe Test of Auditory Discrimination
Authors: R. Goldman, M. Fristoe, and R. Woodcock
Publisher: American Guidance Service, Circle Pines, Minnesota. 1970.
Age range: 4 years and up

General Description

This test assesses the listener's ability to distinguish among common speech sounds under both quiet and distracting noise conditions. The format includes a series of test plates containing 4 drawings and a prerecorded audiotape. The child responds to a stimulus word by pointing to 1 of 4 pictures simultaneously presented on the plate. Subtests include the auditory selection attention test, the diagnostic auditory discrimination test, the auditory memory test, and the sound symbol test.

The test was standardized on 745 subjects from which percentile norms by age level were developed for persons to 74 months old. Extensive reliability and validity data are presented. Items were constructed on everyday tasks, and the test is viewed as sound by educators and speech clinicians.

Title: The Houston Test for Language Development
Author: M. Crabtree
Publisher: Houston Test Company, Houston, Texas. 1963.
Age range: Part I: 6–36 months; Part II: 36 months–6 years

General Description

This test is designed to assess language development skills in children. These include self-identity, vocabulary, body parts and gestures, communicative behavior, counting objects, geometric designs and drawings, and sentence length. The test takes 30 to 60 minutes and is adminstered by a speech clinician. Reliability and validity data are sketchy and the standardization sample is not representative of many groups in the U.S. population. Despite these drawbacks, the Houston Test is widely used as an assessment and screening device.

Title: Indiana Preschool Developmental Scale (IPDAS)
Authors: B. Bateman, J. Henn, J. Wilke, R. Wilson, C. Muslin, and W. Bragg
Publisher: Developmental Training Center, Bloomington, Indiana. 1976.
Age range: 0–6 years.

General Description

The IPDAS provides a profile of 300 items describing the level of the child's functioning in the motor, personal autonomy, communication, and pre-academic areas. It is designed to help teachers formulate for the child a program to be implemented by either the teacher or the parent. The IPDAS is a criterion-referenced instrument with corresponding curriculum objectives for each item. It provides alternative equivalent response modes for visually impaired, hearing impaired, physically/multiply handicapped, and deaf-blind children.

The IPDAS is administered and scored by the teacher. A 5-point rating scale is provided for each item. No reliability or validity data are reported, and the authors provide no discussion regarding the development and selection of items. The items, in general, are similar to those on other profiles and the information related to the assessment procedures is clearly presented and well-organized.

Title: Kindergarten Evaluation of Learning Potential (KELP)
Authors: J. A. Wilson and M. C. Robeck
Publisher: Webster Division, McGraw-Hill Book Company, St. Louis, Missouri. 1967.
Age range: 5–7 years

General Description

KELP is designed to predict success in the early grades based on kindergarten learning. Items include color identifica-

tion, head design, bolt board, number boards, safety signs, writing one's name, and social interaction. Items from KELP are taught by the teacher, who observes and records the learning of the tasks over the kindergarten year. Classroom materials, teaching tips, and summary retention tests are available. Test scores have been correlated with Stanford-Binet scores, and the manual reports surveys by teachers who have used KELP.

Title: Learning Accomplishment Profile (LAP)
Author: A. R. Sanford
Publisher: Kaplan Press, Winston-Salem, North Carolina. 1974.
Age range: 0–74 months

General Description

LAP is designed to provide a criterion-referenced record of a child's skills. It enables the teacher to (1) identify learning objectives, (2) measure progress through changes in the rate of development, and (3) provide information relevant to student learning. LAP measures the child's development in 6 areas: gross motor, fine motor, social, self-help, cognitive, and language. The items, stated in behavorial terms, were extracted from instruments widely used in the field. The scoring sheet restates each item and the developmental age or age range. Examiners, who are usually the classroom teachers, record the assessment date and the child's achievement for each item. A comments column can be used to record data regarding criteria, materials, or problems.

LAP is administered over a period of days and actually in a series of steps. Long-range objectives and short-term objectives are developed. Teaching effectiveness is assessed. No reliability or validity information is provided, and there are no reports of a standardization group. Still, items are clearly stated, easily scored, and fairly comprehensive. Teachers may need to further analyze some of the items to fit the needs of more moderately impaired children.

Title: Minnesota Preschool Scale
Authors: F. Goodenough, K. Maurer, and M. J. Van Wagener.
Publisher: American Guidance Service, Circle Pines, Minnesota. 1940.
Age range: 6 months to 6 years

General Description

The Minnesota Preschool Scale is designed to assess the mental abilities of young children. The scale consists of 26 verbal and nonverbal items. The test can be individually administered by a trained professional in approximately 30 minutes, and scoring procedures can be completed with a minimum of difficulty. Testing procedures are well described as are standardization procedures and norm groups. Extensive reliability and validity data are reported.

Title: Peabody Individual Achievement Test
Authors: L. M. Dunn and F. Markward
Publisher: American Guidance Service, Circle Pines, Minnesota. 1970.
Age range: 5 years and up

General Description

This is an individually administered measure of mathematics, reading, spelling, and general information. The test, which requires 30 to 40 minutes to administer, yields 6 scores—mathematics, reading recognition, reading comprehension, spelling, general information, and a total—all of which have norms presented as grade equivalents, percentile ranks, and standard scores. The test requires only oral or pointing responses. The manual reports extensive reliability and validity data as well as a detailed description of standardization procedures and norm groups.

Title: Peabody Picture Vocabulary Test, Revised (PPVT)
Author: L. M. Dunn
Publisher: American Guidance Service, Circle Pines, Minnesota. 1981.
Age range: 2.5–18 years

General Description

The PPVT provides an estimate of verbal intelligence by measuring the child's hearing vocabulary. It is an individually administered criterion-referenced test administered by a testing professional and requiring from 10 to 15 minutes. This test provides a measure of only one aspect of intelligence—receptive vocabulary. It provides adaptations for nonreaders and low readers, speech impaired, cerebral palsied, partially sighted, and perceptually impaired children. The testing manual contains extensive data on the standardized procedures and the norms groups, and it reports extensive reliability and validity data.

Title: Portage Guide to Early Education, Revised Edition
Authors: S. Bluma, M. Shearer, A. Frohman, and J. Hilliard
Publisher: The Portage Project, Portage, Wisconsin. 1976.
Age range: 0–6 years

General Description

The Portage Guide was designed to help educators assess child behavior and plan curriculum goals. This criterion-referenced instrument contains three parts: (1) a checklist of 580 items sequentially arranged in 5 behavioral areas—socialization, language, self-help, cognitive, and motor, (2) a card file listing possible methods of teaching related to these behaviors, and (3) a manual of directions. Skills listed on the checklist are behaviorally stated, and the child may be assessed by an individual with minimum training. Children are assessed in a variety of settings so that a representative sample of their behavior is taken. Scoring procedures are simple, but no reliability or validity data are reported.

Title: Preschool Attainment Record (PAR) (Research Edition)
Author: E. Doll
Publisher: American Guidance Service, Circle Pines, Minnesota. 1966.
Age range: 0–7 years

General Description

PAR is an expansion of the Vineland Social Maturity Scale designed to measure the physical, social, mental, and language attainments of young children. The record includes 8 areas: development-ambulation, manipulation, rapport, communication, responsibility, information, ideation, and creativity. There is one item for each area per 6-month interval. The test is individually administered by a professional in 20 to 30 minutes. Extensive reliability and validity data are reported but no information is given on standardization procedures or norms. Validity data suggests that items are not developmental in nature and the predictive validity for the instrument is questionable.

Title: Primary Mental Abilities Test (PMAT)
Author: T. G. Thurstone
Publisher: Science Research Associates, Chicago, Illinois, 1963.
Age range: Kindergarten–first grade

General Description

PMAT is designed to provide multifactored and general measures of intelligence. The instrument consists of 5 tests—verbal meaning, number facility, reasoning, perceptual speed, and spatial relations. It takes a little over an hour to administer and may be given to small groups. The perceptual speed test is timed. The test is given from a test booklet (no other materials are required), and mental age equivalents for each part and for the total test are given.

Title: Skills Inventory
Authors: D. Brown, V. Simmons, and J. Methvin

Publisher: Jackson County Education Service District, Medford, Oregon. 1978.
Age range: 0–6 years

General Description

The Skills Inventory provides a criterion-referenced assessment and curriculum guide for children with visual deficits. It contains 693 skills, and serves 3 purposes: (1) to assess the child's developmental level in cognition, language, self-help, socialization, fine motor, and gross motor domains, (2) to select appropriate teaching goals, and (3) to record the child's acquisition of new skills. The test is individually administered, preferably by a school psychologist, but no data on testing time is provided. No information is provided on standardization, reliability, or validity procedures. Scoring procedures are well-described and easily implemented. This is one of the few comprehensive checklists available for visually impaired children.

Title: Stanford Early School Achievement Test (SESAT)
Authors: R. Madden and E. F. Gardner
Publisher: The Psychological Corporation, Atlanta, Georgia. 1970.
Age range: Kindergarten–first grade

General Description

SESAT measures cognitive abilities upon entrance into kindergarten or first grade. Subtests include the environment (social and natural environments, social science, natural science), mathematics (conservation of number, space, volume, counting, measurement, numeration, classification, simple operations), letters and sounds, and aural comprehension. The test is group-administered in 5 sessions. Groups of 5 to 6 children per assistant are recommended for beginning kindergarteners and groups of 15 per assistant for older children. The test takes approximately 90 minutes to administer over several sessions. Split-half reliability data on the subtests are available but no validity studies are reported.

REFERENCES

Almy, M., and Genishi, C. *Ways of studying children: An observational manual for early childhood teachers.* rev. ed. New York: Teachers College Press, 1979.

Asher, S. R., Oden, S. L., and Gottman, J. M. Children's Friendships in School Settings. In L. G. Katz et al. (Eds.). *Current topics in early childhood education.* Vol. I. Norwood, N.J.: Ablex Publishing Company, 1978.

Boehm, A. E., and Weinberg, R. A. *The classroom observer: A guide for developing observation skills.* New York: Teachers College Press, 1977.

Cartwright, C. A., and Cartwright, G. P. *Developing observation skills.* New York: McGraw-Hill, 1974.

Cooper, J. O. *Measurement and analysis of behavior techniques.* Columbus, Ohio: Charles E. Merrill, 1974.

Gessell, A., and Ilg, F. L. *Child development: An introduction to the study of human growth*. New York: Harper, 1949.

Goodwin, W. L., and Driscoll, L. D. *Handbook for measurement and evaluation in early childhood education*. San Francisco: Jossey-Bass, 1980.

Hall, R. V. *Behavior modification: The measurement of behavior*. Lawrence, Kansas: H and H Enterprises, 1971.

Irwin, D. M., and Bushnell, M. M. *Observational strategies for child study*. New York: Holt, Rinehart and Winston, 1980.

Lowenbraun, S., and Affleck, J. Q. *Teaching mildly handicapped children in regular classes*. Columbus, Ohio: Charles E. Merrill, 1976.

Preschool profile. Unpublished. Model Preschool Center for Handicapped Children, Child Development and Mental Retardation Center, University of Washington, Seattle.

Risley, T. R. Spontaneous language in the preschool environment. In J. Stanley (Ed.). *Research on curriculums for preschools*. Baltimore, Md.: Johns Hopkins University Press, 1971.

Salvia, J., and Ysseldyke, J. E. *Assessment in special and remedial education*. (2nd ed.). Boston: Houghton Mifflin, 1981.

Sattler, J. M. *Assessment of children's intelligence and special abilities* (2nd ed.), Boston: Allyn & Bacon, 1981.

Wallace, G., and Larsen, S. *Educational assessment of learning problems: Testing for teaching*. Boston: Allyn & Bacon, 1978.

Seven

CREATING A SUPPORTIVE SOCIAL ENVIRONMENT

It is difficult to overestimate the importance of the social environment in which children learn. The types of relationships they form with teachers and classmates can affect not only their academic performance but also their feelings about themselves, their attitudes toward others, and ultimately, the social patterns they will adopt. Teachers who are aware of the social climate in their classrooms can prevent behavior problems that might arise and provide opportunities for optimum social growth. They are also better prepared to identify children who need special help.

Factors that create the social climate in a class include the curriculum (both its content and its presentation), the teacher's influence, and the influence of the children. In this chapter the influences of teacher and children are discussed. The importance of the various areas of the curriculum is extensively discussed later in this book.

TEACHER INFLUENCE

Of all the factors that contribute to the social environment in which children are educated, the teacher is by far the most critical. The teacher's attitude toward children and their education determines to a very great extent how children perceive school, themselves and each other, and eventually, how much progress they make. Teachers can make learning pleasant or punitive; they can motivate or they can induce fear; they can produce excited anticipation or dread. Teachers can also greatly influence the extent to which handicapped children will be accepted by their nonhandicapped peers. A teacher's personal style and approach, perhaps more than anything else, creates the climate and mood that characterize the classroom.

Brophy and Putnam (1979) have identified the following attributes of effective teachers. They should be liked by their students, and therefore, they should have cheerful dispositions, be friendly, emotionally mature, sincere, and well adjusted. They should have the ego strength to stay calm in a crisis, be able to listen to children without becoming authoritarian or defensive, avoid conflicts, and maintain a problem-solving orientation to their classrooms. Teachers with these attributes can use a variety of techniques to effectively manage their classes.

The impact of the teacher's behavior on the classroom has been supported by a great deal of recent research that illustrates the relationship between teachers' behavior and pupils' behavior (see, for example, Peterson and Walberg, 1979). In light of the critical role played by teachers, it is important to consider the characteristics of teachers that are conducive to a healthy social classroom environment. Such areas include self-concept, positive behavior, understanding, planning, and knowledge about behavior problems and solutions to these problems.

Teachers' Self-Concept

Although research has customarily focused on the relationship between the child's self-concept and development, some writers have directed their attention toward the effects of the teacher's self-concept on the child's social development. Jersild (1965), for instance, asserts that the personal problems of teachers frequently interfere with their performance in class and can influence the attitudes of their pupils. A similar view has been expressed by Combs (1965), who found that effective teachers are distinguished by their positive attitudes toward themselves and others. Combs (1965) also suggested that efforts to foster positive self-concepts among beginning teachers should be an important component of teacher training programs. Indeed, Combs asserts that the attitude of teachers toward themselves and others is as important in enhancing the self-concept of their pupils as the procedures they use. Moreover, research suggests that teachers with positive attitudes toward themselves promote a positive classroom atmosphere, while teachers with negative attitudes toward themselves promote negative feelings among pupils (Hart, Allen, Buell, Harris, & Wolf, 1964).

As these studies illustrate, teachers need to view themselves as respected and liked by others. When teachers have favorable attitudes toward themselves, they are in a much better position to build a supportive environment for learning.

Positive Behavior

When people are in a good mood, their behavior will have a ripple effect; those around them usually begin to show some of the same feelings. This happens in classrooms as well as in other social situations. The classroom status of teachers increases the likelihood that their behavior will be imitated by their children (Bandura, 1971). If teachers are positive and enthusiastic, their students will be positive and enthusiastic. Although everyone has some bad days, these should not outnumber the good.

Negative teacher attitudes and behavior can affect children, often making them passive, withdrawn, and even fearful. In addition, a teacher's expectations can influence students' academic achievement and social behavior. If low IQ scores or personal perceptions of inadequate performance cause a teacher to be negatively biased toward a child, these expectations may result in a self-fulfilling prophecy: influenced by the teacher's expectations, the student may perform poorly. By contrast, the student whose teacher exudes optimism and challenges him or her to perform well should enjoy more success (Rosenthal & Jacobson, 1968).

Positive attitudes and expectations for all children, but especially for the handicapped, must be combined with praise, support, and encouragement. By emphasizing children's good points, teachers can build their students' confidence and their persistence in completing more difficult learning tasks. The development of healthy social interaction in the classroom cannot be accomplished through criticism and ridicule.

Understanding

Teachers in an integrated classroom must be aware of differences in their students' abilities and must be sensitive to the conflicts or misunderstandings that can result from them. The negative stereotypes and prejudices that even young children can develop are dangerous in the classroom and often stem from ignorance. Whether expressed openly in the teacher's words or actions or more subtly, a lack of tolerance for diversity affects any child

who differs from the norm. By gathering information from a number of sources, both in school and in the child's home, interested teachers can gain a better understanding of the differences that do exist within the class and use this knowledge to design a relevant program for each child. An accepting atmosphere will not only promote integration but also support the development of an optimum setting for the social growth of the entire class. At the same time it will provide all children with a model of understanding too often absent in their world.

Planning

Teachers must continuously plan, evaluate, and modify the daily educational program to promote the participation of every child in the learning experience. All materials must be readily accessible, with guidelines for their use and limitations clearly spelled out, and the duties and responsibilities of the children must be clearly delineated. Teachers must also use information obtained from individual assessments to select materials and activities that will stimulate thinking and enhance learning without causing excessive frustration. The lack of such preparation can lead to failure for the handicapped child, which in turn can produce undesirable social behaviors and thwart healthy social and emotional growth.

Regardless of the age of the students or the type of educational program, teachers must be consistent in their relationships with both individual children and the group as a whole. Consistency is especially important in working with handicapped children.

This can be accomplished by clearly specifying both the rules or standards for classroom behavior and the consequences for noncompliance. Guidelines that teachers establish for classroom behavior can help in avoiding numerous social problems that otherwise might erupt. Unanticipated changes can produce misunderstandings and a wide range of testing behavior, especially among handicapped children. A discussion of techniques for planning and organizing for instruction in an integrated classroom is presented in Chapter 4. Proper planning can help avoid behavioral problems in the classroom.

In teaching, as in most professions, success demands continued growth and a willingness to change as the situation warrants. Each year brings new students, and handicapped children will certainly create new and different problems. Indeed, handicapped children are characterized best by their diversity. While some teachers react to handicapped students with unwarranted concern or with fear that they will not be able to serve these children adequately, most teachers quickly learn to deal with such students in diverse ways, learning new techniques and modifying those they have used before.

An open attitude can be reflected in the teacher's active search for ideas and suggestions that will improve performance. Regular classroom teachers can call in special resource persons to discuss and explain teachniques and principles with which they are unfamiliar. Teachers must also recognize that they can learn by watching children, just as children can learn from them. Having the flexibility and security to incorpo-

rate student ideas into the daily routine will also help promote a high level of interest and participation in the classroom.

There is no one best way of teaching all students. Teachers need to identify instructional approaches best suited to achieving educational objectives and best utilized by children with different learning styles and abilities. Discussions concerning the advantages and disadvantages of open versus structured teaching, for example, are meaningless unless they are related to children's individual styles and abilities. In the early childhood years emphasis must be given to the development of social and expressive skills as well as basic academic skills, such as reading, writing, and arithmetic. These are all prerequisites to school success.

Regardless of the instructional approach used, teachers must remain constantly aware of the effect of their own behavior on that of the children. Studies of teaching contain many examples of how teachers have inadvertently caused children to behave inappropriately. Teachers must realize that children's behaviors can often be changed simply by their reaction to them. Teacher's behavior that is directed toward approving desirable activity will increase children's willingness to engage in such activity.

The development of a healthy social environment in the classroom depends largely on the ability of teachers to gain the willing involvement and participation of the children. This must be achieved through affection and sincere concern that tells students that their teachers are working in their students' best interests. The positive climate of a classroom, however, can only be effective when teachers are consistent from day to day and child to child.

Knowledge About Behavior Problems And Solutions To These Problems

Behavior problems can arise even in the most carefully planned social environment. Teachers must be able to recognize and cope with them. Handicapped children may act in ways that interfere with, prohibit, or compete with school-related activities and useful social and work skills. To maintain a positive social climate, regular classroom teachers must know what type of problem behaviors to expect and how to deal with them.

Spodek (1978) has identified the following guidelines to help teachers develop an approach to discipline:

1. Children should know the behaviors expected of them.

2. Children should be told why rules are in effect.

3. Children should have opportunities to observe and practice proper behavior.

4. Behavior expected of children should be possible for them.

5. Children cannot be expected to behave properly at all times.

6. Teachers should behave with consistency toward the children in their class.

These guidelines are as important with handicapped children as they are with nonhandicapped children.

The problem behaviors typically manifested by young handicapped children in mainstream settings may be classified as (1) behavioral excesses, (2) shy and withdrawn behaviors, (3) behavioral deficits, and (4) behavioral ineptitudes (Bijou, 1976). Children with behavioral excesses are frequently described as hostile, aggressive, continually out of their seats, having tantrums, crying, and creating conduct problems. These children often elicit the greatest concern from regular class teachers because they can disrupt the entire classroom. The objective for teaching these children is to help them develop positive social behavior.

Children who are shy and withdrawn are variously described as isolated (Weinberg, 1976), having adjustment problems (Ullmann, 1957), or friendless (Shure, 1963). These children, because they represent no immediate threat to classroom control, are often ignored at great expense to their future development. Children who are socially isolated, for example, are more likely to drop out of school (Ullmann, 1957), to be later identified as juvenile delinquents (Rolf, Sells, & Golden, 1972), and to have mental problems later in life (Cowen, Pederson, Babijian, Izzo, & Trost, 1973). A few authors (e.g., Asher, Oden, & Gottman, 1977) have suggested that the consequences of low peer acceptance may be more severe than the consequences of low achievement. Socially isolated children are often physically unattractive, low achievers, and tend to move frequently from school to school (Asher et al., 1977). The objective of teaching isolated children is to help them develop positive social behavior that will lead to positive and sustained contact with peers.

Children with behavioral deficits include those who are underdeveloped in self-care, language, social skills, academic abilities, and basic knowledge (Bijou, 1976). These children often display inappropriate classroom behavior out of a sense of frustration stemming from inability to keep up with others in the classroom. In teaching these children, the primary objective is to help them develop skills and abilities in their areas of deficits.

Children with behavioral ineptitudes often have many appropriate behaviors but use them at the wrong time or place. Children who can talk but do not direct conversation to people, children who have acquired manners but do not apply them at the proper time, and children who react to people as objects and do not address them directly would be included in this group. The goal in working with these children is to help them learn under what circumstances certain social behaviors are acceptable or unacceptable.

DEALING WITH BEHAVIOR PROBLEMS

Over the past decade several strategies for dealing with classroom behavior problems have been developed. Many of these come out of a behavior analysis framework. Others come from social learning theory, psychodynamic theory, and ecological psychology. Methods for dealing with behavior problems include behavior analysis techniques, psychodynamic approaches, and ecological approaches.

Behavior Analysis Techniques

Positive Reinforcement.   Positive reinforcement for appropriate social behavior is by far the most widely used and easily implemented technique. A reinforcer is a positive event, such as a smile, approval, recognition, a good grade, or affection, that follows a behavior and is likely to strengthen that behavior. Many events in the classroom can serve as reinforcers, and not all

children will find the same materials or events reinforcing. Various materials and events common to preschool, kindergarten, and primary classrooms serve as reinforcers. Reinforcement for desirable social behavior is a strong management technique.

There are a variety of types of reinforcers. Whatever is used should be something that is valued by the child. Some programs have used edible reinforcers, such as candy, cookies, or fruit that children enjoy, given in small quantities. Toys or other small, inexpensive objects have also been used as reinforcers. Sometimes activities have been used as reinforcers. Children are allowed to play with certain materials or engage in certain activities, if they have performed appropriately. Often when activities are used as reinforcers, a token economy (described below) is established. This prevents the reinforcing activity from becoming disruptive in a class and keeps

---

EXTINCTION

Mabel, a first grader, was constantly attempting to obtain Mr. Green's attention by jumping up and down in her seat, frantically waving her hand and whispering in a loud voice, "Mr. Green, Mr. Green, me, me, call on me." Mabel exhibited this behavior an average of 11 times a day—55 times during a one-week data collection phase. Mr. Green also discovered that he responded to Mabel's inappropriate behavior almost 90 percent of the time by either permit-

ting Mabel to answer the question, telling the child to be quiet and sit still, or signaling his disapproval nonverbally. Regardless of the specific reaction, Mr. Green realized that he was attending to Mabel's attention-getting behavior.

Mr. Green decided he would ignore Mabel's behavior until she exhibited acceptable behavior in response to questions directed to the class. Mabel's attempts to obtain attention subsequently decreased.

---

children from immediately changing activities. In selecting materials or activities as reinforcers, the teacher can use things that have educational value in themselves.

Teachers often use social reinforcers, including praise, attention, and affection. When these are made contingent on children's appropriate behaviors, they can be extremely influential. Whatever reinforcers are selected, teachers should be careful to use them for only a limited time, fading them (using them less and less frequently) and allowing appropriate behaviors to provide their own satisfactions over time.

Extinction. Extinction, a technique used to weaken inappropriate or disruptive behavior, involves ignoring behavior. This procedure is useful only when a child is not likely to be reinforced by peers for that behavior. In addition, the use of extinction proce-

dures generally take time to be effective and thus requires much patience on the part of teachers. Some behaviors such as those in which the child inflicts self harm or harms others cannot be ignored; thus, this technique cannot always be used.

Time-Out. Time-out refers to withholding access to reinforcers as a response to inappropriate behavior. In most early childhood classrooms, time-out involves withdrawing a child from a group instruction or play situation for a brief period of time. When using time-out it is important for teachers to calmly explain to the child the reason for being removed from the group and that it will only be for a brief period of time. There is a danger that teachers may overuse time-out as a management strategy. Frequently, asking a child to behave appropriately, explaining why appropriate behavior is important, and then reinforcing the de-

---

TIME-OUT

Sam was a hyperactive kindergarten child having great difficulty remaining in his seat and refraining from grabbing persons and objects near him. He would also grab and eat his classmates' lunches. Sam's teacher, realizing that these behaviors were interfering with his learning and with that of his classmates, attempted several procedures to help Sam, including verbal reprimands, ignoring, and reinforcing appropriate behavior. None of these procedures was effective, and the teacher, on advice of the school psychologist, decided to implement a time-out procedure.

Each time Sam left his seat at an inappropriate time, he was to be placed in a time-out area for 2 minutes. In implementing this procedure, Sam's teacher followed these simple steps:

1. Out-of-seat behavior was defined as any time Sam's posterior was not in contact with his chair during appropriate times during work periods.

2. When Sam was out-of-seat, the teacher's aide escorted Sam to the time-out area for 2 minutes, during which time he had to be quiet and remain seated. The time-out area with a chair was created in the corner of the classroom by rearranging two filing cabinets. A chair was provided outside the area so the aide could monitor Sam during the time-out period.

3. At the end of 2 minutes of quiet sitting, Sam was allowed to reenter the classroom.

---

sirable social response, is as effective as or more effective than time-out (Martin & Pear, 1978).

Token Economy Systems. Token economy systems are employed when immediately available reinforcers such as praise are not sufficient to maintain appropriate classroom behaviors (Kazdin, 1975). Typically, tokens consist of poker chips or paper stars that are earned for good work and measureable improvement. Tokens are exchanged for other reinforcers such as a toy or material or the opportunity to participate in some enjoyable activities. When using token economy systems, there are 6 essential steps: (1) specify what

behaviors will earn tokens; (2) develop a menu of back-up reinforcers specifying what the tokens will buy; (3) set prices and wages: how many tokens are earned by each goal behavior and what each activity, privilege, or object costs in tokens; (4) select tokens that can readily be given, are handy, and will cause minimum interference; (5) establish the value of tokens through instruction ("This token is given for good work."); and (6) keep records of points each child earns and spends each day.

While tokens can be effective in maintaining appropriate classroom behavior, there are several problems inherent in using token systems. One problem is the amount of teacher time

A TOKEN ECONOMY SYSTEM

Mrs. Cain, the third grade teacher, was having difficulty with three boys—Brad, Burt, and Bob—each of whom displayed various behavior disorders that interfered with their learning in the regular class. After consulting with the resource teacher, school psychologist, and principal, it was decided a token economy program might be useful. The resource teacher explained a token program in a memo to Mrs. Cain:

MEMO

TO: Mrs. Cain

FROM: Alice Tolkin

RE: Token System

A token economy program consists of ten basic steps. These are listed below along with suggestions to use with Brad, Burt, and Bob.

Steps	*Suggestions*
1. Select a target behavior.	1. Focus on in-seat, compliance with requests, or coming in on time after recess.
2. Present the idea to the child.	2. Sit down with the three boys and explain what the system is, why it is being used, and how it will work.
3. Select an appropriate token.	3. You could use poker chips, points, stars, smiling faces, point cards, trading stamps, animal stickers, or play money. Use the same token with everybody.
4. Establish rewards for which tokens can be exchanged.	4. There are several possibilities you can use, including library time, time in the book corner reading a favorite book, or additional recess.
5. Develop a reward menu.	5. Set up a menu such as: *Item:* 10 minutes free time. *Cost:* 4 tokens *Item:* 10 minutes of listening to records. *Cost:* 7 tokens *Item:* 5 minutes of cutting and pasting. *Cost:* 5 tokens Post the list of activities in the classroom. Be prepared to increase

	costs so that more and more good behavior will be required to engage in good activities.
6. Implement the program.	6. Initially introduce the token system on a limited basis. Build an understanding of its use, explaining the system to the children clearly and precisely. Be patient and answer all children's questions.
7. Provide immediate reinforcement for acceptable behavior.	7. Dispense tokens at the appropriate time to limit frustration. You can delay the delivery of tokens gradually.
8. Pair delivery of the token with a more natural social reinforcer.	8. We want the child to respond to the same social reinforcers as others. First present the social reinforcer and then the token; then present more social reinforcers and fewer tokens.
9. Provide time for the children to exchange tokens for rewards.	9. Allow the child to have 5 exchange times daily at first. Reduce this to 1 daily, 3 times weekly, and so on.
10. Revise the menu frequently.	10. Change back-up activities periodically and gradually raise the price for activities as the time goes by.

it takes to implement. Records must be kept and tokens dispensed, and children must be carefully monitored. Another, more serious, problem involves the necessity to fade out the use of tokens. Since behavior in the regular class is not typically maintained by tokens, children must learn to respond in time to such natural reinforcers as praise and approval rather than tokens. Most teachers are not trained in the subtle procedures needed to effectively fade out the use of tokens.

Response Cost. Response cost refers to a situation in which behavior results in the loss of reinforcing events (Sulzer & Mayer, 1972). Loss of a specified amount of recess or gym time for undersirable classroom behavior is a common example of response cost. This technique is a form of punishment and can easily be overused by teachers.

Shaping. Shaping involves using positive reinforcement to change behavior gradually. The first step is to wait until the child's behavior somewhat approximates the behavior to be learned or to prompt such behavior and then give the child a reinforcer. As the child's behavior further approaches the de-

RESPONSE COST

Sylvia, a preschooler, was a behavior problem. She would often kick and scream at the teacher, other adults, and on occasion, at peers. Mr. Kemp, Sylvia's teacher, decided to implement a response cost technique whereby Sylvia would lose 1 minute of playtime for kicking or screaming (not to exceed a total of 10 minutes). On the first day of the intervention, Mr. Kemp showed Sylvia 10 cards, with one through ten circled on them, arranged on a bracket similar to that of a daily desk calendar. He told Sylvia that each time he heard her kick or scream he would flip down one card which meant that she would lose 2 minutes of playtime.

sired behavior, he or she is again reinforced. This shaping process continues until the new behavior is learned. For example, Allen et al. (1964) conducted a study on an isolated 4-year-old nursery school child. After six weeks of school, the child remained isolated from other children and engaged in a variety of behaviors to gain the teacher's attention. After observing the child for a baseline period to determine the child's natural functioning, the teacher praised the child for interacting with other children. At first, the subject was reinforced for standing close to another child or playing beside another child. Later she was reinforced only for direct interaction. The researchers discovered that reinforcing statements that focused on the subject

SHAPING

Chris, 4, a moderately retarded child, was having difficulty playing circle or ball games that required running from one specific location to another. Whenever he engaged in a game of this type, he ran about at random, dashing here and there, jumping up and down, and in general confusing himself and his playmates.

Ms. Kale, the physical education teacher, determined that Chris did attend to the action of the game and did attempt to play by the rules. To help Chris, Ms. Kale modified the rules by having all team members run hand-in-hand in pairs from one location to another. Chris was Ms. Kale's partner until he was used to the new running pattern. Once Chris developed acceptable skills, the traditional rules were again enacted.

MODELING

Mr. Simmons, a second grade teacher, provides special help during work periods for Susan and Martha. He notices that while Susan works on her assigned tasks, Martha seldom attempts to complete assignments. He also notes that both children respond to his attention. Therefore, he decides to use his attention as a reward for completing work. Susan was reinforced in Martha's pres-ence for attempting and completing assignments, as well as for paying attention to instructions; Martha's inappropriate behavior was ignored. After a few sessions in which Susan's behavior was rewarded, Martha began to imitate Susan to receive Mr. Simmons's attention. Mr. Simmons concluded that Martha learned appropriate behavior by modeling Susan who was reinforced by Mr. Simmons.

---

as a member of the group (e.g., "You three girls have a cozy house.") were successful and resulted in a high level of sustained interaction with other children.

Modeling.   Modeling involves learning something by watching someone do it. Teachers or other peers can use modeling to teach an exceptional child appropriate social behaviors by showing the child how to behave. For example, a teacher might sit next to a child and play with another child to demonstrate how to share. Too often teachers fail to recognize that handicapped children need to be explicitly shown how to do things that other, more normally functioning children learn through informal observations on their own. Modeling is an especially effective procedure for withdrawn or behaviorally inept children (Bijou, 1976).

An interesting application of modeling to promote social behavior is reported by O'Connor (1969), who identified socially isolated children in 9 nursery school classes. Half of the children saw a film modeling appropriate behavior while the other half saw a film about dolphins. Post-film observations showed that the social interaction of children in the modeling group greatly increased while the control group hardly changed at all. Subsequent follow-up studies with similar groups of children showed that film modeling also produced results that maintained over time (O'Connor, 1972; Evers & Schwarz, 1973).

Verbal Instructions.   Verbal instructions involve telling or explaining to children what is expected of them. Verbal instructions alone can be effective with mildly handicapped young children, but are most generally used in conjunction with other techniques such as positive reinforcement, punishment, modeling, or shaping.

Coaching.   Coaching is a procedure developed for use primarily with socially isolated children. It consists of

---

CONTINGENCY CONTRACTING

Sally, a mildly handicapped third-grader, is having difficulty completing reading assignments during work periods even though she has the skills necessary to do the assignments. Mr. Anderson, her teacher, notes that Sally is often out of her seat during work periods, talking and bothering others. Mr. Anderson has tried several strategies ranging from depriving Sally of recess time to keeping her after school, but with no success. On the advice of the resource teacher, Mr. Anderson met with Sally and together they developed the following contract:

This Contract is between <u>SALLY LANGE</u> and MR. ANDERSON

About *Completing Assignments During Work Periods.*

TASK: Sally will read one chapter in her reading book and provide full written answers to all the questions at the end of that for five consecutive days.

TIME: Within the 30-minute period assigned for work on reading.

CRITERION: Sally will get at least 70% of the answers correct.

REINFORCER: 10 minutes of free time during any other work period.

PENALTY: If less than 70% correct, Sally will come in after school to make corrections.

BONUS: 70% for 10 consecutive days = one day of no written work.

SIGNED: Student _____

Teacher _____

Date   _____

Sally and Mr. Anderson also agreed to renegotiate the contract if the need arose.

---

three components. First, a child is provided with a rule or standard of behavior; in simple terms, that child is told what to do. Second, the child has opportunities to rehearse or practice the behavior. Finally, there are opportunities for feedback in which the child's performance is discussed, approval is given, and suggestions for improvement are made.

Zahavi (1973) used coaching to modify aggressive behavior in nursery school children. Initially, the teacher met with four of eight aggressive children for approximately 15 minutes, during which time she explained to the children that hitting others causes harm, that no one likes to be hit, and that there are alternative behaviors to hitting such as sharing and taking turns. The teacher also asked questions so that the children would participate in formulating concepts. Children were then given opportunities to play with others while the teacher waited and afterward the teacher provided feedback. Four children served as controls. Results indicated a dramatic decrease in the aggressive behavior of those children receiving the coaching condition

---

GROUP CONTINGENCY

Mrs. Wienke, the kindergarten teacher, had problems keeping her 25 students quiet in the hall as they passed from their classroom to the multipurpose room for physical education. She noted that the children talked loudly, walked out of line, and occasionally started to push and fight in the hall. She also noted that all her students enjoyed the gym activities. Mrs. Wienke decided to implement a group contingency contract to reduce talkouts, pushing and fighting, and other out-of-line behavior.

Initially, she met with the students,

discussed the problem with them, and told them they could *all earn* five extra minutes of gym time activities if everyone was quiet and walked in a straight line while going from the room to the gym. If anyone was noisy or got out of line, the *whole class would lose* five minutes of gym time. The group contingency led to immediate compliance with the teacher's request, and over a two-week period, the teacher was gradually able to eliminate the extra gym time as a reinforcer.

---

and continued high levels of aggression on the part of the control children.

Contingency Contracts. Contingency contracts involve an explicit agreement between the teacher and child specifying the relationship between the child's behavior and the consequences that will follow (Homme, 1977). This procedure, used primarily with older children, is effective with handicapped children who have difficulty associating a behavior with its consequences. Typically, a contingency contract defines the task, when it will be done, how it must be done, the reinforcer to be earned, the penalty for noncompliance with the contract, and a bonus that can be earned for extra good work.

There are several advantages to contingency contracting. When a child has some input, performance may improve. Moreover, contingencies are not as

likely to be aversive since the child negotiates for them. In addition, contracts are flexible and can be renegotiated and revised to fit the needs of the individual. Contracts also provide a way to structure a relationship between individuals and thus can help handicapped children understand the impact of their behavior on others. A child has to understand the nature of a contract for this to be used, however (Wilcox & Pany, 1976). Group contingency contracts can also be developed with the entire class. In such cases, a single individual, a small group, or the entire class can earn consequences, as illustrated.

Psychodynamic Approaches

While the approaches described above focus on the behavior of children, psychodynamic approaches focus on the underlying causes of that behavior.

Dreikurs (1968), for example, suggests that children misbehave for one of four reasons: to gain attention, to display power, to gain revenge, or to display a deficiency in order either to seek special services or to be exempted from certain expectations. Teachers need to find out why children misbehave. The last of these reasons suggests that a misbehavior may be a call for help from a handicapped child and needs to be treated differently from a misbehavior that results from other causes.

Dreikurs suggests that teachers use logical consequences rather than punishment or reinforcement to deal with misbehavior. Logical consequences express the reality of the social order, involve no moral judgments, and are concerned only with present circumstances. If a child deliberately creates a mess, for example, the consequence might be that that child stays in and cleans up, possibly missing a valued activity. The child should also be told why the particular consequence has been selected.

Often the negative feelings children have are not given legitimate outlet in school and are therefore expressed in negative behavior. Legitimizing these feelings and helping children cope with them, as well as providing children with skills for expressing their feelings verbally rather than behaviorally can lessen disruptive behavior in a classroom. The teacher should make clear that he or she understands the child's feelings but will not permit the negative behaviors associated with them. In addition, group meetings can be used to deal with children's feelings about having a handicapped child in class. This can lessen fear and ignorance that may occur, eliminate stereotyping, and help children deal directly with issues that confront them.

The group process might also be used to deal with problems in social behavior. A number of programs have been designed to aid early childhood teachers in helping their children deal with personal feelings and concerns. These include: *DUSO: Developing Understanding of Self and Others* (Dinkmeyer, 1970), *Dimensions of Personality* (1970), *First Things—Values* (1972), and the *Human Development Program* (Bessel & Palomares, 1970). Martorella (1975) has compared these four in terms of basic teaching used, basic affective themes addressed, and key student and teacher roles.

The *DUSO-1* program is designed for kindergarten–primary grades. It includes storybooks, recordings, posters, activity cards, role-playing cards, discussion cards, props and puppets, along with a teachers' manual. It is designed to help children understand themselves, their feelings, and the feelings of others and to comprehend the interdependence of the group. Teachers are expected to read stories, lead discussion groups, and help children engage in role playing and puppet dramatizations. The materials are designed to help children understand social and emotional behavior and develop desirable behavior responses.

Dimensions of Personality is a primary grade program that makes use of student and teacher manuals, activity sheets, and ditto masters. Children participate in group discussions and work on individual exercises. The function of the program is to develop social competence skills, including skills in working with groups, and to build positive self-concepts.

The *First Things—Values* program consists of a set of records or cassettes, filmstrips, and teachers' manuals. Moral dilemmas are posed to children through the audiovisual material. These are related to truth, fairness, rules, promises, and notions of right and wrong. Children are asked to take a position related to one of these dilemmas and provide a rationale for that position. The material is built on Kohlberg's concept of stages in moral development (e.g., Turiel, 1973).

The *Human Development Program* provides materials for children beginning at age 4. The program focuses around "Magic Circle" activities in which children participate in group process discussions, with the teacher functioning as group leader and structurer, discussion stimulator and clarifier, and rule enforcer. The program is designed to improve communication in the group, develop children's self-concepts, and improve personal self-control.

Each of the programs described can help teachers deal with the social climate of the class by helping children become better aware of their own feelings and the feelings of others, by helping them develop a more positive sense of self, and by providing a medium wherein class difficulties can be discussed and possible solutions explored. In each of the programs the teacher functions as a discussion leader as well as an observer of social conditions in the classroom. In some of the programs the teacher also serves as a diagnostician and behavior reinforcer. Teachers may review the programs and

select the one that conforms to their views of how social behavior is best modified in the class and how children's social development is best supported. Whichever program is selected, it is important that what occurs within the program is supported in the total social life of the class.

Ecological Approaches

Another approach to dealing with behavior problems in early childhood classrooms is by looking at ways to modify the environment to diminish the possibility of conflict. Swap (1974) views many of the problems that emotionally disturbed children have in school as resulting from the fact that they are still resolving conflicts associated with earlier developmental stages. Because the classroom environment is often designed for children with greater emotional maturity, the regular classroom setting contributes to social conflict and behavioral problems for those children. Teachers need to become careful observers of their children, capable of judging their emotional as well as academic maturity. By modifying academic requirements, varying work space, using different kinds of groupings, and matching instructional materials to the capabilities of the students, inappropriate behaviors can be diminished.

Kounin (1970) also views discipline and classroom management from an ecological point of view. His early studies on the "ripple effect" demonstrated that the way a teacher corrects one student's behavior influences the behavior of the other students in class.

This seems especially so with young children. He also found that the teacher's awareness of classroom processes is conveyed to students and contributes to their effectiveness as classroom managers. Thus teachers with eyes in the back of their heads, who are able to attend to a range of activities and are aware of the goings-on in the classroom, are most effective in managing the group process.

Similarly an alert teacher can establish an adequate flow of classroom activities, pacing them properly for the children, maintaining the momentum of the activities, and attending to the need for proper transitions. Activities for all children, including handicapped children, need to be varied and challenging and should help them feel they are making academic progress. By using the social, physical, and academic elements of the classroom environment to meet the educational needs of all the children, more manipulative and direct forms of discipline and punishment can be avoided.

Each of the techniques reviewed above can be effective, either singly or in combination, in dealing with the behavior problems of young exceptional children.

PEER INFLUENCE

Young children learn a lot from one another. Interacting with each other daily in a variety of activities and settings, children learn to see themselves as leaders, followers, or isolates. When they are accepted and liked by peers, children gain confidence and self-assurance and perform better in school. Uncertain or partial acceptance, on the other hand, produces anxiety and self-doubt. When students are totally rejected, they can experience trauma, act out aggressively, or withdraw into apathy or fantasy.

The extent to which children are affected by their peers depends on several factors including age, social and ethnic background, and the child's handicapping condition. Preschool-age children, for example, tend not to be as strongly influenced by their peer group as older children. During the preschool years, home and adult praise are more important than peer approval. According to Winkler (1975), however, beginning in the early primary years the effect of peer group composition increases with the age of the child. In addition, physically disabled children at any age tend to be less well accepted by peers.

Considering the impact that children's peers have on their social and academic development, teachers in integrated settings must learn to understand and use the classroom social environment. There are things that a teacher can do to increase the chances for healthy social interaction among children in integrated early childhood settings. These include: being sensitive to peer norms and values, being able to understand peer roles and relationships, and being aware of social interactions between handicapped and nonhandicapped children.

Peer Norms and Values. In any classroom where children learn and play together, an extensive system of norms, expectations, and values quickly develops. As with all social groups, this system stipulates what will be accepted and admired. Children want to be popular and accepted by their peers. If they perceive that such activities as participating in class, cooperating with the teacher, or accepting differences in individuals are acceptable, they will conform to these group standards. Peer support for these behaviors can be effective in motivating individual children.

Teachers can explain the importance of cooperation and sharing. They can help children understand that while individuals differ in their abilities and personalities, they still deserve the respect of all. Teachers can also look for opportunities to model appropriate social responses and to reinforce other children for their appropriate behavior.

Peer Roles and Relationships. The peer group in every classroom, no matter how large or small, has some degree of organization. For example, groups have leaders who attain their popularity and status through actions and attributes considered important by the group. Peer group leaders are frequently instrumental in determining group activity, establishing cooperation with the teacher, and initiating acceptance of new members. By obtaining the cooperation of group leaders, teachers are better able to promote acceptance of and interaction with handicapped children.

Social Interactions Between Handicapped and Nonhandicapped Children. In order to promote integration, it is important that teachers determine, early in the year, the extent to which handicapped children are accepted by their nonhandicapped peers and the extent to which they interact with them.

Because results have been equivocal, research on the nature of social interaction in integrated early childhood settings provides little guidance for the teacher. Some studies (e.g., Peterson & Haralick, 1977) have shown substantial spontaneous peer interactions between handicapped and nonhandicapped children. Other studies (e.g., Porter, Ramsey, Tremblay, Iancobo, & Crawley, 1978) show a consistent preference by nonhandicapped children for other nonhandicapped children. Since teachers cannot assume that positive peer interactions will occur naturally in integrated early childhood settings, procedures to encourage and support such interactions should be used.

Teachers have several options as to ways to increase social interactions among young children in integrated settings. These include teacher reinforcement, peer attention, peer tutoring, role playing, and seating and work assignments.

Teacher Reinforcement

Teacher praise, contingent upon the child's positive interactive behavior, increases social integration among preschool children. Strain and Timm (1974), for instance, applied contingent teacher attention to reinforce an isolate preschool child and her peers for attempts at social interaction, measuring interactive behavior under two conditions of contingent teacher attention. In the first condition, verbal praise and physical contact were directed to a target subject's peers for appropriate interaction with the target subject. In the second condition, verbal praise and physical contact were directed to the target subject for appropriate interaction with peers. Results indicated increased appropriate social behaviors for both the target subject and her peers. The recipients of contingent adult attention also initiated more appropriate social contacts than did their peers.

Teacher reinforcement, however, can also interfere with ongoing social interaction that occurs naturally between children. Shores, Hester, and Strain (1976) found that structuring dramatic play or role-playing activities was more successful in producing social interaction between handicapped and nonhandicapped preschool children than was continued adult attention alone. Similarly, Strain and Wiegernick (1976) found that sociodramatic activities (e.g., having handicapped and nonhandicapped children act out favorite stories) were far more effective in promoting social interaction than teacher attention alone. These studies suggest that teachers should be no more obtrusive than necessary in promoting positive social interactions between handicapped and nonhandicapped children.

Peer Attention

Teachers need to promote constructive use of peer attention. This involves three things: (1) eliminating peer rein-

forcement for undesirable social behavior, (2) encouraging peer attention for appropriate behavior, and (3) encouraging peer acceptance of handicapped children. Each of these objectives can be accomplished in a variety of ways. One is through promoting social interaction that should encourage peer acceptance of handicapped children by their nonhandicapped peers.

Several studies have demonstrated ways of using peer attention to eliminate undesirable social behavior. Barrish, Saunders, and Wolf (1969) attempted to eliminate inappropriate talking and out-of-seat behavior in a third-grade class by dividing the class into teams and establishing a point system whereby teams earned privileges. Points were lost when team members acted inappropriately. The children often actively discouraged any behavior that would result in loss of privileges for all. As a result, all students had to abide by class standards.

This study and others (e.g., Patterson, 1965) clearly show that teachers can influence the kind of attention and encouragement that children give to each other. Few consequences are more powerful than peer attention, and an imaginative teacher should be able to redirect numerous socially inappropriate behaviors as well as promote social acceptance of handicapped children by using a variety of strategies.

Peer Tutoring

Another strategy, useful in promoting social interaction between handicapped and nonhandicapped children is peer tutoring. This strategy is discussed in Chapter 4.

Role Playing

One strategy to improve social interaction of children is role playing. In role playing, children act out brief episodes that involve problems of interacting with one another. Role playing provides a nonthreatening circumstance in which to encounter reactions of others and to learn ways to cope with such experiences.

Several situations can be presented through role playing. Teachers can ask children to reenact problems that frequently arise during class. They also may want to introduce situations that have not yet been encountered but that will arise in time. In either instance, when using role playing the teacher should remember to select situations that are concrete and relevant, to keep role-playing sessions brief and to the point, to explain to children observing a role-playing situation what they should watch, and to strategically choose the children who play the various roles.

Seating and Work Assignments

All classrooms are characterized by patterns of friendship and social interaction. When teachers have identified children or subgroups who only minimally participate with others, they can make changes in seating and work assignments to encourage more involvement.

Rearranging seats may involve moving a handicapped child closer to the center of the class or next to a friendly nonhandicapped peer who is likely to accept him. If, on the other hand,

groups of children are on the fringe of activity, the teacher may want to use a seating arrangement that supports interaction of members with each other. In any case, the teacher should consider using a seating plan that promotes rather than hinders social interaction among students.

Teachers can also use work assignments to stimulate social integration among handicapped and nonhandicapped children. The teacher can select children for group reports, art projects, or gym activities that provide handicapped children with an opportunity to participate actively. Whenever possible, the teacher should assign duties and responsibilities to handicapped children to further enhance their role and status in the classroom. If a handicapped child has special skill or knowledge, the teacher should design situations in which those skills can be shared with the group.

Each of the above strategies can be useful in promoting the social acceptance of handicapped children by their peers. The teacher should also help children become more aware of their own feelings about themselves and others and help them develop social skills related to expressing those feelings in socially sanctioned ways. This must be done at the same time as the classroom is redesigned to limit disruptive behavior and a program is implemented to change the behavior of the children in the class. Some children who are affected by more serious problems may need specialized help. Teachers can receive assistance from specialists in identifying effective ways to deal with such problems.

SUMMARY

Teachers are as concerned with children's social learning as they are with their academic learning. The ability of a handicapped child to function in a regular classroom is determined to a great extent by the social climate in that classroom and by the child's social skills. Teachers can become aware of the social interactions that take place, using specific strategies to improve the social climate and the level of acceptance that handicapped children might feel. They can help all children develop skills to better understand themselves and others and to learn how to work and play with others.

In this chapter, we have considered some of the factors that are associated wih developing a positive social climate in integrated early childhood classrooms. Teachers, peers, and the classroom program can affect the social environment of the classroom in diverse and subtle ways. By carefully considering the skills needed to influence these factors, teachers can increase their chances of developing a healthy social climate.

There are a range of techniques available for teachers to use in their classrooms. These include behavior analysis techniques as well as techniques rooted in psychodynamic theories. They can also use group process techniques in modifying peer influences in the classroom. Teachers should consider a range of alternative approaches in dealing with the social environment of the classroom and experiment to find those approaches that best fit their particular situation and their view of what is appropriate in an educational setting. Teachers can also experiment with classroom organization to provide support for the social interactions they wish to nurture.

A good resource teachers can use in reviewing various models of classroom discipline, both from a theoretical and practical view, is *Building classroom discipline: From models to practice* (Charles, 1981).

Disruptive behavior can be devastating in a classroom. Teachers are more often shaken by their inability to control the behavior of pupils than with pupils' inability to learn. Appropriate social behavior is learned, however, just as academic behavior is learned. If disruptive behavior does occur, it is important that teachers view appropriate classroom behavior as a goal that can be achieved, rather than as something to be expected from all children from the onset.

REFERENCES

Allen, K. E., Hart, B., Buell, J. S., Harris, F. R., and Wolf, M. M. Effects of social reinforcement of isolate behavior of a nursery school child. *Child Development*, 1964, 35, 511–518.

Asher, S. R., Oden, S. L., and Gottman, J. M. Children's friendships in school settings. In L. G. Katz (Ed.). *Current topics in early childhood education (Vol. 1)*. Norwood, N.J.: Ablex Publishing Company, 1977.

Bandura, A. Psychotherapy based on modeling principles. In A. Bergin and S. L. Garfield (Eds.). *Handbook of psychotherapy and behavior change: An empirical analysis*. New York: John Wiley and Sons, 1971.

Barrish, H., Saunders, M., and Wolf, M. M. Good behavior game: Effects of individual contingencies for group consequences on disruptive behavior in a classroom. *Journal of Applied Behavior Analysis*, 1969, *2,* 79–84.

Bessell, H., and Palomares, U. *Methods in human development*. San Diego, Calif.: Human Development Training Institute, 1970.

Bijou, S. W. *The basic stage of early childhood*. Englewood Cliffs, N.J.: Prentice-Hall, 1976.

Brophy, J. E., and Putnam, J. G. Classroom management in the elementary grades. In D. L. Duke (Ed.). *Classroom management*. 78th Yearbook of the National Society for the Study of Education. Chicago: University of Chicago Press, 1979.

Charles, C. M. *Building classroom discipline: From models to practice*. New York: Longman, 1981.

Combs, A. W. *The professional education of teachers: A perceptual view of teacher preparation*. Boston: Allyn & Bacon, 1965.

Cowen, E. L., Pederson, A., Babijian, H., Izzo, L. D., and Trost, M. A. Long-term follow-up of early detected vulnerable children. *Journal of Consulting and Clinical Psychology*, 1973, *41*, 438–446.

Dinkmeyer, D. *Developing understanding of self and others*. Circle Pines, Minn.: American Guidance Service, 1970.

Dimensions of personality. Dayton, Ohio: Pflaum/Standard, 1972.

Dreikurs, R. *Psychology in the classroom* (2nd ed.). New York: Harper and Row, 1968.

Evers, W. L., and Schwarz, J. C. Modifying social withdrawal in preschoolers: The effects of filmed modeling and teacher praise. *Journal of Abnormal Child Psychology*, 1973, *1*, 248–256.

First things—values. Pleasantville, N.Y.: Guidance Associates, 1972.

Hart, B. M., Allen, K. E., Buell, J. S., Harris, F. R., and Wolf, M. M. Effects of social reinforcement on operant crying. *Journal of Experimental Child Psychology*, 1964, *1*, 145–153.

Homme, L. *How to use contingency contracting in the classroom*. Champaign, Ill.: Research Press, 1977.

Human development program. El Cajon, Calif.: Human Development Training Institute, 1970.

Jersild, A. T. Voice of the self. *NEA Journal*, 1965, *54*, 23–25.

Kazdin, A. *Behavior analysis in applied settings*. New York: Dorsey, 1975.

Kounin, J. *Discipline and group management in classrooms*. New York: Holt, Rinehart and Winston, 1970.

Martin, G., and Pear, J. *Behavior modification: What it is and how to do it*. Englewood Cliffs, N.J.: Prentice-Hall, 1978.

Martorelli, P. H. Selected early childhood affective learning programs: An analysis of theories, structure and consistency. *Young Children*, 1975, *30*(4), 289–301.

O'Connor, R. D. Modification of social withdrawal through symbolic modeling. *Journal of Applied Behavior Analysis*, 1969, *2*, 15–22.

O'Connor, R. D. Relative efficacy of modeling, shaping and the combined procedures for modification of social withdrawal. *Journal of Abnormal Psychology*, 1972, 79, 327–334.

Patterson, G. R. An application of conditioning techniques to the control of a hyperactive child. In L. P. Ulmann, and L. Krasner (Eds.). *Case studies in behavior modification*, New York: Holt, Rinehart and Winston, 1965.

Peterson, N. L., and Haralick, J. G., Integration of handicapped and nonhandicapped preschoolers: An analysis of play behavior and social interaction. *Education and Training of the Mentally Retarded*. 1977, 12, 235–246.

Peterson, P. L., and Walberg, H. J. *Research on teaching: Concepts, findings and implications*. Berkeley, Calif.: McCutchan Publishing Co., 1979.

Porter, R. H., Ramsey, B., Tremblay, A., Iancobo, M., and Crawley, S. Social interactions in heterogeneous groups of retarded and normally developing children: An observational study. In G. T. Sackett (Ed.). *Observing behavior*, Vol. I. Baltimore, Md.: University Park Press, 1978.

Rolf, M., Sells, S. B., and Golden, M. M. *Social adjustment and personality development in children*. Minneapolis: University of Minnesota Press, 1972.

Rosenthal, R., and Jacobson, L. Teacher Expectations for the disadvantaged. *Scientific American*, 1968, 218–19 ff.

Shores, R. E., Hester, D., and Strain, P. S. The effects of amount and type of teacher-child interaction on child-child interaction during free play. *Psychology in the Schools*, 1976, 13, 171–175.

Shure, M. B. Psychological ecology of a nursery school. *Child Development*, 1963, 34, 979–992.

Spodek, B. *Teaching in the early years* (2nd ed.). Englewood Cliffs, N.J.: Prentice-Hall, 1978.

Strain, P. S., and Wiegernik, R. The effects of sociodramatic activities on social interaction among behaviorally disordered preschool children. *Journal of Special Education*, 1976, 10, 71–73.

Strain, P. S., and Timm, M. A. An experimental analysis of social interaction between a behaviorally disordered preschool child and her classroom peers. *Journal of Applied Behavior Analysis*, 1974, 4, 583–590.

Sulzer, B., and Mayer, G. R. *Behavior modification procedures for school personnel*. Hinsdale, Ill.: The Dryden Press, 1972.

Swap, S. M. Disturbing classroom behaviors: A developmental and ecological view. *Exceptional Children*, 1974, 41, 163–172.

Turiel, E. Stage transition in moral development. In R. Travers (Ed.). *Second handbook of research on teaching*, Chicago: Rand, McNally, 1973.

Ullmann, C. A. Teachers, peers and tests as predictors of adjustment. *Journal of Educational Psychology*, 1957, 48, 257–267.

Weinberg, N. Social stereotyping of the physically handicapped. *Rehabilitation Psychology*, 1976, 23 (4), 115–124.

Wilcox, B. and Pany, D. Group contingencies: A review of research. Unpublished manuscript, Urbana: University of Illinois, 1976.

Winkler, D. R. Educational achievement and school peer group composition. *Journal of Human Resources*, 1975, 10, 189–204.

Zahavi, S. Aggression-control. Unpublished Master's Thesis, Urbana: University of Illinois, 1973.

Eight

WORKING WITH PARENTS

Parent education has always been an important element in early childhood programs. Indeed, the history of parent education in the United States is intertwined with that of early childhood education. Early kindergartens included work with parents as well as activities for children, and one of the first nursery schools established in our country was a parent cooperative.

The importance of parent involvement in the education of young children has been underscored in the many research and development programs designed in the 1960s and 1970s for children of poor and minority group backgrounds. The Head Start and Follow Through programs that resulted from this work, as well as other federally funded programs, have mandated parent involvement as an integral element of these programs. This involvement often takes the form of parent education in which parents are helped to deepen their understanding of child development and develop new skills related to educating and rearing their children. Parents also help in classrooms. And they have been

brought into the decision-making process through creation of parent advisory boards and other mechanisms that give parents a voice in determining their children's educational programs and in selecting staff.

In teaching handicapped children, the teachers' work with parents needs to be underscored. Involving parents in decisions about their handicapped children's education has a legal base under Public Law 94-142. The requirement that parents understand and approve the educational plans designed for their handicapped children means that teachers will have to spend more time on and give more attention to interpreting their programs to parents.

There are also significant moral and professional reasons for supporting a high level of parent involvement. This chapter discusses the importance of working with parents of handicapped children, describes some of the problems confronted by parents of handicapped children, presents a rationale for parent programs, and describes the various types of programs that can be offered.

LINKING HOME AND SCHOOL

In most states all children above the age of seven are required to attend school, and public funds are used to support those schools. The basic control of schools is in the hands of lay persons, generally elected members of boards of education, who represent their community and who establish educational policy.

Although parents have always been able to influence school policies, this has been enhanced by their right under Public Law 94-142 to accept or reject Individual Educational Programs created for their handicapped children. This requirement highlights the need for good communication and a good working relationship between home and school. This new relationship with parents brings them into the decision-making process, allowing teachers to make use of knowledge and understanding parents have about their own children—knowledge and understanding that should prove useful to teachers in creating the best, most appropriate educational plans for any child. Bronfenbrenner (1974) has suggested that involvement of the child's family is critical to the success of an intervention program. When parents are considered partners, the program's effects are reinforced and its achievement sustained beyond the end of the program. Parents can help the handicapped child apply what has been learned in school in a variety of settings, providing the child with opportunities to extend his or her learning (Stokes and Baer, 1977; Marholin, Siegel, & Phillips, 1975). The program's

effects are likely to be severely limited without it.

Parents are the first teachers of their children. While their teaching is usually informal and often indirect, it is usually effective. This informal teaching, however, may not be enough for handicapped children who might need more explicit and more varied forms of instruction than normal children. These might not be discovered intuitively, and specific teaching strategies might have to be taught to parents of handicapped children. Handicapped children continue to be the responsibility of their parents over a significantly longer period than do their normal counterparts (Shearer & Shearer, 1977); thus, helping parents learn skills for teaching their children can effect the learning process over an extended period of time.

By establishing a working relationship with parents the school can improve communications between parents and teachers and develop agreement about educational goals and ways to achieve these goals for the handicapped child. This can make what happens to the child at home more consistent with what happens at school, limiting unnecessary conflict and confusion.

Lillie (1976) has identified four different dimensions of parent programs: providing social and emotional support, exchanging information, improving parent-child interactions, and having parents participate in the school's program.

Activities in a parent program can be designed to reduce anxieties caused by the family's emotional reactions to the child's handicapping condition and to make the family feel more positive about themselves as a social unit. A similar need for support may be found in all family units, but the need is often more critical when a handicapped child is present.

In any educational program, information needs to be shared among parents and teachers. Parents can learn about their child's program and about the progress being made. Parents can also gain information about principles of child growth and development, and learn specific things they can do to help their child. Teachers, too, need to have information about the child's background and home behavior to improve their understanding of that child's school behavior. This information can be used to build a better educational program for each individual child.

A range of approaches is available to help improve parent-child interactions. Some programs are designed to teach parents systematic structured ways of working with their children (e.g., Becker, 1971; Linde-Kopp, 1974); others are designed to help parents develop insight into why their children behave the way they do (e.g., Ginott, 1965; Gordon, 1970). Still others provide experiences to support optimal interactions between parents and children (Gordon, Guinagh, & Jester, 1972; Sparling & Lewis, 1979).

The final dimension of parent involvement relates to having parents engage in activities related to their child's program. They may participate in advisory groups, act as aides in the classroom, or become involved in making materials for the program.

Schools might develop parent programs containing only some of the dimensions just mentioned. Given the availability of resources, schools and teachers might evolve a program using just one or two of these dimensions. Also, not all parents will become involved in all dimensions of a parent program that has been developed, nor will they all be involved to the same extent. Work and other considerations may limit the time they can give to and the degree to which they can become involved in the program. Teachers need to be as accepting of the abilities and needs of parents as they are of children.

There are definite benefits to be derived from this increased parent involvement. Parents can provide a pool of talent, often untapped, for the class. Many parents have special skills or knowledge related to their employment, hobbies or special backgrounds and interests. Parents can also supplement resources provided by the schools by donating materials such as wrapping paper, scraps of cloth, egg cartons, paper tubes, and other items found in the home. These can be used in a variety of classroom projects.

Parents can be aides and helpers in the classroom, either on a regular basis or for specific projects or excursions. Adding these adults to the classroom can allow greater individual attention to be given to children. In the classroom parents can help with working on projects, cleaning up, observing, and tutor children with special needs. Providing experiences with more and varied adults may help children who need to develop skills in interpersonal relations, which may be especially important to some handicapped children.

Once parents know the program and feel good about it, they can become good public relations resources, providing information to the community at large about what is happening to chil-dren in school. They can also become effective advocates of the school program. In many cases parent advocacy has been directly responsible for altering policies and laws relating to children, especially handicapped children, through their work with school boards, advisory councils, and state and federal legislatures (Lillie, 1974).

PARENTS' REACTIONS TO THEIR CHILDREN'S HANDICAPPING CONDITIONS

Teachers need to be sensitive to parents' reactions to their handicapped children and to their levels of acceptance of their children's conditions. Parents differ in their reactions to their children's handicaps. Some accept the problem more easily than others. And the initial reaction changes as they live with their child who is different from normal children. The range of parental reaction has been described by Gardner (1973), Love (1970), and others. They have been summarized into stages of denial, anger, guilt, blame, shame, overprotection, and adaptation by Karnes and Lee (1980).

A common parental reaction to the diagnosis of a child's handicap is to *deny* the problem exists. The diagnostician's competence may be questioned and opinions of other experts sought. The feelings of parents must be understood at this stage. While teachers try to help them accept their child's condition, parents' feelings of helplessness and frustration can lead to *anger* toward their child and themselves. Teachers should attempt to direct parents' hostile feelings into useful channels, such as working to benefit children with similar handicapping conditions.

Parents' sense of *guilt* may lead them to be preoccupied with mistakes they feel they have made that they believe may have caused the problem. Often these "mistakes" have little to do with the child's condition. Parents may *blame* the doctor for faulty prenatal care, others for creating the handicapping condition, and/or the child's teacher and school for inappropriate education. While it may be difficult, teachers should attempt to help parents see the reality of the situation.

Parents may feel *shame* about the birth of an impaired child, anticipating disapproval of others and fearing they and their child will be judged as inferior. Talking to other parents of handicapped children can be helpful at this stage. Counseling may be the best strategy in this situation.

Parents often *overprotect* their handicapped children, denying them the opportunity to play with other children and encounter challenge. This prevents them from developing in as normal a way as possible with other children and may be a further handicap. Parents may have to be convinced to involve handicapped children in educational programs and extracurricular activities.

In most cases parents will accept their children's handicapping condi-

tions and will *adapt* to them. At this stage parents develop positive attitudes toward themselves and their children. They are then able to learn the skills needed to contribute to their children's futures. Parents may manifest attributes of several stages at one time and might shuttle between one stage and another in dealing with their concerns.

ASSUMPTIONS UNDERLYING PARENT INVOLVEMENT PROGRAMS

In developing a parent involvement program, a teacher must assume the support of the school and its administration and that there are other persons in the school who are willing and able to help. The teacher must also assume both that she or he has or can develop the skills necessary to carry out the program and that the parents for whom the program is designed are able and willing to become involved and to learn from their involvement.

Most parents are sincerely interested in the education of their children and will work to promote that education. In most parent involvement programs it is at the onset of the program that the most time must be committed by the professional staff and the greatest amount of support and help must be given to the parents. Parents will generally find the time to give the program, if teachers communicate their willingness to give of their time and energy and if mutually agreeable times are scheduled. Teachers must be seen as willing to give support to parents if parents are to be expected to give support to handicapped children.

In establishing programs of parent participation, teachers need to assess the parents' concerns for their children's education. They need to be aware of the values of the school community and whether those are the values held by the parents involved; and they must also discover the goals parents have established for their own children's education. When there is inconsistency or conflict between the goals and values of the parents and those of the teachers, there is little hope for cooperation. Sometimes apparent inconsistency is the result of misunderstandings or a lack of communication. Once the teacher has become aware that this has happened, lines of communication can be established and teachers can help parents understand what the school wants for their children. Improved communication may require increased effort and use of new resources, but it can be a vital basis for establishing parent cooperation.

When real differences exist between the values of the school and those of the home, programs of parent participation are more difficult. Parents may be unwilling to become involved in school activities and may feel uncomfortable in school settings. An adversary relationship may develop between teachers and parents. In such cases it may be helpful to try to negotiate agreements between parents and children whereby schools begin to accept some of the values and goals of the parents in the hope that parents may become more understanding and more accepting of the school's point of view.

Parents must feel their participation will be worthwhile, both meeting their own needs, interests, and desires and supporting their children's learning and development. Using parents only for routine classroom cleaning tasks will lead them to feel they are not making a meaningful contribution to their children's education. While they may ease the burden for the teacher, they learn little that they can use with their children; nor do their children benefit directly from their involvement. On the other hand, if parents are taught how to read stories to their children, to play educational games with them, or to carry on conversations with them—activities that are significant in extending the child's language—they are likely to feel more satisfied because they gain a sense of contributing directly to their children's learning.

Parents should be given specific tasks and shown how to engage in those tasks. They should also be shown how those tasks are related to the goals of the program and how those goals are in turn related to the needs of the children.

Teachers should show appreciation and enthusiasm for the contribution being made and provide parents with feedback on their own performance. Telling parents they have read a story particularly well, or have engaged a child successfully in a difficult interaction, will help the parents appreciate the contributions they are making. Feedback to parents should be positive and instructive. Parents will make errors in their work with children, especially in the beginning, and so they should also be told or shown, tactfully, how to improve.

Teachers' suggestions about how parents work with the children should be specific. Showing a parent exactly how to hold a book, where to sit in relation to a child or group of children, and how to ask particular questions about a story read will be of greater help to parents than telling them to be warm and responsive. The results of parents' work with children, and especially the progress shown by those children, should be pointed out regularly and consistently.

Parents come from different backgrounds, and thus have different values and conceptions of what is good and useful for children. They also have different views of what their role should be in relation to children. Not all parent activities will be of equal interest to all parents, nor will they all need to be involved in all the activities planned. Parents who cannot be involved in the classroom during the day because of work responsibilities can be involved in other ways. Parents with little education can instruct children if they are shown what to do. Each contribution should be valued. Mutual trust and respect should provide a basis for a joint support for the child's continued learning and development.

PATTERNS OF PARENT INVOLVEMENT

Although the involvement of parents of handicapped children will differ little from that of all other parents in the school, there will be some activities designed specifically for parents of the handicapped.

In all schools, teachers are expected to use both written reports and parent conferences to report to all parents about their children's progress. Parents may also be invited into the school periodically to view the program. Often schools have parent or parent-teacher associations that hold meetings during the school year and sponsor other parent activities. Schools may invite parents to view class performances or to share in various school observances. These limited forms of participation may not be enough to have a major impact on their handicapped children's education. Only by a joint effort of parents of the handicapped and their teachers can the optimum educational effect be achieved, and this means going beyond the traditional, limited role of the parent in school. Care should be taken, however, that these parents are not isolated from the rest of the school's parent group.

Sharing Information with Parents

Federal and state legislation requires all parents to have available to them all information that the school has concerning their children. Since decisions made about each child by the school are based on this information, and since parents are expected to be involved in these decisions, it seems reasonable to make all this information available.

Teachers need to interpret this information to parents. Test scores, for example, mean little by themselves, but when test scores and records of observations of children in class are interpreted together, the parent can gain a full picture of the child's school performance. Only when many different kinds of information are pooled, including teacher observations, the results of standardized and nonstandardized tests, and the judgements of professionals and informed parents, does a full picture evolve that can become the basis for educational plans and decisions. The typical report card is usually too general and nonspecific in its grading system to communicate the basis for educational decisions. Thus, regular parent-teacher conferencing becomes an important part of the reporting system. Information is usually also shared with parents through written reports and newsletters, as well as orally through parent conferences.

Written Reports. Written reports can take a variety of forms; *report cards* are one of these. Typically, report cards are standardized forms used by schools to report pupil progress to parents. They are used in primary grade classes and in many kindergartens, but are seldom found in nursery schools and day care centers. Report cards cover categories of academic learning (e.g., reading, language arts, music) as well as social behavior (e.g., getting along with others, sharing, cooperation). The cards are designed so that teachers can complete them for an entire class fairly quickly, since one must be completed for each child at regular intervals during the school year. Reports of children's progress may be reported simply with a letter grade (A, B, C, D) or a judgement of how a child meets a criterion (S = satisfactory, U = unsatisfactory).

Report cards, by their nature, deal with general expectations for an entire class. Since handicapped children in a classroom have learning expectations that are different in some ways from other children, report cards alone are not adequate for sharing information with parents. Some other supplementary written report, specifically related to the goals established in the child's Individualized Educational Plan must also be provided. This could take the form of a checklist or a narrative letter, either of which might also be used with all the children in a class.

The *checklist* generally consists of items more specific to what is learned in a particular class than those on a report card. Statements of particular accomplishments can often be denoted by a simple mark in a column. Examples of observation checklists were presented in Chapter 3. The reporting checklist is not much different in form. The actual content of a checklist can be determined by the individual teacher or school and can thus be designed to provide parents with a better idea of what each child is specifically accomplishing.

A *narrative letter* is another way of sharing written information with parents about their particular child. Letters can communicate the qualitative aspects of a child's work better than re-

port cards or checklists since they can be used to describe activities more fully. Such a letter can describe a child's learning style and pattern of interaction with other children, as well as the books read or the materials used. Descriptions of specific incidents can be included. To save time, some teachers duplicate a letter describing activities of the whole class and supplement this with a few paragraphs specific to each child.

No one form of sharing information about individual children is totally satisfactory in all ways. The more specific and descriptive a report is, the more time it takes to complete. Teachers are often caught in a dilemma about which form to use. Compromises often need to be made. A combination of different types of individual reports may provide the best balance.

Report cards and individual letters to parents share specific information with individuals. *Newsletters* can be used to share information of general interest with all parents. They can describe incidents and activities of the entire class that would be interesting to all.

A newsletter might be sent home at the end of each semester, each quarter, or each month. How often it is sent depends on how much time a teacher can devote to its production as well as how much help is available. Newsletters can describe special events (such as a field trip or the visit of a resource person) as well as ongoing activities of special interest (such as a cooking experience in a nutrition unit). They can include articles highlighting a particular staff member, describing her or his academic background and professional experience as well as personal information related to family, hobbies, or travel. Short vignettes describing individual children's products or activities can also be included, with care taken to mention each child at some time during the year. Notices of community or school activities, reports on articles or books that might be of interest to parents, information about community resources, and requests for materials or help for the classroom might round out the content of a newsletter.

Newsletters for mainstreamed classrooms should be of interest to parents of both handicapped and non-handicapped children. They should be written in understandable language. Parents can often be used as resources in publication of a newsletter, writing items, typing copy, and reproducing material.

Parent Conferences. Many teachers share information with parents orally through parent conferences, either to substitute for written reports or to supplement them. Because parent conferences are a form of face-to-face contact,

---

GUIDELINES FOR PARENT-TEACHER CONFERENCES

Before the conference

1. Identify the purposes for the conference (e.g., reporting, information-sharing, problem-solving).

2. Prepare an agenda.

3. Review the child's record.

4. Prepare specific materials to show parents (e.g., observation notes, test results, work samples).

5. Set a time for the conference that is convenient for all.

6. Invite both parents, if possible.

7. Find a comfortable, relaxing, quiet place for the conference.

During the conference

8. Be friendly—establish a positive atmosphere.

9. Inform parents about the class program, schedule, and routines.

10. Make positive comments about the child; talk about strengths as well as problems.

11. Be specific about the problems you present.

12. Use language that parents can easily understand.

13. Provide opportunities for parents to speak as well as listen; be a good listener.

14. Work cooperatively with parents on specific solutions and activities for the child; identify responsibilities.

15. Summarize the meeting; make sure you and the parents are clear about the next steps.

After the conference

16. Make a brief record of the content of the meeting.

17. Plan for follow-up.

they often enhance positive communication. If messages are misunderstood by either party, questions can be asked and meanings can be clarified immediately; in addition, a wide range of communication can be covered in a relatively short period of time. Also, since there is dialogue between parents and teacher, communication can be shared both ways in parent conferences, which is not true of written communication.

In order for parent conferences to be effective, they must be carefully planned and implemented. The teacher should set up an agenda for the conference and bring together materials to be discussed with the parent(s). The conference agenda needs to be handled flexibly, however, so that concerns raised by parents can be responded to as well as concerns that become evi-

dent to the teacher as a result of the dialogue that takes place within the conference.

Conferences need to be followed up. A brief written record should be made of a parent conference, noting topics discussed, parent reactions, and any follow-up that needs to take place. It is helpful to involve both parents of a child in a conference, although this is not always possible and sometimes a child has only one parent. If, however, decisions are made that involve more than one parent, it is important that all those involved participate somehow in the decision. Sometimes telephone calls or letters can supplement parent conferences.

Other Ways of Sharing Information. A range of other methods can be used for sharing information with parents. Schools often set up *bulletin boards* especially for parents. Notices of meetings or activities of interest to parents along with newspaper and magazine articles might be posted on them. Requests for help might also be posted there. The advantage of a bulletin board is that it is relatively easy to set up and can be changed fairly often, since teachers do not have to develop what they put on them. Care should be taken that a parent bulletin board be placed where it can easily catch the attention of parents, that it be maintained attractively, and that its contents be changed regularly to keep it interesting.

If space is available in the school building, a separate room or alcove might be set aside as a *parents' center*. Such a center might contain comfortable chairs for parents to sit in, as well as firmer chairs and a table to facilitate work. The room might have a coffee pot going to encourage parents to spend some time there as well. This might be where the bulletin board is located. It also might have a small library, including magazines, flyers, pamphlets, and books of interest to parents. Among books that might be especially useful to parents of young handicapped children are:

Becker, W. C. *Parents are teachers.* Champaign, Ill.: Research Press, 1971.

Bicklen, D. *Let our children go.* Syracuse, N. Y.: Human Policy Press, 1974.

Braga, J., and Braga, L. *Children and adults.* Englewood Cliffs, N. J.: Prentice-Hall, 1976.

Brehm, S. S. *Help your child: A parent's guide to mental health services.* Englewood Cliffs, N. J.: Prentice-Hall, 1978.

Brown, D. S. *Developmental handicaps in babies and young children.* Springfield, Ill.: Charles C. Thomas, 1972.

Buscaglia, L. *The disabled and their parents.* Thorofare, N. J.: Charles B. Slack, 1975.

Croft, D. *Parents and teachers: A resource book for home, school, and community relations.* Belmont, Calif.: Wadsworth, 1979.

Fredericks, H. D., and Baldwin, V. *Isn't it time he outgrew it?* Springfield, Ill.: Charles C. Thomas, 1976.

Isaacs, S. *Troubles of children and parents.* New York: Schocken, 1973.

Jeffree, D. M., and McConkey, R. *Let me speak.* New York: Taplinger, 1976.

Jeffree, D. M., McConkey, R., and Hewson, S. *Let me play.* New York: Taplinger, 1977.

Jeffree, D. M., and Skeffington, M. *Let me read.* London: Souvenir Press, 1980.

Jenkins, J. K., and McDonald, P. *Growing up equal: Activities and resources for parents and teachers of young children.* Englewood Cliffs, N. J.: Prentice-Hall, 1979.

Leitch, S. M. *A child learns to speak: A guide for parents and teachers of preschool children.* Springfield, Ill.: Charles C. Thomas, 1977.

Mopsik, S. I., and Agard, J. A. *An education handbook for parents of handicapped children.* Cambridge, Mass.: Abt Associates, 1979.

Patterson, F. G. *Families.* Champaign, Ill.: Research Press, 1975.

Wender, P. H. *The hyperactive child—A handbook for parents.* New York: Crown, 1973.

Additional opportunities to share information with parents are available through a range of *informal contacts* a parent might have with the school. Especially in nursery schools and day care centers, parents may drop their children off in the morning and pick them up at the end of the school ses-

GUIDELINES FOR PARENT MEETINGS

Before the meeting

1. Involve parents in planning the meeting.

2. Establish a convenient time for the meeting.

3. Find a comfortable, convenient place to meet.

4. Announce the topic and format of the meeting well in advance; inform parents of what they should bring.

5. Send out notices of the meeting with return slips.

6. Follow up on parents who do not return slips.

7. Arrange for transportation and baby sitters if necessary.

8. Check with parents about refreshments.

During the meeting

9. Start and end the meeting on time.

10. Establish ground rules early (e.g., smoking, breaks, confidentiality).

11. Be flexible in following the agenda.

12. Vary program activities (e.g., discussion, role-playing, lecture, film, games).

13. Provide opportunities for everyone to be involved in the discussion.

14. Allow some time for informal interaction at the end of the meeting.

After the meeting

15. Make a brief record of what happened.

16. Plan for follow-up activities.

---

sion. These short periods provide limited but useful opportunities for teachers to share information "on the fly." Teachers who plan so that one staff member is available to greet the children and send them off can spot particular parents with whom they might want to converse briefly and develop a short exchange. Such opportunities should not be overused, nor should they be seen as a substitute for parent conferences.

Telephone conversations and *brief notes* sent home with children also offer opportunities to share bits of information. Teachers should not overdo these since, if they are used too often, parents may stop paying attention to messages sent.

Parent Education Programs

Teachers, often with the help of other school personnel, may be given the responsibility of developing a parent education program to help parents develop specific skills in educating their handicapped children. To avoid reteaching skills they already have, the teacher must identify what parents already know about their handicapped child and about how to work with them.

Since parents have limited time and competing interests and their ability to commit themselves to a parent education program may be limited, the programs developed should be of relatively short duration. In establishing a program, the teacher should attempt to identify common interests and goals. Both parents and teachers should agree on the areas of parent education and on expected outcomes. Once goals are established and skills to be taught are clearly defined, skills and understandings should be taught to parents as simply and concisely as possible. Parents should be shown what they should do and should be given an opportunity to practice what they learn. It is important to provide feedback on parents' performance. Tell them what they are doing right; help them correct errors.

In working with parents, teachers should speak simply, avoiding educational terms if possible. It is also helpful to run the program in the type of setting in which children and parents will operate. The child's home or classroom are appropriate settings.

Skills and activities that parents use at home should be consistent with the way in which the teacher works with the children in school. Open lines of communication can help parents and teachers know what each is doing and create a consistent set of home-school learning expectations, activities, and environments.

Parents as Program Advocates

Parents of handicapped children have a special stake in the education of these children. They can become advocates of the programs in which their children are enrolled and involve themselves in public relations activities. Parents can talk about their children's programs to friends and neighbors within the community. Parents can also help to run fund-raising activities to purchase materials and equipment not provided by public funds. Parents can represent the school on local radio and television programs, provide press releases, or inform the local paper of activities that might be worthy of press coverage.

Parents of handicapped children can also be effective advocates in the political arena, meeting with public officials, writing letters to legislators, and attending local school board meetings. They can testify at public hearings in support of specific programs. The parents' knowledge and commitment will serve to enhance their role in the area of public policy. Teachers should not provide scripts for parents to use at hearings or in media presentations; the parents' own words are usually most effective. Rather, teachers should provide parents with the information they will need in their advocacy role, make parents aware of the opportunities that arise for establishing advocacy relations, and help parents develop the skills they may need. While parents must speak for themselves, they may need help in developing the skills needed to speak out in public.

Helping Parents Help Parents

Parents who discover that their children have handicapping conditions often suffer from a sense of isolation. This may be caused by the feeling that their children are different from other children and that their responses to their children are different from other parents' responses in similar situations. Knowing that others have had similar experiences and have responded in similar ways can do much to alleviate such feelings of isolation. Persons who have shared similar experiences are also better able to communicate with one another about similar inner thoughts and feelings. Such sharing, the basis for many self-help groups, can be the basis for establishing supportive relations among parents of handicapped children. A parent of a handicapped child can often be an effective counselor to another parent of a handicapped child, providing emotional support and encouragement and sharing ways of dealing with practical problems.

Teachers can encourage parents to consult with one another by introducing parents to other parents and by setting up parent meetings and discussion groups, which they take care not to dominate. Parents should be allowed to determine for themselves the content and purposes of these meetings and discussions, with the teacher providing mainly technical assistance. If desirable, a school social worker might be recruited to provide insight and support to a group. As parents feel more comfortable about themselves, they will feel more comfortable about their children and the program provided for them in school.

Parents in the Classroom

The ways parents can be included in the activities of the classroom are usually limited only by the desire, willingness, and ability of the teacher to use other adults in the classroom and

to supervise them. Most parents can learn the techniques needed to support children's programs, such as reading stories to children, helping in craft activities, or working with manipulative materials or paper and pencil activities. Parents with particular talents or hobbies may be invited to share these with the children as a special activity. Parents are a helpful addition on a field trip. They can also be used to observe and record children's behavior.

Parents may be volunteers or they may become part of the paid staff of early childhood programs. In terms of regular attendance and responsibility, more can be expected of a paid parent aide than of a volunteer participant. But parents will do many of the same things whether they are employed or volunteer their services.

Parents involved in classroom activities must be aware of classroom organization and routines and know what will be expected of them. They should be given tasks that they are able to perform reasonably well. Individualizing the parent's involvement is just as important as individualizing the children's program. A helpful handbook for parents participating in early childhood classes is *The Aide in Early Childhood Education* (Todd, 1973).

Parents on Advisory Councils

Many federal programs require that parents serve on advisory councils to ensure that they have a role in educational decision-making. Such councils can be effective in helping determine the nature of children's programs. Too often, however, these councils become rubber stamps to the program's administration and parent involvement becomes more mythic than real. The effectiveness of a council will depend to a great extent upon how the council is allowed to operate and the way in which school professionals deal with the council.

Successful advisory councils create conditions that allow parents to be effective members. Adequate information is provided so that parents have a basis for making decisions. The information given to parents is organized so that they can use it easily. Reports are written in language parents can understand, and statistical reports are summarized and interpreted. All reports are sent to parents well ahead of scheduled meetings so that they have time to read and think about the material.

Meetings should be scheduled when the majority of members of the council can attend. Whenever possible, a schedule of meetings should be established for the semester. Meetings should be long enough to allow discussion of all agenda items, or when necessary, a series of meetings might be scheduled. Many parents cannot spend long evenings at a meeting, and few persons can be very effective decision makers working into the early hours of morning. Reports and proposals need to be given to councils well in advance of their deadlines so that the council will feel they have the ability to modify a request or report without scuttling a program. Minutes of all meetings should be kept and distributed soon after a meeting so that members can remember what transpired and make necessary corrections.

Most important, an advisory council should be taken seriously. Administrators and staff should heed the advice given, and when that advice cannot be followed, the council should be helped to understand why. If an advisory council is not listened to, its members will give up trying to be effective. They will stop coming to council meetings or they will attend but not offer suggestions or participate in discussions. At that point an advisory council exists in name only.

Parents have serious concerns about the education of their children. They see their children and their children's schools from a different vantage point than do professionals and they have different interests at heart. An advisory council should advise, not determine a program, and not all of its suggestions will ever be implemented; but if advice is continually disregarded or manipulated by professionals, then the parents involved will feel disparaged and insulted. Relationships between parents and teachers are never completely without problems or differences of opinion. But when parents are respected and their contributions are valued—whether contributions to decisions or to classroom practice—then an effective partnership can be established between home and school that can serve the best interests of the children.

PLANNING AN EFFECTIVE PARENT PROGRAM

Working with parents requires planning to achieve effectiveness. A well-thought-through plan of action allows a teacher to identify goals and to gather and utilize resources so that optimum use can be made of his or her time and energy. Following are some elements that go into a good plan for parent participation.

Establishing Mutually Determined Goals

One of the first things that should be done in planning a parent program is to determine exactly what purposes are to be served. Parents might want a program that helps them be better informed. Administrators might want a program that gives the school public visibility. Teachers might want parents to serve as classroom aides. All of these goals are legitimate and might be possible to some extent, but priorities must be established.

The first task in designing a parent program is to determine what goals are considered desirable by all parties: parents, administrators, and other professionals. A variety of techniques can be used to identify desirable goals. The teacher could send questionnaires, interview people from each group, or call small group meetings to gain this information. The teacher should make it clear that while suggestions are being solicited, it might not be possible to address everyone's interests and that priorities need to be established. The final determination of goals, however, should reflect the concerns of all parties.

The final goals of the year's program might be varied. For a single program the goals might include, for example:

○ Helping parents become more effective in working with their own children

○ Improving communication between teachers and parents

○ Improving communication among parents

○ Helping parents develop better ways of managing their lives and the lives of their children at home

Developing the Program

Program goals are generally stated in broad forms that must be translated into more specific objectives designed to move the parents toward these goals. In developing objectives, teachers need to identify the skills, attitudes, and understandings that will become the focus of the program. Given the focus of improving communication among parents at school, for example, the teacher needs to determine what activities will in fact improve that communication. This could include increasing the number of parent meetings held during the school year, increasing attendance at school meetings, increasing the number of parents participating in meetings, or changing the quality of parent interactions at meetings. Each objective would move the program toward the same goal but would require the teacher to take a different line of action.

The teacher who can think of observable events that would indicate the achievement of an objective will be better able to judge whether that objective has been reached. Counting the number of meetings held, the number of persons attending meetings, the number of people speaking up at meetings, or the number and kinds of interactions between parents during meeting and comparing those figures with observations of the program during the past year can help determine the degree to which the situation has changed.

Based on the program goals and objectives set, the teacher can begin to develop a set of program activities. The teacher needs to consider each activity in relation to the objective(s) it is designed to meet, determining who will do the activity, where it will be done, how it will be done, and for how long. She or he must gather the necessary material, identify the appropriate space, and schedule the required time.

Strategies that can be used in teaching parents of handicapped to deal with problems they encounter at home have been presented by Heward, Dardig, and Rossett (1979). They suggest using behavior management techniques in helping parents teach new behavior to their children, weaken the dysfunctional behavior that may exist, and increase their children's positive behaviors. Suggestions for adapting the home environment to the needs of their handicapped children and planning for future situations are also provided. An excellent resource directory is included.

EVALUATING PARENT PROGRAMS

Teachers must know how well they have been able to implement the programs they have planned and how effective the programs have been. This requires collecting information about the program from its inception and analyzing this information to make judgements about it. Program records can include simple descriptions of how program goals were identified, how objectives were generated, and how activities were planned and implemented, as well as what happened to those involved during the course of the program. Teachers need to assess the program while it is in process to allow modifications to be made early enough to make a difference. The information collected can also be used in planning programs in the future.

QUESTIONS FOR PROGRAM EVALUATION

○ Are methods of reaching parents successful?

○ Could alternative methods be used to better advantage?

○ Are materials required for the activities available when needed?

○ What other sources of materials could be found?

○ How do parents respond to activities planned for them?

○ Is there adequate parent participation in the various sessions?

○ Do the activities seem to make a difference?

Formal and informal techniques can be used in gathering information for evaluation. Although other school personnel such as school psychologists or principals can help collect information, parents are the prime source of information about program outcomes. Judgements made about the program based on the information collected must be related to how well the program was implemented and to the degree to which the program's goals and objective were met. Problems that arise in implementing a program may result in limited outcomes. It may be that while the activities developed seemed to be good ways to achieve the goals and objectives, they were not as effective as the teacher thought they would be. It may also be, however, that the goals and objectives could not be achieved by any group of parents. Being sensitive to all dimensions of the program will allow the teacher to make the best analyses and judgements based upon the information available.

Parent programs are not ends in themselves, but are developed as another way of improving the education of the child. To the extent that the child's education is improved, the parent program is successful. If it does not effect the education of the child, then the parent program, no matter how satisfying to those involved, cannot be considered successful. This indirect impact is hard to assess, since the difference teachers wish to make may be hard to observe. Therefore judgements about the impact of parent programs are difficult to make.

MAINSTREAMING PARENTS

By the very nature of mainstreaming, parents of handicapped children represent only a minority of those with whom teachers work. Although these parents do have distinct needs that must be met in particular ways, they also need to be integrated into the program provided for all parents in the school. The teacher's specialized program should not be so overwhelming that it keeps parents of handicapped children from participating in more general activities. In addition, teachers of mainstreamed classes will have to respond to the concerns of parents of nonhandicapped children regarding the impact of mainstreaming on their children.

Most parents have had little contact with handicapped children. Too often the lack of contact and the resulting absence of knowledge can create fears on the part of parents of normal children. The teacher will have to cope with both the ignorance and fears of these parents. Parents may be afraid that including handicapped children in a normal classroom will be harmful to their children. They may be concerned that the handicapped child, especially if there is some behavior disorder, may physically hurt their children or that their children will begin to model the behavior of handicapped children, leading to inappropriate behavior repertoires and the possibility of arrested development. They may also be afraid that the time and attention the classroom teacher must give to a handicapped child will be time and attention taken away from their own children, causing their learning to suffer.

Teachers need to understand the sources of parental fears. Since one of these sources is often ignorance, teachers should help parents learn about the nature of handicapping conditions in childhood. Parent meetings that deal with child development and handicapping conditions can prove helpful. Teachers can use community resources, including spokespersons from various community organizations, in planning these meetings. It also helps to provide parents with simple articles or pamphlets describing the particular disabilities that are represented in the class.

Another way of allaying parents' fears is to have them see what is happening in the classroom. If a teacher can have an open door policy, allowing parents to visit the class without a great deal of fuss or red tape, parents will find that many of their fears are groundless. Parents of normal children can also serve as resource persons in the classroom, working with handicapped children

and, through this activity, becoming aware of the nature of the handicapping condition.

Other forms of parent involvement that are as important for parents of the nonhandicapped child as for parents of the handicapped include parent participation in the classroom and participation on advisory boards. Neither parents of handicapped children nor those of nonhandicapped children should become the only group that participates in these activities.

Children's special needs have, in the past, led to segregated programs. The move toward mainstreaming is an attempt to eliminate this segregation. The program that a teacher and school staff designs for parents can either support or thwart integration. All parents of all children are concerned about what is happening to their children in the school. The parent program should help all parents move beyond concern for their children alone, understanding that what happens throughout the class, and indeed throughout the school, affects each child.

SUMMARY

Recent laws, especially Public Law 94-142, have made parent involvement in education mandatory for the handicapped. This concern for parent involvement should carry over to the parents of all children in the school. All parents should feel that they are participating members on an educational team. This requires that all parents should be informed as to what is happening to their children and should be involved, to the greatest degree possible, in educational decisions about their children and even in the implementation of those decisions. A long-term working relationship, built upon mutual trust and understanding, can result from an effective program of working with parents in the school.

A strong parent program is especially important in working with young children in a mainstreamed classroom. It can help extend the learning of handicapped children beyond the confines of the classroom. It can also help parents of nonhandicapped children understand how children with disabilities develop, learn, and function.

Parents of handicapped children have the right to know about and approve their children's educational program. Contact with these parents should begin early. Parents may have different reactions to the knowledge that their child is handicapped. At different points in their own development they may be willing and able to participate in the educational programs in different ways and in varying degrees. A range of program alternatives should be available to parents so that a proper match can be made between what they can do and what the school offers.

Teachers can share information with parents through conferences, newsletters, and informal contacts. They need to provide programs to help parents cope with their children's needs and extend their children's education. Parents need to be helped to become effective program advocates at various levels in the community and effective members of advisory councils. In addition, parents need to be provided with a support system that is responsive to their needs. Opportunities for parents to work in their children's classrooms should also be provided.

In developing an effective parent program, teachers should work together with parents in establishing program goals, then develop activities to achieve these goals. Evaluating the program will help teachers improve it throughout the year as well as plan future parent programs.

REFERENCES

Becker, W. C. *Parents are teachers*. Champaign, Ill.: Research Press, 1971.

Bronfenbrenner, U. *A report on longitudinal evaluations of preschool programs (Vol. 2). Is early intervention effective?* Washington, D.C.: Department of Health, Education and Welfare, 1974.

Gardner, R. *M. B. D.: The family book about minimal brain dysfunction*. New York: Jason and Son, 1973.

Ginott, H. *Between parent and child*. New York: Avon, 1969.

Gordon, I. J., Guinagh, B., and Jester, R. E. *Child learning through child play*. New York: St. Martin's Press, 1972.

Gordon, T. *Parent effectiveness training*. New York: Wyden, 1970.

Heward, W. L., Dardig, J. C., and Rossett, A. *Working with parents of handicapped children*. Columbus, Ohio: Charles E. Merrill, 1979.

Karnes, M. B., and Lee, R. C. Involving parents in the education of their handicapped children: An essential component of an exemplary program. In M. J. Fine (Ed.). *Handbook on parent education*. New York: Academic Press, 1980.

Lillie, D. Dimensions in parent programs: An overview. In I. J. Grimm (Ed.). *Training parents to teach: Four models*. Chapel Hill, N.C.: Technical Assistance Development Systems, 1974.

Lillie, D. L. An overview of parent programs. In D. L. Lillie and P. L. Trohanis (Eds.). *Teaching parents to teach*. New York: Walker and Company, 1976.

Linde, T. F., and Kopp, T. *Training retarded babies and preschoolers*. Springfield, Ill.: Charles C. Thomas, 1974.

Love, H. D. *Parental attitudes toward exceptional children*. Springfield, Ill.: Charles C. Thomas, 1970.

Marholin, D., Siegel, L., and Phillips, D. *Treatment and transfer: A search for empirical procedures*. Unpublished Manuscript. Urbana: University of Illinois, 1975.

Shearer, M. S., and Shearer, D. E. Parent involvement. In J. B. Jordan, A. H. Hayden, M. B. Karnes, and M. M. Wood (Eds.). *Early childhood education for exceptional children: A handbook of ideas and exemplary practices*. Reston, Va.: The Council for Exceptional Children, 1977.

Sparling, J., and Lewis, I. *Learning games for the first three years*. New York: Walker, 1979.

Stokes, T., and Baer, D. M. An implicit technology of generalization. *Journal of Applied Behavior Analysis*, 1977, *10*, 349–367.

Todd, V. E. *The aide in early childhood education*. New York: Macmillan, 1973.

Part Three

MODIFYING CLASSROOM PROGRAMS FOR MAINSTREAMED CHILDREN

Nine

TEACHING READING

Through reading we acquire meaning from the printed or written word. The goal of reading instruction is to teach children the necessary skills to interpret the written code to gain meaning. Smith (1971) identifies two ways of achieving comprehension in reading: (1) immediate comprehension in which the visual features of writing allow the reader to interpret meaning, and (2) mediated comprehension, which requires a prior identification of words. Most children who read fluently use mostly immediate comprehension, which is facilitated through the availability to them of alternative sources of information, including word forms, syntactical structures, and the context of words. Readers who have problems with immediate comprehension can use mediated comprehension.

Children who lack experience with the reading process may have problems in achieving comprehension. If they have not been read to, for example, they may focus more on word calling than on the flow of meaning. Having a rich background of related experiences such as having been read to and told stories helps beginning readers associate reading with language and thinking processes.

PROBLEMS ENCOUNTERED BY HANDICAPPED CHILDREN LEARNING TO READ

Teachers in integrated early childhood classrooms may encounter children with handicapping conditions that impact in different ways on their ability to learn to read. Unfortunately some reading specialists assume that all handicapped children are slow learners and that essentially the same instructional techniques should be used with them all. Handicapped children, they argue,

need constant motivation; instruction that is simple, clear and direct; and procedures that provide much practice (Williams, 1979). Such methods, which are successful with some learning disabled children, may be inappropriate for others. Orthopedically handicapped children who may have difficulty in moving from one place to another, may not have any learning problems when it comes to reading. Similarly the visually impaired and hearing-impaired may learn at the same rate as their normal peers if provided with adaptations to instruction such as sign language and braille.

Teachers with handicapped children in their classrooms are bound to encounter a variety of challenges. Mentally retarded children need to be taught at a very slow pace with much repetition. Reading-disabled children need special instruction to develop strength in their areas of weakness. Emotionally disturbed children need assistance in controlling behaviors that block their learning. A reading program that mainstreams handicapped children must provide the appropriate range of methods to accommodate those differences.

PREPARING CHILDREN TO READ

Learning to read is neither learning to match sounds to printed symbols nor memorizing words; meaning is impor-tant. Children begin to acquire reading skills long before they experience instruction with books in a school setting.

Hillerich (1977) identifies the skills needed to learn to read as (1) the ability to think in the language being read, (2) the ability to manipulate the sounds of words in the language, and (3) the ability to understand and use the spoken language. The process that teaches these skills is called reading readiness.

Reading Readiness

Reading readiness identifies and defines prerequisites that allow young children to profit from reading instruction. Getting ready to read starts when children make their first visual and auditory discriminations, when they associate words with objects in their listening and spoken language, when they understand the world around them and their place in it, when they begin to symbolize objects and events, when they socialize with other children and adults, and when they start to know themselves as persons and to build their own individualities.

Kirk, Kliebhan, and Lerner (1978) have identified the components of reading readiness as mental maturity, thinking skills, visual abilities, auditory abilities, speech and language development, physical fitness and motor development, social and emotional development, and motivation.

Mental maturity indicates the level of intellectual development the child has achieved. It is influenced by both the child's maturation and the education experiences that have been provided. Thinking skills are the specific cognitive abilities that the child uses to organize the world and deal intelligently with the information he or she possesses.

Visual abilities are the child's capacity to perceive, identify, and discriminate among visual shapes and forms. Since vision develops through exploration, recognition, and discrimination of objects or forms, manipulating objects helps develop the child's visual discrimination skills (Spache & Spache, 1977). Once children can visually identify and discriminate shapes and forms, practice with tasks that require them to identify differences and similarities in regular geometric forms as well as irregular squiggles becomes unnecessary. Discrimination of letters becomes important since children must discriminate between letters to be able to read.

Auditory abilities are the child's capacity to deal with sounds and to perceive likenesses and differences in sounds, including identification of differences in highly similar pairs of words that are presented orally. The best indicators of auditory ability are children's speech and conversation, since auditory problems are often related to speech problems.

Auditory abilities are particularly important to visually handicapped children who necessarily rely on their auditory skills to learn reading. Although reading readiness for these children includes many of the same factors as for sighted children (e.g., chronological and mental age, emotional maturity, and background experience), their handicap creates special problems related to language development, opportunities for experiences, progress toward independence, and emotional stability within the family.

The teacher needs to demonstrate or explain to blind children the countless tasks and experiences sighted children learn and participate in through visual observation (Lowenfeld, Able, & Hatlen, 1969). Since blind children learn about these tasks and experiences by listening to descriptions of others, their auditory ability is a major means of learning.

Motor development begins when the infant kicks, crawls, walks, runs, and jumps. Although the relationship of motor development to reading is vague, the assumption is that motor skills at least help children do simple copy work and turn pages. Motor development is especially important to visually handicapped children's reading skills. Reading is principally a visual procedure with the reader reacting visually to graphic symbols. Visually impaired children who are unable to see these symbols must learn to read braille, using touch rather than sight. This reading approach requires tactual discrimination to differentiate between sizes, shapes, and textures of objects. Blind children need a wide range of motor experiences to develop their fine tactual discrimination skills. They also can use sensorimotor materials such as sandpaper letters, letter form boards, and movement exercises. The regular teacher, although expected to provide the visually handicapped child with tactile experiences, is not expected to teach braille reading.

Working at learning activities in a classroom is a social activity. In order for children to function well in learning activities they must be able to work with others in a cooperative manner and be able to control their own behavior, meeting realistic standards established for their classroom. They also must be able to work independently when not under the direct supervision of the teacher. These elements of **social and emotional maturity** are as important in reading instruction as they are in any other form of instruction. In addition, learning to read is a difficult task that at times can create a degree of frustration for any child. If there is a sense of failure or if a child does not meet expectations, emotional difficulties can result.

Helping Children Develop Readiness

In a real sense, any rich early childhood program prepares children to read. It provides a wide range of intellectually stimulating activities, and is filled with rewarding language activities. Science experiences help develop intellectual as well as auditory and visual skills. There is strong social and emotional support as children learn about themselves and others and develop an increased ability to work with others, including adults. Physical activities in the classroom and in outdoor play areas support physical development and social skills. In addition, the children broaden their range of knowledge and learn to communicate that knowledge in a variety of media. They have opportunities to hear stories told and read and thus develop a desire to learn to read. Although informal, these are elements of a strong reading readiness program.

A readiness program, though informal, should still be systematically planned. Teachers must carefully analyze the elements in the teaching-learning situation that can support reading readiness activities. These can be highlighted in planning, and the teacher can carefully see that all the children, including those with handicaps, participate in those activities. Story reading, discussion times, and other times in which expressive and receptive language are highlighted are examples of these activities.

When a child does not seem to be learning from informal activities, the teacher needs to analyze the nature of the problem. Sometimes a child's handicap is such that it is not possible to gain what others do from an informal activity. The activity may need to be modified or the teacher might have to use some form of direct instruction. Learning-disabled children, for example, may not be able to identify similarities and differences in sounds unless they are clearly pointed out to them. After initial training and practice, they may be successful in identifying such similarities and differences in informal situations.

At times, a teacher may have to break up a complex learning activity, simplifying it so the child can learn its component parts before putting them together again into their complex whole. Thus, in helping children with auditory discrimination skills, a teacher might first provide a child with a set of Montessori Sound Boxes, or their equivalent. The child can hear the sound made by shaking the boxes, then match it to the sound of a comparable box in the set. The discrimination is easier to make because the child hears the sounds in isolation. Later children can listen to sounds of other objects in the room as well as in the neighborhood, comparing them to one another. Finally the

teacher can help the child focus on the sounds of words that are alike or different.

Some handicapped children are easily distracted and for them the teacher might need to isolate the learning environment to reduce possible distractions. Creating a partially secluded section of the room by using furniture or equipment as a screen can help. Using headphones to listen to records rather than listening through a phonograph's speaker might also help. Instruction given to these children should be simple, clear, and free from irrelevancies and distractions.

Once the child has gained a skill or a concept, it is important that opportunities are provided for practice. The teacher should also check back regularly to be certain the child retains the skill or concept.

Whatever readiness activities are planned for the children, the teacher should try to match them with what the child can do. Learning opportunities should be characterized by success, which will lead the child to wish to continue with similar activities. Readiness activities should also be related to the children's interests so that they will want to continue to engage in language learning.

In addition to being provided with a rich array of oral language experiences, children can be helped to acquire knowledge of the written language and to begin to understand the nature of the reading process. Reading to children individually or in small groups is one way of doing this. As the adult or older child reads, the words that are being read should be pointed out. If the same story is read repeatedly, the children will be able to anticipate the words and even be able to point to the correct words in the text, thus learning to associate the word seen with the word heard. The children will also see that letters are organized into words with spaces between and that these words are followed from left to right on the page. They will become aware of the association of the sounds read aloud with the written referent on the page and thus gain a sense of what occurs in the reading process.

Children can also dictate stories to adults to be read back to them or the class at a later time. This will help them associate the written word with the spoken word. As children learn to make letters, they can begin to write their own stories, inventing spelling before they learn to spell properly. The letter-sound associations they establish will be fairly regular, and if incorrect, will be easily replaced when children learn to spell (Chomsky, 1971). Thus, the transition between readiness activities and beginning reading instruction can become a smooth, natural one as children move in stages into reading.

Before beginning reading instruction, the teacher must assess two features of the child's understanding of the spoken language. Children need to be able to listen to and understand both the stories found in early readers and the specific words and phrases used to teach reading. It is essential that the prereading program focus on these specific factors of language and communication.

Before they learn to read, children must also learn that our oral language can be broken down into a range of linguistic units including phrases, words, syllables, and distinctive sounds (phonemes). This skill requires knowing the oral language intuitively and gaining an analytic sense of the way language is arranged. These oral segments are later matched to written segments as children learn to read. Grapheme discrimination, the ability to distinguish among letters of the alphabet and other graphemic symbols, is also important. While most nonhandicapped preschoolers can distinguish and name most of the letters in the alphabet, many handicapped children cannot.

To establish a desire to read in children as early as possible, teachers may need to support whatever interest the children already have for such activities as picking up a book and looking at pictures. Eventually the act of reading itself will become enjoyable, but handicapped children may need more help in learning to enjoy reading because of the problems they may encounter in the learning process.

Young children come to the task of learning to read with a great deal of information about written language. These children know about the graphic features of the written language and can distinguish words and letters from nonwriting graphic displays. During their preschool years children also increase their knowledge about what one does while reading, learning the characteristics of words and about the relationship between printed words and written words. They also begin to perceive words as combinations of sound segments (Schickedanz, 1982). It is this knowledge of the reading process that makes beginning reading instruction meaningful to young children.

In summary, a prereading program must make sure that : (1) the student has both adequate intellectual, motor, and language competence and an awareness of the special modes in which language is utilized to teach reading; (2) the student can segment spoken language into words, syllables, and phonemes; (3) the student knows and can discriminate among the letters of the alphabet; and (4) the student is interested in learning to read.

TEACHING CHILDREN TO READ

The movement from reading readiness to beginning reading is a gradual process. A beginning reading program must individualize instruction and be flexible, especially when handicapped children are in the class. Only those children who are ready for, or are already, reading can benefit from formal reading instruction. Thus, the teacher should provide reading instruction for those who are ready and help other children develop their prerequisite skills.

Word Recognition Skills

Word recognition skills are designed to help children become independent readers by learning to pronounce and understand new words. The main methods for teaching children to analyze words include the language experience approach, whole word methodology, phonics, and contextual analysis.

The Language Experience Approach. The two words *language* and *experience* best describe this approach to reading instruction (Stauffer, 1980). Reading is integrated with the other language arts as children listen, speak, write, and read. The students' own ideas and personal experiences are used to produce reading materials, which helps them see the relationship between the written word and spoken language. Since students differ in language and experiences, the content of such a reading program varies from child to child and from group to group. The child's speech represents language patterns, while experiences provide the content.

This approach is meaningful because it is based on the student's own personal language and experiences (Hall, 1976). Children first dictate stories about their experiences to the teacher who writes them on experience charts, which are then used for teaching reading. As children learn to write, they produce their own stories rather than dictating them to the teacher. Since the children create the instructional material, there are seldom problems with vocabulary; even difficult material is remembered. Children will then move from reading their own material to reading the work of other children as well as books that are available in the classroom.

The language experience approach does not deny the need to learn to crack the code of letter-sound associations, but suggests that this is learned best through organic activities. This process of learning to read more closely parallels learning a native language than learning a second language (Spodek, 1978).

The language experience approach to reading can be used even with children who have sensory impairments. Hearing-impaired children are deprived of some of the feedback children normally get from the language of others as they test out their developing sense of language structures, processes, and concepts. However, language experiences can be planned to amplify their vocabulary. Hearing-impaired children can have a person in front of the group interpret for them during language experiences. As the teacher records children's experiences and goes over the chart, the interpreter signs the language for the hearing-impaired child. A child who is partially hearing-impaired may gain this experience by sitting nearer to the chart with a classmate close by to help out informally.

Although visually impaired children may not be able to see the writing on the chart, they can also participate in the language experience approach and contribute to it. A partially sighted child, for instance, might be placed in a position from which it is possible to see and hear better and can either write experiences in braille or have the teacher/resource person record them. When braille is introduced to children in class through the language experience approach they will perceive it as an exciting new tool to help store ideas. The language experience approach cannot simplify learning the braille code system, but it can make learning the code important to the child who becomes motivated to read his or her own dictated words. Short stories and words stored in word banks for later use can also be recorded in braille. As these children learn to read braille, they can gain access to interesting books.

The language experience approach, besides facilitating reading instruction, promotes independence in visually impaired children. These children gain self-respect and independence as they manipulate, add to, and interact with their word banks and as they are able to function independently at the learning centers. The ability to manipulate words and to construct sentences or label objects gives them a feeling of control over their environment. The visually impaired child's independence, self-respect, and sense of control motivate continued learning (Curry, 1975).

Reading experience charts helps develop a wide range of word-recognition skills. The content of the chart, based on the child's recorded experience, makes it easy to teach the use of context clues. The child's intuitive knowledge of sentence structure and the shared experiences recorded on the chart make this approach effective. Individuals and small groups of children who have been writing their own stories and charts can easily be introduced to simple, short reading charts. A good foundation builds on each child's language knowledge and stimulates reading. As the child progresses, the reading charts can become longer and more elaborate. Children can also write their own stories on smaller sheets of paper and can start writing and reading books.

Whole-Word Methodology. The whole-word method enables the child to look at, think, and say a word, identifying the word on sight without any kind of analysis. Whole word methodology promotes vocabulary and word identification through labeling high frequency words and identifying words commonly needed for reading comprehension. Whole word methodology requires developing three subskills: (1) visually discriminating letter strings, which demands letter recognition, attention to letter order, and focus on the entire word, (2) relating and remembering labels for the letter strings, and (3) retrieving and articulating labels as the strings are observed (Venezky, 1975). This method does not require the child to analyze words or their component sounds but rather requires rote learning of a large number of specific words and letter patterns, which is limited by a person's memory capability (Williams, 1979). Some children are able to increase their reading vocabulary with this approach while others, because of a short memory span, are not.

Children with learning handicaps who have poor memories have particular problems using this approach. Children with strong visual memory abilities but poor auditory analysis skills are better able to use the whole word approach. However, they may not be able to rhyme or to generalize from known to unknown words. They may also have comprehension problems, recognizing and reading words but not being able to interpret what they read.

Many language- and learning-disabled children may have difficulty with word retrieval. They will understand words but be unable to retrieve them for spontaneous communication. This problem is especially evident in oral reading. Some of these children may interchange meaningful words such as dog for puppy; others will be able to define the words but not pronounce them. Still others may examine a word like *inspection* and say, "I know that it means to look over something very carefully, but I can't say it." Children may identify letters or sounds correctly, but be unable to retrieve the name or sound. Cuing techniques such as multiple choice questions or presenting the initial sound of the word can be helpful with these children. In regular reading instruction these children should receive extra opportunities to recognize and associate responses. Initially, the sight vocabulary should be composed of nouns and verbs to help them associate objects or pictures with the printed form (Johnson, 1979).

Whole-word methodology is of benefit to sensory impaired children when it is taught in context and when skills are taught analytically. This may require more time and experiences to build concepts, learn sight words, and read selections. Hearing-impaired children need to learn sight words and sound/symbol associations visually within meaningful contexts. Although the visually handicapped child uses auditory cues to compensate for limited vision, that child should also acquire sight words in meaningful contexts.

The teacher must help the child develop concepts before teaching sight words. Activities that promote new concepts and sight vocabulary and expand ideas are beneficial to these children.

Children with severe visual handicaps can be provided with brailled materials in an expendable form. Multiple thermoform copies of brailled material in a wide variety should be available to them. The teacher can place words from the word bank on top of the children's desks and encourage them to read them in proper order as well as in mixed order, reading the sentence aloud to their peers. Resource pages on which they can find words and objects to cut, label, and sort can be made available to visually impaired children.

Mentally retarded children can benefit from whole-word methodology. Brown, Huppler, Pierce, York, and Sontag (1974) designed several programs to teach trainable retarded students to verbally label sight words, to functionally read nouns and adjective-noun phrases, to spell printed words, to complete sentences that include the verb form *to be* and nine different prepositions, and to indicate they understand the meanings of words by touching the objects to which the words or sentences refer. The results of this study indicated that the whole word methodology is a practical approach for trainable mentally retarded students and could be used with educable mentally retarded students as well. When used with these children the whole-word method should exclude odd materials, unfamiliar language, abstract concepts, isolated skills, and items in workbooks. Instead, the materials pro-

vided should contain simple, familiar words.

Phonics. Phonics uses letter-sound relationships to help children sound out words they have not seen before in print but that are in their speaking and listening vocabulary. Five subskills for decoding with phonics are: (1) letter differentiation, (2) association of sounds and letters, (3) blending sounds, (4) identification of sounds within a word, and (5) sound matching within words (Venezky, 1975). Teaching phonics can help improve the reading achievement of most children. Some educators believe that phonics methods or part-word approaches are the only proper methods for teaching reading while other educators caution against their overuse. Guszak (1972) found that some children fail to use context clues in reading and thus neglect to attend to the meaning of the passage, because too much attention is placed on analysis of the individual words. Goodman (1968) suggests that an overemphasis on phonics in reading instruction leads children to believe that word analysis is an end in itself rather than a tool to assist them to acquire meaning.

Most reading programs use phonics to introduce reading. The phonics approach utilizes the "sound-out" method; it isolates every sound of the English language and represents it with a special symbol. The teacher presents these symbolized isolated sounds to the children. Teachers without specialized speech training may have difficulty giving each sound its accurate pronunciation. They may not, for example, place their tongues in the exact proper position when saying isolated sounds. It is difficult to pronounce the *p* without adding a vowel utterance to it. Thus, teachers' mispronunciations may provide the wrong examples to their students. In addition, teaching a sound in isolation may cause children to have difficulty identifying the same sound in the context of words.

The phonics approach is an inappropriate teaching strategy for hearing-impaired children who may be unable to distinguish speech sounds and who may produce inaccurate sounds in their own speech. They will probably fail to hear clearly structure words such as *and* and morphological endings such as *ed* or *ing*, because these are usually unaccented. They may become confused and experience difficulty with words that have minimal sound differences and words having multiple meanings. Colloquial expressions or unclear input from the language of others can compound the problem for the hearing-impaired.

Friedman and Gillooley (1977) suggest focusing on the use of artificial orthographies, that is, special alphabets that simplify letter-sound associations such as *ita* (the initial teaching alphabet) with hearing-impaired and deaf students. These orthographic approaches help beginning readers acquire a rapid mastery of sound-symbol correspondence by using sets of symbols that may bear little resemblance to the familiar letters of the alphabet. Friedman and Gillooley (1977) examined whether the limited availability of a sound system and its mediational cues would affect the perception of letter sequences by deaf students as well

as the age at which such an effect would be manifest. They found that the influence of orthographic structure begins at the earliest stages of learning to read (first- and second-grade levels) and continues throughout a more advance stage (fourth-grade level). Deaf children learned the rules of orthography as well as the hearing children with whom they were compared. They also developed a compensatory skill that allowed them to have a superior perception of unstructured items.

The prelingual deaf, those who have been deaf before the acquisition of language, are generally far behind their age-matched counterparts in reading achievement. Since they lack experience with the acoustic components of language, they must presumably decode written materials to meaning directly, without the mediation of acoustic cues—"hearing the word in their head"—which is essential in developing phonic skills in young hearing readers.

Contextual Analysis. Contextual analysis teaches word recognition by using the passage as a clue to the meaning of a word. Context clues help identify unfamiliar words through syntactic, semantic, pictoral, typographic, and stylistic prompts. Contextual analysis helps develop vocabulary and is an integral part of reading comprehension. Children learn to employ both verbal and nonverbal symbols and to process multiple messages (Johnson, 1979). Materials used in teaching contextual analysis should be familiar and brief and should include simple words from the children's sight vocabulary. Teachers should place words in their meaningful context immediately after they have been decoded, employing the word in a phrase or identifying the word as a nonsense word (Williams, 1979).

Teachers can also provide several stories, each consisting of a series of four pictures with one or two short sentences under each picture. This process, however, may create problems for children with memory disorders. Studies of memory indicate that reading-disabled children often have difficulty with temporal sequencing. Burns (1975), who investigated the differences in sequential memory according to modality input and output, suggests that the reading-disabled children had difficulty with serial memory, irrespective of mode of input or output. Johnson (1979) showed that during remediation, most reading-disabled children could learn a series through rhythmic patterns in groups of three.

Educable mentally retarded (EMR) children do not perform as well as nonretarded children of the same chronological ages on tasks requiring short-term memory. This short-term memory failure can cause these children to lose their train of thought in the course of reading a passage or to show semantic or syntactic inconsistencies between the early and later parts of their conversations (Deese, 1970). Since they can process a smaller number of units than nonretarded children and cannot group information into categories, EMR children have difficulty using context effectively in reading. They are also limited by their level of language development, their abilities to attend and to learn by discovery, their motivation, and the amount of practice they have had in reading.

However, EMR children can learn to use context analysis (Estes, 1970; Spitz, 1973). These children need to receive additional instructional material that teaches the same words in the context of varied sentences (Ramanauskas, 1972). Smith (1971) argues that children can discover ways of using context themselves. Using environments which emphasize context utilization skills can be more effective than teaching the use of context directly.

Milgram (1973) found that EMR children have difficulty with problem-solving tasks of a verbal nature and with learning tasks involving verbal mediation. EMR children were unable to utilize relevant cues and employ information-processing strategies. Thus, EMR children probably have difficulty discovering rules for analyzing context in reading, selecting relevant information, and maintaining attention. This may lead to problems in reading, causing the children to perform below their potential. To benefit from contextual redundancy, the child must discover relevant cues. Because EMR children fail to find the relevant dimension of a task, they do not have the redundant ability to learn by discovery.

The printed language is the hearing-impaired person's main medium of communication that is held in common with all persons. Reading stimulates the hearing-impaired child intellectually, but the reading process may be found difficult. Reading is based on spoken language; symbols that make up reading are based on language patterns. Hearing-impaired children cannot hear these language patterns and thus cannot easily convert written symbols into oral symbols. Many written words have no meaning to them since they lack the

oral referents. Hearing-impaired children can learn to use contextual analysis if they experience language and are provided with concepts that will help them to meaningfully recognize printed symbols. These direct experiences are provided by children participating actively in the events and activities of school life. Hearing-impaired children learn the concrete words that name objects and visible things in their environment in their formal reading programs.

Using context in reading provides an effective means to obtain meaning from reading through an understanding of the language. The child internalizes the rules of language structure and the necessary conceptual background to respond to the meaning of the context. Children's ability to predict from context using syntactic cues is less well developed than their ability to utilize semantic cues.

Basal Readers

The basal reading program is probably the most common framework for teaching reading in the kindergarten-primary grades. In this approach, a series of reading texts is used to help the child learn to accurately recognize and understand the words being read. The child learns to read single words in isolation and then to read with greater meaning and speed by grouping words. In addition to making provision for word recognition techniques, basal readers offer children opportunities and experiences for developing comprehension skills, including reading for information, reading to organize, reading to evaluate, reflective reading, and reading for appreciation.

Basal readers are written for sighted students and transcribing them into braille only compounds the blind child's problems, since the language content of basal readers is heavily dependent upon illustrations (which cannot be clearly seen by the visually impaired) and the stories in transcribed books are senseless without these pictures. Any possible comprehension cues and interest-arousing aspects are lost and the stories lose their appeal. In addition, basal readers have a sense of verbal unreality for blind children because most of their language refers to objects and concepts that visually impaired children have not experienced and that, therefore, convey no meaning (Cutsforth, 1951). For example, the visually impaired child who reads about green grass and a blue lake may be compelled to memorize terms for which he or she has no referent. The complicated descriptions of these abstract concepts are difficult for such children to understand and can cause visually impaired children to lose the incentive to read (Curry, 1975).

Children are placed in graded basal readers and their accompanying workbooks based on an assessment of their performance. Bradley (1976) examined the grade equivalent scores on two standardized reading tests to estimate instructional placement in a basal reading series. Students' scores on the reading tests were matched with their instructional reading levels in the Harper and Row basal reading series. In comparing instructional placement with test scores, Bradley (1976) found that the *Wide Range Achievement Test* over-

estimated the students' achievements when compared with the instructional placement in the basal reader. More than 90 percent of the students were being asked to read materials assessed as above their level.

Since most basal readers are geared to children at reading levels equivalent to their grade levels, retarded children, who usually read below their grade level, may find the content of these readers inappropriate, uninteresting, and even humiliating. Hillerich (1974) suggests a way of evaluating reading programs and textbook series that is useful to teachers. Some readers such as the *Functional Basic Reading Series* (1963, 1964, 1965) written specifically for retarded children, or the *Bank Street Readers* (1965), may be more meaningful to the retarded reader and may better help her or him learn even though they are somewhat dated.

Appropriate basal readers, in addition to teaching reading, can help children in the socialization process by providing them with realistic experiences that prepare them for their roles in society. The content of readers affects children: if they read intelligent content, they are more likely to act intelligently (Sanders, 1967). The content of basal readers can help children solve problems. Since they can learn to deal with difficulties by reading about them, basal readers can nurture independent behavior.

The characters in the basal readers can become role models for retarded children. However, achievement themes for males are found with greater frequency in the basal readers than for females. Achievement imagery in basal readers needs to be equalized for both sexes (McCloud, Mitchell, & Ragland, 1976). Without this change, other role-modeling materials must be considered for female students in the class.

Instructional Reading Materials

Stimulating instructional reading materials, including books, worksheets, and audio-visual materials can improve children's reading. Materials should be evaluated in relation to reading difficulty, interest, relevance, and their potential for helping to achieve reading goals.

The Federal Act on the Education of the Blind, as amended by Public Law 91-230 (1970), provides blind students who are enrolled in educational programs below college level with textbooks and educational aids through the American Printing House for the Blind. These materials are dispensed to the various educational programs through quota allocations, determined by dividing the total number of blind pupils registered in schools into the total amount of funds allocated by Congress.

The teacher can use the services of the American Printing House for the Blind and select the best types of educational materials, including textbooks and recordings. An assessment of the types of school programs visually handicapped students are attending, the degree of vision they possess, and the reading media and materials they are using, can be helpful in this process. For example, partially sighted children employ more of their residual vision by using regular ink and large-type readers and decreasing the use of braille.

Instructional materials that help children organize arrays of objects, explore patterns in systematic fashion, and schematize figures and patterns help develop the children's visual perception. Visually impaired students may need to use their fingers to follow reading words to foster their perceptual skills.

Braillers.   Braillers, which are machines that produce braille characters on paper, can be stored in the classroom on shelves within children's reach. Ideally there should be a brailler at the desk of each visually impaired child in a primary class who needs to use one, just as sighted children have pencils and paper available. The opportunity to experiment and practice with the brailler is essential to the blind child's reading growth and to learning the keys of the brailler. The brailler can be used to write stories, copy words for the word bank, or write sentences.

Some classroom teachers may have reservations regarding blind children's instruction in reading and writing braille. Braille is difficult, but it is possible to learn to read it visually, and sighted children are curious about it and think using it is fun. Teachers and sighted children decode braille visually by using the braille chart. Specialists should assume responsibility for teaching braille reading and writing as well as providing appropriate books and reference materials. The State Commission for the Blind or the Department of Social Services may pay the special reading teacher to help the handicapped children and may also provide instructional material.

The blind child will also need other supplies. The braille alphabet is important for the severely visually impaired. Each blind child should have a copy of the braille alphabet and her or his braille name should be taped to the desk for reference. An abundant supply of braille paper (heavy bond paper) should be available in the classroom. Blind children must have a supply at their desks and know where to get more when they need it. They should have their own binders for braille paper, along with a hole puncher to allow them to file their papers and have them at their disposal.

Braille words are small and are easily kept in envelopes or deposited in a file box which becomes their word bank. Each school with blind children should own a thermoform machine that uses a heat process to make copies of brailled pages. Teachers can copy dictated stories or instructional materials for the blind children on thermoform machines (Curry, 1975).

Cassette Tape Recorders. Cassette tape recorders provided in the classroom allow blind children to listen to taped stories while reading along in braille. Children can make recordings for others to listen to and to follow along with thermoform copies. Recorders can also be placed in different learning centers to provide more elaborate instructions for the blind child parallel to those that might be written on assignment cards for sighted children. These recorders should be accessible to both handicapped and nonhandicapped children. The children's personal recordings can be used to record lessons as well as to help the teacher assess their work. The teacher may use the same content and concepts in these recordings as would be used in a textbook, but the material should be revised so that the concepts are presented using simple language and at the social level of the child.

Several other pieces of equipment can be used to strengthen concepts. Audio-tutorial lessons, for example, allow students to learn at their own pace. Such lessons may include an audiotape accompanied by a workbook, a filmstrip, a slide, or an eight millimeter film loop. Pacing machines for reading, electronic readers, and computers can also be used with handicapped children. The expense of such equipment, however, limits their availability.

ASSESSING READING ABILITIES

Screening and assessment programs identify children who need reading remediation early in their lives, identifying each pupil's strengths, limitations, and needs and helping the teacher develop a reading program to foster reading growth compatible with each student's skills, needs, and educational progress. Accuracy is important in early identification, which should be concerned with motor development, auditory acuity, and visual acuity.

Gross motor development may be assessed by observing children's movement, while speech may be assessed with an articulation test as well as through informal conversation. Task-oriented tests can also be used; they might require drawing a person, copying geometric forms, or writing names. Drawing tasks requiring gross and fine motor coordination, speech, and expression of feelings can also be used.

Loss of hearing affects reading, especially if it involves the loss of higher frequency sounds, or if the type of instruction used puts a premium on auditory factors. A child with poor auditory discrimination will need extra help in learning to read phonics. Children's hearing should be tested at the beginning of the year. If it is not, teachers need to watch for such symptoms as inattentiveness, confusion in following directions, overly loud speech, distorted speech, rubbing or cupping of the ear, and frequent complaint of earaches.

Formal and informal visual screening tests can identify the need for a professional visual examination. Informal observations must also be part of the screening process for vision problems. A vision specialist should examine all children who seem to have visual problems, including those who persistently complain of headaches, dizziness, burning eyes, or blurred vision; move close to the chart, television screen, or chalkboard; rub or press their eyes frequently; have reddened eyes or eyelids; squint or scowl a great deal; have styes, excessive watering, or imbalance of the eyes; or have eyes that are not working together. An eye specialist should be consulted if one or more of these problems exist.

A child's visual problems should not be ignored until the results of the visual screening test or the diagnosis of the vision specialist has confirmed a deficiency. Visual stress can be reduced immediately by placing the child where he or she is best able to work and by providing reading materials with suitable print. The young child should have material with relatively large print and words that are printed far enough apart to be seen without stress. Books that are held in a slightly slanted position are often easier to read and raised boards or desk lecterns can be provided to slant reading material for children who need it. Reading tasks should be varied to provide several degrees of visual stress. Working with one type of task, even if different material is used, can cause fatigue that may accentuate visual problems.

TEACHERS' MANAGEMENT SYSTEMS

Once teachers have assessed their students, developed appropriate instructional methods, and selected materials, a workable management system should be designed to meet the range of individual differences in the classroom.

Teachers' Assistants

Additional adults might serve as resources including reading specialists, parent volunteers, college students, or teacher aides. Children with reading disabilities can also serve as tutors.

Tutoring gives the handicapped child a feeling of importance and can increase self-esteem while providing repetition and a review of reading material at the reading level in which that child is working. In the process, the handicapped reader will encounter tasks that require some skills that need to be developed. These tasks may challenge, excite and stimulate the child to the degree that she or he initiates a learning plan and seeks out the necessary help.

The Buddy System

Another successful approach in mainstreaming is the buddy system, using teams of two members each. The younger team member may be in grades one to three, while the older team member is usually of junior high school age. During their meetings, the older buddies help the children select books, listen to them read, help them with difficult words, and read aloud to them. The buddy is also a friend (Himmelsteib, 1979). The reading teacher and the classroom teacher serve as consultants for these volunteers, recommending suitable activities and games and providing inservice workshops for them.

A good management system is critical to a successful program when a number of people are involved. Individuals must work together to meet the needs of handicapped children. Careful planning can provide the basis for effective reading instruction for handicapped children within the regular classroom. Children's special services in reading should be scheduled during the reading period in order that they be away from their class during a time when they usually experience failure, rather than during other class activities when they may be experiencing success. This can be done if the children are grouped for reading at the same time. The classroom teacher should work closely with the special reading teacher to coordinate these children's programs.

Grouping

Grouping is one way of individualizing instruction. Hall, Ribovich, and Ramig (1979) suggest that since many students may have common needs, it is more effective to teach them in a group than individually. For instance, six children who need to learn to use initial consonant substitution may be grouped together for that topic and taught at the same time. In addition, some children usually learn better in a group than individually, learning from each other's responses. Many children seem less pressured and more relaxed in a group setting.

Children can be grouped for reading instruction within classrooms and/or by means of interclass grouping arrangements within a school based on a specific criteria such as achievement level, age, or interest. According to Wilson and Ribovich (1973), the most common ways that teachers group children include:

1. *heterogeneous grouping*, where children are instructed in the same grade disregarding ability or achievement

2. *homogeneous grouping*, where children are divided based on academic ability

3. *special grouping arrangement*, where children are grouped across grades based on reading or other achievement levels regardless of age

4. *team teaching arrangement*, where children are grouped based on the strengths of individual teachers and where a team of teachers plan together for the instruction of children assigned to them.

Wilson and Ribovich (1973) suggest using alternative grouping patterns, including *open grouping*, *flexible skill grouping* and *paired grouping*.

Open grouping, in which children have the freedom to select their own groups, can be used to avoid rigidity. Children may decide to participate in a certain reading group because they want to be challenged or because they are interested in the story being read. This type of grouping requires that the activities and stories be announced ahead of time so that children are able to plan their selections. Before the group meeting, the teacher can have the story read to visiting children who may have difficulty reading it themselves. Thus, visiting children will be able to successfully engage in the discussions as they will already know the story.

Flexible skill grouping, in which children are grouped temporarily according to similar skill strengths or skill needs that have been identified through assessment, can also be used. Children in a group are similar in one criterion, though not necessarily similar in all skill areas. Children's status in relation to a particular skill changes; therefore, a continuous readjustment of educational provisions for those children becomes essential. Flexibility is employed when children's differences are perceived as being considerable and dynamic.

A third alternative is *paired grouping* in which children are divided flexibly and temporarily in pairs in order that one child may teach the other and they both learn together. Paired grouping, like skill grouping, is based on the assumption that strengths and needs are often independent of general ability level or reading level. An individual's strengths can be demonstrated and internalized through the process of teaching someone else, while each individual's needs are met by receiving help from someone else. All children must have the opportunity to teach and be taught. For instance, Michael may help Janie with sounds and may receive assistance from Dahlia on syllabication. Pairing can cross ages with other students at one level and assist younger children at another level.

Multi-age grouping, also called family grouping, offers an enriched intellectual community for children and permits cross-age tutoring (Spodek, 1978). Children assist and instruct one another, the pressure of age expectations are alleviated, and the individual's own performance abilities are the basis for judgements about programs.

Another way to provide for individualization is by creating a wide range of learning alternatives for children's selection. Independent and group learning is encouraged through an environment in which children are permitted to behave freely and reasonably. A classroom organized into interest centers encourages children by supporting activities in which they participate. Experimentation and continuous modification of the physical setting can support a dynamic learning situation.

PERSONALIZING READING THROUGH DISCOVERY AND INVESTIGATION

Children can learn to read through discovery and investigation. Teachers can plan reading lessons for the day in relation to their instructional goals. Reading becomes personalized by having children actually experience and internalize reading materials.

A group of first graders may be fascinated with the story of the Gingerbread Man. The teacher provides a series of activities related to the Gingerbread Man. Such activities can include reading the story, telling the story, listening to the story, viewing a film of the Gingerbread Man, learning a song, and dramatizing the story of the Gingerbread Man so that he becomes almost real to them. This can be done by first having the children discuss the character of the Gingerbread Man and asking the children questions such as "What type of character is the Gingerbread Man?" "How does he run?" "How does he walk?" Then they will be ready to imitate the Gingerbread Man and develop their own dialogues based on the familiar story. They can then write stories about or draw pictures of the Gingerbread Man.

One morning they can bake a Gingerbread Man and then go for a walk. When they return to their classroom, they will find that the Gingerbread Man is gone. In his place they find a note which says, "I went to the principal's office." The class goes to several places, each time finding a different note, and finally, they read one that sends them back to their room where they find the Gingerbread Man. Every time the children discover a note, it should reflect their reading vocabulary. When they arrive at their classroom, they discuss the experience and eat the Gingerbread Man.

Follow-up activities can include reading more about baking. Other stories and other interests about the Gingerbread Man may develop. The teacher can construct a chart for children to plot their working location, plan their activities, and record their progress. For example, John and Joe may be conducting research in the library, Frances may be discussing the Gingerbread Man with a group of children, and Pablo may be writing a book on the Gingerbread Man with another group of children. Using the children's interests can promote reading skills because the reading material will be relevant and interesting. Teachers need to be careful that topics are changed once children lose interest.

SUMMARY

Reading, the process of abstracting meaning from the written language, is one of the most important academic skills taught to young children. Anyone who expects to function independently in our society, whether handicapped or normal, must acquire this skill. Before children begin to learn to read, they must have achieved a degree of readiness. This includes acquiring basic knowledge of the language and developing auditory discrimination skills, visual discrimination skills, and motor skills.

There are many different approaches in use today for teaching reading to children, including the whole-word approach, the phonics approach, the language-experience approach, and the basal reader approach. No one approach is best for all children with all types of learning characteristics in all situations. Most teachers use a combination of approaches.

In working in mainstreamed classes, teachers must be acutely aware of the advantages and disadvantages of each approach for teaching reading. They must assess the competencies of the children they teach and tailor individual programs so each child has a program made up of the most relevant elements of each approach. Careful preparation of the learning environment and the selection of appropriate teaching material is vital. Most important, the reading program should be carefully coordinated with the total language arts program in the classroom, a topic that is addressed in Chapter 10.

REFERENCES

Bank Street Readers. New York: Bank Street College of Education, 1965.

Bradley, J. M. Evaluating reading achievement for placement in special education. *Journal of Special Education*, 1976, *10* (3), 237–245.

Brown, L., Huppler, B., Pierce, L., York, B., and Sontag, E. Teaching trainable-level students to read unconjugated action verbs. *Journal of Special Education*, 1974, *8* (1), 51–56.

Burns, S. An investigation of the relationship between sequential memory and oral reading skills in normal and learning disabled children (Doctoral dissertation, Northwestern University, 1975). *Dissertation Abstracts International*, 1975, *36*, 439A.

Chomsky, C. Write now, read later. *Childhood Education*, 1971, 47, 296–299.

Curry, R. G. Using LEA to teach blind children to read. *The Reading Teacher,* 1975, *29* (3), 272–279.

Cutsforth, T. D. *The blind in school and society*. New York: American Foundation for the Blind, 1951.

Deese, J. *Psycholinguistics*. Boston: Allyn & Bacon, 1970.

Estes, W. K. *Learning theory and mental development*. New York: Academic Press, 1970.

Friedman, J. B., and Gillooley, W. B. Perceptual development in the profoundly deaf as related to early reading. *Journal of Special Education*, 1977, *11* (3), 347–354.

Functional Basic Reading Series. Pittsburgh: Stanwix House, 1963, 1964, 1965.

Goodman, K. S. *The psycholinguist nature of the reading process*. Detroit: Wayne State University Press, 1968.

Guszak, F. J. *Diagnostic reading instruction in the elementary school*. New York: Harper and Row, 1972.

Hall, M. A. *Teaching reading as a language experience approach*. 2nd. ed. Columbus, Ohio: Charles E. Merrill, 1976.

Hall, M. A., Ribovich, J. K., and Ramig, C. J. *Reading and the elementary school child*. New York: D. Van Nostrand Company, 1979.

Hillerich, R. L. *Reading fundamentals for preschool and primary children*. Columbus, Ohio: Charles E. Merrill, 1977.

Hillerich, R. L. So you're evaluating reading programs. *Elementary School Journal*. 1974, *75*, 172–182.

Himmelsteib, C. Buddies read in a library program. *Reading Teacher*, 1979, *29* (1), 32–38.

Johnson, D. J. Process deficits in learning disabled children and implications for reading. In L. B. Resnick and P. A. Weaver (Eds.). *Theory and practice of early reading* (Vol. 2). Hillsdale, N.J.: Lawrence Erlbaum Associates, 1979.

Kirk, S. A., Kliebhan, J. M., and Lerner, J. W. *Teaching reading to slow and disabled learners*. Boston: Houghton-Mifflin, 1978.

Lowenfeld, B., Able, G. L., and Hatlen, P. H. *Blind children learn to read*. Springfield, Ill.: Charles C. Thomas, 1969.

McCloud, B. K., Mitchell, M. M., and Ragland, G. G. Content analysis of basal reading texts for normal and retarded children. *Journal of Special Education*, 1976, *10* (3), 259–264.

Milgram, N. A. Cognition and language in mental retardation: Distinction and implications. In D. K Routh (Ed.). *The experimental psychology of mental retardation*. Chicago: Aldine Publishing Co., 1973.

Ramanauskas, S. Contextual constraints beyond a sentence on close responses of mentally retarded children. *American Journal of Mental Deficiency*, 1972, *77*, 338–345.

Sanders, J. Psychological significant of children's literature. In S. I. Fenwick (Ed.). *A critical approach to children's literature*. Chicago: University of Chicago Press, 1967.

Schickedanz, J. A. The acquisition of written language in young children. In B. Spodek (Ed.). *Handbook of research in early childhood education*. New York: The Free Press, 1982.

Smith, F. Twelve ways to make learning to read difficult. *Psycholinguistics and reading*. New York: Holt, Rinehart and Winston, 1971.

Spache, G. D., and Spache, E. B. *Reading in the elementary school*. (4th ed.) Boston: Allyn & Bacon, 1977.

Spitz, H. The channel capacity of educable mental retardates. In D. K. Routh (Ed.). *The experimental psychology of mental retardation*. Chicago: Aldine Publishing Co., 1973.

Spodek, B. *Teaching in the early years*. (2nd ed.) Englewood Cliffs, N.J.: Prentice-Hall, 1978.

Stauffer, R. G. *The language experience approach to the teaching of reading*. New York: Harper and Row, 1980.

Venezky, R. L. *Prereading skills: Theoretical foundations and practical applications*. (Theoretical Paper No. 54). Madison: University of Wisconsin, Wisconsin Research and Development Center for Cognitive Learning, 1975.

Williams, J. The ABD's of reading: A program for the learning disabled. In L. B. Resnick and P. A. Weaver (Eds.). *Theory and practice of early reading* (Vol. 3).

Hillsdale, N.J.: Lawrence Erlbaum Associates, 1979.

Wilson, R. M., and Ribovich, J. K. Ability grouping? Stop and reconsider! *Reading World*. 1973, *13*, 84–91.

Ten

TEACHING THE LANGUAGE ARTS

Children come to school having learned a great deal about their native language and how to use it. They have developed an extensive vocabulary and have learned most of the important grammatical rules. They have also learned to use language for many purposes in a number of settings. Although the language of children is significantly different from that of adults, it generally reaches a high degree of competence before the onset of formal instruction.

An early childhood language program needs to build on what children have learned about language in their preschool years. It should extend that knowledge in a systematic way and fill in whatever gaps exist in the areas of reading, listening, speaking, and writing. This chapter addresses both the expressive and receptive language arts and discusses ways of modifying regular classroom programs to meet the needs of handicapped children in a regular classroom.

The goals of early childhood education language arts programs include:

1. *Developing basic oral language skills*—learning to speak in sentences, express ideas in logical sequence, enunciate clearly, and pronounce words correctly

2. *Developing listening skills*—learning to attend, increase attention span, and understand what is said

3. *Building a meaningful vocabulary*—developing a vocabulary to use in a variety of contexts

4. *Developing writing skills*—learning to express thoughts in writing as well as in speech

To achieve these goals the teacher should build upon what children already know while developing new understanding. For example, children from bilingual backgrounds can continue learning their native language or dialect, and learn standard English as well. Their repertoire of words and meanings can be extended through opportunities to talk about objects, events, and ideas in their expanding

world. Children should also be allowed to use language to express private thoughts and for social communication in ways that are satisfying to them.

The goals of a language arts program for handicapped children should be the same as those for nonhandicapped children. The degree to which these goals can be achieved may vary, however, depending on the nature of a child's problem. While language usage is learned, most children develop language skills early in life without direct or deliberate teaching. At times, however, most children will exhibit some problems in language development. They may not respond to queries unless the verbalizations are accompanied by gestures. Their verbal responses may not make sense: the words they use may be inappropriate or their syntax wrong. Or they may seem to have

difficulty understanding when others are communicating to them.

A number of handicapping conditions are associated with problems in children's language development. Children who are developmentally delayed, for example, are often delayed in speech and language development. Such delays may be associated with mental retardation as well. Blind children, especially in the preschool years, may manifest a different pattern of language development than do sighted children, although the differences will fade as the children mature. Children with speech and hearing problems will also have problems in achieving the goals of a language arts program to the extent that normal children might.

A teacher who senses that a child is having a language problem and who suspects that other problems might exist could arrange a hearing examination for the child using an audiometer. Deafness and hearing losses account for a large number of learning disorders and, if not diagnosed during the early years, can lead to difficulties in academic skill acquisition later on (Hare & Hare, 1979). If there is no problem identified by such an examination, further assessment should be done. The teacher should determine whether the child hears different speech sounds; has delayed motor control of the tongue, jaws, and palate (which can affect articulation); or has a neurological problem. A proper assessment of the nature and cause of the problem will suggest appropriate treatment as well as appropriate instruction. A speech and language specialist should be consulted in such cases.

THE LANGUAGE ARTS PROGRAM

Language arts include the receptive activities of listening and reading as well as the expressive activities of speaking and writing. In preschool and kindergarten the focus will be on oral language activities. These activities interrelate with one another as children observe the world around them, evolve and express ideas, and gain ideas from others. Gradually children become aware of the relationship between spoken and printed language. They learn to receive ideas and impressions through both listening and reading; they learn to share their own ideas, impressions, and feelings through speaking and writing. Many experiences can be offered to young children to enhance skills in listening, speaking, reading, and writing and to make them aware of the beauty and function of language. This can be done through activities such as children's literature, choral speaking, puppetry, creative dramatics, and discussions in which children describe sensory experiences and interpret pictures. As children move through the primary grades there is increased emphasis on written language skills. The mechanics of handwriting, spelling, and grammar are taught along with an emphasis on writing as another form of language communication.

Children's Literature

Many beautifully illustrated and well written books are available for young children. The following guidelines by Jacobs (1972) can be used in selecting literary materials for children:

1. *Provide a balance of contemporary literature and classics.* Contemporary literature considers the minds of modern children, the tempo of their world, their delights and enthusiasms, and the language patterns appropriate for their developmental level.

2. *Provide a balance of realistic and fanciful literature.* Realistic literature refers to feasible events, projecting children into possible time and place settings with seemingly real people. Incidents and events in-

vented by the author seem actual. "Make-believe" stories should also be included.

3. *Provide a balance of fictional and informational reading matter.* Fiction and informational reading present children with two modes of knowing about the meanings and promises of life.

4. *Provide a balance of popular and precious materials.* An abundance of popular books as well as books of high-level literature reflecting both the teacher's and children's individual preferences should be available.

5. *Provide a balance of expensive and inexpensive books.* Many inexpensive books are written by reputable writers and illustrated by excellent artists. These books should be carefully selected and offered in class. However, children need to experience high quality, expensive books as well.

6. *Provide a balance of periodical and book reading.* Children need to be presented with the best current children's newspapers and magazines appropriate for their age group, as well as books.

7. *Provide a balance of prose and poetry.* A rich and balanced contact with literature offers a developmental language program through books, reading stories, storytelling, poetry, dramatizing literature, choral speaking and reading, puppetry, and creative dramatics.

Books. Good picture-story and story books transmit the mores, attitudes, and values of the culture. They also help children experience other people's emotions. Factual, realistic, and imaginative literature extends and satisfies children's curiosity and nurtures their interests. Books provide children with opportunities to learn the language, free them to explore the meaning of language, and stimulate them to use their higher mental processes: thinking about meanings, seeing relationships, remembering similar feelings and occurrences, developing concepts, generalizing, and abstracting.

Reading Stories. Reading stories to young children helps the reader share the joy and wonder of a broadening acquaintance with the world of books. The reader takes the children into a literary journey, often stretching their experience and extending their world of words and feelings. This activity develops children's desire for more stories and poems and influences their literary taste.

Storytelling. Telling stories, rather than reading them, provides intimate contact and rapport with children since there is no barrier between the teller and the children. The content of the story can be adapted to the children's needs and interests while the pace of the story can be adjusted to the children's attention and developmental levels. Difficult words or phrases can be explained in context. Stories can be personalized by substituting children's names for those of characters.

Poetry. Arnstein (1962) defines poetry as an art that is intended for enjoyment, as are music and painting. Of course, just as some people are not responsive to music or graphic arts, some will not be responsive to poetry. Many people (including children) however, enjoy listening to music, examining paintings, and hearing or reading poetry.

Poetry can be easily introduced to young children. They enjoy the sound and feel of words and are intrigued with their rhythmic qualities. As children search for harmony in their own lives, their rhythms and rhythmic interpretations become poetic in nature.

Expressive Language Arts

Dramatizing Literature.   Through dramatization children can bring the printed world created by authors closer to a world they know as they assume the roles of the characters in the story or poem. To achieve this the teacher reads the story and makes children aware of its dramatic potentiality, but does not directly prescribe dramatic activities. Children can easily capture the dramatic quality of the literature and make their own dramatic presentations.

Choral Speaking and Reading.   Choral speaking and reading takes place when a group of children read a story or a poetry selection together. Choral reading can help children become more aware of the sounds and cadence of literature. In choral speaking and reading activities, children can help choose selections they most enjoy although some degree of teacher guidance is necessary and teachers must be responsive to what children can do and what they like.

Puppetry.   Puppets have been around for centuries. They provide children with opportunities to enrich and expand their language skills and challenge their imaginations. Children are often less self-conscious with puppets than in a dramatic performance. Children can perform puppet shows for each other, which can lead to asking questions and experimenting with the puppets after the show. Puppet presentations should be varied, based upon the children's developmental levels. Young children may have spontaneous dialogues with puppets while older children (ages 6 to 8) may put on a formal play.

Simple puppets to be used with the youngest children can be made out of a paper bag or a sock.

Creative Dramatics.   Creative dramatics are informal dramatic experiences, including pantomimes, improvised stories and skits, movement and body awareness activities, and dramatic songs and games. Their purpose is more to support children's growth and development than to entertain an audience. Children create plays by improvising action and dialogue rather than by memorizing written scripts. Or they can compose written scripts and record their improvised product. Children may wish to share their creations with an audience, especially if they have spent a great deal of time preparing them. Creative dramatics develops language skills, improves socialization skills, stimulates creative imagination, helps develop an understanding of human behavior, and fosters group work and group problem solving.

Discussion Sessions.   Discussion sessions are group interaction periods

during which a child usually speaks to a group or the whole class while the others listen, ask questions, and make responsive comments. Examples of these activities are "show and tell" and "sharing time." An object from home or even an event may be shared during these activities. Discussions can also be less formal, taking place between the teacher and a child or a small group of children.

Some good topics for discussion sessions can include classifying objects by shape, texture, or sound and then using them in manipulative games. Opportunities to smell, touch, see, taste, and hear are firsthand experiences that need to be described and often provide a good basis for discussion sessions. Describing sensory experiences helps extend children's vocabularies as they search for proper words or seek analogies.

Children might also tell a story illustrated by a single picture, a picture book, or a sequence of pictures during a discussion session. Appropriate pictures can be obtained from magazines, discarded schoolbooks, or picture dictionaries. Discussion pictures, published by a number of firms, can also be used.

MODIFYING THE LANGUAGE ARTS PROGRAM FOR HANDICAPPED CHILDREN

Types of language activities handicapped children need and can benefit from depend on their physical, motor, sensory, cognitive, and social abilities. Impairment in one or more of these modalities affects the child's language in different ways. Physical disabilities such as cerebral palsy affect muscle coordination and can create speech disorders as well as problems in writing. Sensory disabilities that create difficulties in hearing-impaired and visually impaired children affect children's abilities to learn language and limit their developing concepts based upon directly accessable sensory data. These children may also have delayed speech.

Hearing-impaired children, who are unable to associate the sounds of language with their experiences, may have a limited vocabulary; become confused with synonyms, prefixes, and suffixes; arrange words in improper order; omit prepositions and articles in sentences; and create sentences with poor syntax. An intellectual disability can also delay language development. Mentally retarded children's language develops at a slower pace than their normally developing peers. The retarded child's language performance may be only slightly below normal, may appear to be normal or may show a serious deficit as compared to normal children (Lindsley, 1964).

The inadequate language skills of handicapped children during early childhood create two major problems: (1) their inability to communicate effectively during the formative years may have detrimental effects on social skills and life adjustment potential; and (2) their inadequate language skills may limit later academic success in school. Thus, language arts activities must be a high priority for teachers of handicapped children and must support all four language skills: listening, speaking, writing, and reading.

Listening

Listening occurs when children hear, recognize, interpret, and understand. Children's listening can be improved through experiences with children's literature, discussion sessions and classes which help children attend to descriptions, sensory experiences, and pictures. Using audiovisual material can also enhance listening skills. Handicapped children can listen to record players, cassette tape recorders, and machines such as the Language Master. The teacher can create listening stations containing headsets attached to these machines so that listened activities do not disturb others.

Careful selection of materials provided for listening activities is important. They should be of interest to and developmentally appropriate for the handicapped child. The teacher can provide opportunities to interpret materials and experiences in an individualized way and simultaneously provide imaginative experiences as the basis for conceptual thinking. A simple framework must be designed for a child to master enough tasks to feel successful. For example, Burks, Good, Higginbotham, and Hoffman (1967) describe Stephen who was active, had aggressive outbursts, and preferred nonverbal communication. The teacher designed activities to change his attitude toward verbal communication. Formal speech training was postponed and a discrimination program with little direct relation to speech sounds was implemented to acquaint Stephen with the classroom and help him learn to follow verbal directions to which he responded motorically in relation to space discrimination (e.g., "Crawl over the desk and between the chairs"). A special audiotape was prepared to allow him to listen to certain sounds in isolation—a telephone ring, an alarm clock, a window closing, and a vacuum cleaner. Once Stephen could distinguish these sounds, he listened to records and stories. Later he was encouraged to respond to the stories until he began to make up and record his own. The teacher worked with Stephen one-half hour a week for a total of eight sessions and used appropriate group activities to reinforce Stephen's learning.

Learning to follow verbal directions should be part of a listening program. Most young handicapped children who first attend school do not have the necessary direction-following skills. And, although teaching direction-following skills requires considerable time and energy, the attainment of such skills by children is essential for smooth classroom management. Scheuerman, Cartwright, York, Lowry, and Brown (1974) developed a three-phase instructional program addressed to this problem. In Phase 1 students learned to follow a one-component local direction (e.g., "stand up"). In Phase 2 they followed a one-component distant direction (e.g., "go to the door"), and in Phase 3 they learned to follow a two-component local direction (e.g., "stand up, then raise your hands"). Brown, Bellamy, Lang, and Klemme (cited in Scheuerman et al., 1974) offer the teacher three alternative methods for teaching direction-following skills: (1) model the specified directions for the students, (2) physically guide the students through the specified di-

rections, or (3) have students perform tasks implicit in the specified directions.

Hearing-impaired children need specific auditory training to develop listening skills. Mildly hearing-impaired children are probably easily neglected in the regular classroom because these children rarely ask to have a direction repeated. To be able to help such children use their hearing to the fullest extent, teachers should know each child's listening level. The hard-of-hearing need to associate sounds with objects, actions, and people. In addition, these children need to become aware of sounds and develop discrimination skills that help them distinguish various sound and speech patterns. Deaf children can learn to attend through their eyes, speech-reading as well as following nonverbal cues or sign language. Since these children depend more heavily on visual cues, directions must be specific and clear. Hearing-impaired children can enjoy literature through carefully selected picture-story books and other materials. Telling stories with the aid of a flannel board or pictures is also helpful.

Many hard-of-hearing children who can produce normal speech have difficulty understanding the speech of others. These children need to learn to fill in gaps in conversation with speech reading. Children with borderline hearing loss may get along in a normal classroom without difficulty by using speech reading. Some children need hearing aids in addition to speech reading.

Speech specialists or speech-reading specialists teach speech reading. Children, however, practice speech reading

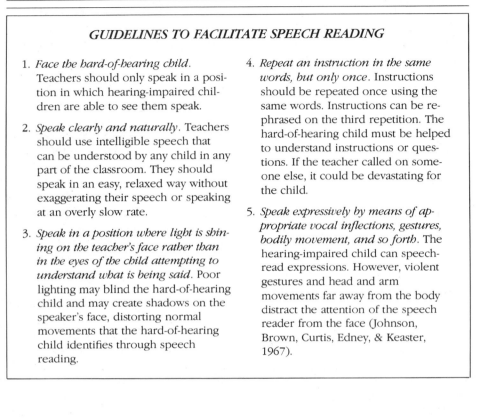

GUIDELINES TO FACILITATE SPEECH READING

1. *Face the hard-of-hearing child.* Teachers should only speak in a position in which hearing-impaired children are able to see them speak.

2. *Speak clearly and naturally.* Teachers should use intelligible speech that can be understood by any child in any part of the classroom. They should speak in an easy, relaxed way without exaggerating their speech or speaking at an overly slow rate.

3. *Speak in a position where light is shining on the teacher's face rather than in the eyes of the child attempting to understand what is being said.* Poor lighting may blind the hard-of-hearing child and may create shadows on the speaker's face, distorting normal movements that the hard-of-hearing child identifies through speech reading.

4. *Repeat an instruction in the same words, but only once.* Instructions should be repeated once using the same words. Instructions can be rephrased on the third repetition. The hard-of-hearing child must be helped to understand instructions or questions. If the teacher called on someone else, it could be devastating for the child.

5. *Speak expressively by means of appropriate vocal inflections, gestures, bodily movement, and so forth.* The hearing-impaired child can speech-read expressions. However, violent gestures and head and arm movements far away from the body distract the attention of the speech reader from the face (Johnson, Brown, Curtis, Edney, & Keaster, 1967).

in the regular classroom and the teacher should provide practice opportunities.

Speech reading is learned through both formal and informal instruction. Speech specialists, classroom teachers, or parents can teach simple speech reading. Sensory perceptions are used to learn and understand language. Speech reading instruction should occur in natural settings and focus on the visual impressions of speech. Beginning instruction requires that speech reading be practiced in isolation so the child can focus on the visual stimuli, eliminating auditory stimuli.

The teacher must whisper or mouth words. This takes practicing silent speech in front of a mirror until the speech feels and looks normal. Instruction and practice in speech reading should have a normal amount of lip movement and be at a normal rate of speech, because that is what the child will find outside the classroom. It is essential for the child to learn to read and understand speech at a normal rate.

Formal speech-reading lessons should be developmentally appropriate and related to the child's interest. Practicing speech reading with several speakers who look different and have different speech patterns is effective. After the child can read voiceless speech, let him or her read speech that can be partially heard and seen. Such children will have to follow conversations with both ears and eyes in normal situations.

Instruction in beginning speech reading is easiest in a context that is familiar to the child. Johnson, Brown, Curtis, Edney, and Keaster (1967) give the following suggestions:

1. Use colloquial expressions, such as "Hello" "Good morning" "How are you?" "Good-bye".

2. Use nursery rhymes, such as *Jack and Jill, Mary Had a Little Lamb, Humpty Dumpty*.

3. Use language in familiar categories, such as days of the week, months of the year, the alphabet, numbers.

Once the hard-of-hearing child has acquired some facility in speech reading with familiar material, less familiar language can be introduced in a variety of ways including units such as the family or zoo animals. Audiovisual materials and simple directions can make instruction more effective. For example, "Find the boys" or "Tell the story about the cat". The unit should be progressive. For instance, the teacher begins with a simple, familiar picture and moves to a complex use of words in sentences and stories.

Telling a story is complex and, like Wanda Gag's *Millions of Cats*, should involve much repetition. Stories should be selected based on the child's interest and attention span. A simple outline

or a set of sequenced pictures to show the sequence of events help children follow the story. Long stories can be condensed or divided into sections to help children keep up with the sequence. The teacher can tell each section separately and emphasize its main points by asking questions. When all sections have been completed, the story is retold in its entirety. It is best to avoid extremely long stories.

Blind children rely upon listening more heavily than other children. Although they use their other senses, their safety and existence depend to a great extent on their ability to hear sounds in their environment. Reading or telling them stories are rewarding experiences that promote listening skills. Sharing a good book with the teacher and classmates enlarges the children's literary world and helps them live vicariously through the literary characters in the story. Visually impaired children may react to the story or may wish to write about it on a braille typewriter.

Beatrix Potter's and A. A. Milne's stories, the *Mother Goose Stories* and other nursery rhymes, and such children's favorites as the Babar, Paddington, Curious George, and Madeleine stories as well as *Charlotte's Web, The Biggest Bear,* and *Winnie-the-Pooh* have all been recorded on readily available long-playing records. If commercial records are not available, the child's own favorite story can be recorded on tape allowing him or her to listen to it as often as desired.

Listening builds memory skills and recall. To help children extend their memories the teacher can read a passage and then ask the children a series of questions about it. Listening activities can also be provided to help children infer, compare, follow directions, and sequence incidents. The teacher can record common sounds to help children discriminate hearing sounds. These sounds can range from simple to complex and from the known to the unknown. The teacher can start with sounds familiar to the child such as car, train, or animal sounds and then go to less familiar sounds. A tape with sounds of different musical instruments or various types of music can be included. As the child's listening skills develop, the tapes can become more complex. Musical instruments can help children discriminate high and low sounds. Sound boxes similar to those developed by Montessori can be used to match sounds that are alike or to seriate sounds from high to low pitch or from loud to soft. Teachers can use their ingenuity to develop materials and activities that extend the listening skills of the visually impaired child. Experience will guide the teacher to continually provide new listening opportunities.

Speaking

Theories of language development do not suggest that handicapped individuals develop language in an abnormal manner. However, language-impaired children develop language at a slower rate and developmental sequences of language behavior can be affected by speech disorders.

In planning and implementing speaking activities, the teacher needs to assess the nature and degree of the children's disorders.

Language training for nonverbal children requires intensive individual attention. However, many educational settings have too many children and too few staff to provide such training. Guralnick (1972) suggests using nonprofessionals such as parents, or college and high school student volunteers. Volunteers should be provided with a training program and be expected to attend training sessions before working with classes.

Writing

Writing, like reading, is based on printed symbols. Handwriting, the most concrete language arts skill, is mainly a motor skill that requires visual ability as well as motor coordination. In writing, the handicapped child, like the normal child, identifies and produces forms including manuscript and cursive letters, punctuation marks, Arabic numerals, conventions for arrangement and spacing, and conventions for margins and headings. Writing develops visual-motor perception and is an important communication skill.

Children may begin to develop writing skills long before they enter the primary grades. Writing manuscript letters entails making vertical, horizontal, and diagonal lines as well as circles or circle segments. Children must learn to hold writing implements and make these forms accurately, combining them into letters. They must also be able to apply enough pressure on the writing instrument to make their marks while holding the paper in place. Art activities offered in preprimary grades have many elements that prepare the

child for writing. While painting and crayoning provide a freer form than does writing, there are elements common to them all. Thus, children can be helped to experience some aspects of writing early, and those children who are having difficulty learning to write may go back to earlier forms.

Teachers need to help children make letter forms carefully. Templates that allow children to draw prescribed forms may help them gain greater control of their strokes. Such forms are available in Montessori programs. Tracing and copying letter forms also helps. Sometimes writing instruments need to be modified to enable children with motor problems to grasp them adequately. Extra thick pencils may be easier to hold than those of normal

thickness, and even these may need to be wrapped in tape or run through a small ball to allow greater ease in handling.

The teacher of handicapped children needs to determine which form of writing to teach. Until the 1960s, special education and learning disabilities specialists recommended teaching cursive writing because words written in cursive were considered to be more easily perceived as whole units: cursive writing, focuses on left-to-right progression, the flowing motion avoids reversals, spacing and alignment are easier to keep, and a transfer to another kind of alphabet is avoided. Special education and learning disabilities specialists have more recently suggested teaching manuscript writing because it resem-

bles book print, it facilitates reading instruction, it seems more legible, and
the shapes are easier to form.

The authors of DISTAR and the *ita*
alphabet favor their own alphabets
which provide a more regular relationship between letters and the sounds
they represent. They affirm that their
special alphabets have the advantages
of manuscript writing and that the use
of additional symbols fosters beginning
reading instruction and creative writing. Another trend that is advocated is
the compromise approach in which
manuscript writing is modified to resemble italic writing that resembles the
print used in books (Hanson, 1976).
Capital letters are written in the block
form familiar to preschool children,
and it is a form of writing based on
natural hand movements. The teacher
needs to make some judgement about

which orthography to use based on an
assessment of what would be easiest
for the children and most acceptable to
others in the school.

LeBlanc, Etzel, and Domash (1978)
suggest using cuing procedures that are
gradually withdrawn with children who
are having learning difficulties. A child
who cannot write the word *red*, for
example, can be given a worksheet on
which the letters *r, e,* and *d* are presented many times. The first presentation would use a solid line with an X at
the point where the child should start
to trace each letter. The X would be
faded and then eliminated, and the
solid line would give way to a dotted
line as the whole letter was replaced by
a smaller and smaller portion of each
letter. As the child works through tracing the form, she or he becomes less
dependent on the cues and more inde-

pendent in reproducing the proper form of each letter, ultimately putting the letters together to create the word. Since developing such a program takes a considerable amount of time and effort, the authors suggest using such procedures only when normal methods do not succeed.

Spelling

Many linguists and early childhood educators (e.g., Chomsky, 1981) suggest that teachers should not concern themselves to any great extent with the correctness of young children's spelling when they begin to write. Children will invent spelling, writing words in a way that sounds right to their ears and thus making their own sense of the relationship between written letters and spoken sounds. As they mature and

gain greater experience with written language, the rules the children originally created will drop out and conventional spelling will fall into place.

Some children will have difficulty with spelling even through the elementary grades, continuing to spell phonetically or making totally inappropriate letter substitutions. Often the errors made are the result of a lack of visual or auditory skills. Analyzing the errors children make can help the teacher identify the child's specific problems. Prerequisite skills in the auditory or visual area may need to be taught. Teachers can then build a program to help children overcome their spelling problems which may parallel their reading problems (Hart, 1981).

For handicapped children the mechanics of writing may cause problems to which teachers must necessarily re-

spond. It is important, however, to be continuously aware that learning to write is not just learning mechanics. Children, handicapped and nonhandicapped, must learn to express meanings through writing (Lebrun & Van de Craen, 1975). To the extent that mechanical problems block the achievement of that goal, they must be dealt with in class before teachers can move the children toward using writing as a form of expression.

CHILDREN WITH LEARNING HANDICAPS

Major problem areas in handwriting include visual-perception-input, visual spatial relationships, visual-motor ability, and short-term visual recall. Visual-perception-input refers to accurate perception of a configuration. Persons with problems in this area are unable to perceive a shape correctly. They may write twisted letters, inconsistently reverse letters, and slant letters diagonally. Children can learn to recognize similarities and differences among letters. Cardboard letters can be used to help children visually recognize like and unlike shapes. Using cut-out letters and shapes along with parquetry blocks helps children learn to discriminate and group shapes. Children can match shapes to form designs that the teacher constructs or pictures of designs. They can also work with shapes made of sandpaper, clay, playdough, crayons, or tagboard with the children ultimately forming letters on paper. Remediation requires visual sequencing such as matching manipulative objects with a row of pictures of the same objects and copying items in proper sequence.

Children form visual-spatial relationships by relating themselves to the space around them and relating two objects in space to each other. This skill helps children write letters on a line, organize letters on paper, space letters appropriately, and proportion the size of letters. Children with visual-motor difficulties may write very heavily or very lightly. They may hold the pencil with a tense grip that causes them to make holes in the paper or with such a light grip that their letters are barely seen. These children may also erase numerous times as they try to write proper letter shapes.

Children with visual-imagery (visual recall) problems are unable to transfer words from one paper to another or from the chalkboard to a paper. As they copy, they omit letters or entire words or write letters out of sequence. They also have difficulty making motor and spatial judgements. These shortcomings may be the result of poor motor skills, unstable and erratic temperament, faulty visual perception of letters, and difficulty in retaining visual impressions.

Handwriting is a visual and motor task; therefore, the teacher needs to carefully plan handwriting activities for visually impaired children. Blind children can use braille, but they must learn to use other types of communication as well. Special devices are available to help them write letters, spell words, and sign their names. Providing darkly lined paper and large pencils makes writing easier for the visually impaired. Sand and clay writing are good exercises to develop motor skills. The ability to type is also a useful skill. An electric typewriter may be more appropriate for a child with severe motor difficulties than a manual one and computers with joysticks may also be used.

Writing disorders can be avoided if children have a good writing foundation (Lebrun & Van de Craen, 1975). Children must be able to learn directionality such as left to right and up and down. Spatial orientation and directional sense are essential with young children. Left-handed children need extra help; they must follow different writing directions. Grapho-

motor skills are enhanced through drawing, painting, or coloring. The development of prerequisite skills with these materials will facilitate writing skills. Gross motor and fine motor skills are fundamental to success in writing. Children need to control their finger and arm movements during writing activity. Movement activities, finger plays, and the use of manipulatives are exciting and help children gain body control. Rhythmic activities increase children's awareness of their bodies. Handwriting activities for children should evolve from meaningful experiences and be integrated with other activities that have definite writing purposes that are individually determined and practical.

ENHANCING DELAYED-LANGUAGE DEVELOPMENT

The teacher should give prompt attention to children with delayed language problems, arranging through a clinic or with a speech pathologist for assessment throughout the year to determine what help should be provided. Referral to a proper resource may be indicated. Psychological and hearing tests as well as a physical examination might be arranged. Home visits or parent interviews can provide additional information.

Children as young as 3 and 4 years of age can be assessed for language disorders and referred for proper treatment. The classroom teacher is responsible for notifying the speech specialist of problems identified in class and for requesting specific suggestions as to how to work with the child.

Serious language disabilities require the help of professionals. A team may include the teacher, speech specialist, psychologist, social worker, and audiologist. Other professionals (such as a dentist, occupational therapist, physical therapist, and one or more medical specialists) may also be involved as needed. The teacher is responsible for identifying the language problems, communicating with the parents, referring the child to the appropriate specialists, and carrying out the recommendations made by the team. The teacher supports the speech specialist by including class activities that serve as a follow-up of the specialist's lesson.

SUMMARY

This chapter has focused on the receptive (listening and reading) and expressive (speaking and writing) aspects of the language arts, including children's literature. It has discussed each area in relation to the modifications necessary for dealing with children's handicaps when teaching language arts. Special attention has been given to children with language related disabilities.

A language program should not be isolated from programs in other learning areas. Language problems often affect other curriculum areas. Delayed language development in a young child will frequently manifest itself later in marked slowness in learning to read and a lack of ability to express thoughts in writing that may continue throughout the years. A language environment should foster the children's optimal language learning. The teacher promotes language functioning through encouraging and actively teaching communication skills including expression in a variety of forms of speaking and listening. A wide range of alternative approaches must be provided in all aspects of the curriculum.

REFERENCES

Arnstein, F. J. *Poetry in the elementary classroom*. New York: Appleton-Century-Crofts, 1962.

Burks, H. L., Good, J. A., Higginbotham, E. S., and Hoffman, C. A. Treatment of language lags in psychotherapeutic nursery school. *Journal of Special Education*, 1967, *1* (2), 197–206.

Chomsky, C. Write now, read later. In C. B. Cazden (Ed.). *Language in early childhood education* (Rev. ed.). Washington, D.C.: National Association for the Education of Young Children, 1981.

Gag, W. *Millions of Cats*. New York: Coward, McCann, 1928.

Guralnick, M. J. A language development program for severely handicapped children. *Exceptional Children*, 1972, *39* (3), 45–49.

Hanson, I. W. Teaching remedial handwriting. *Language Arts*, 1976, *53* (4), 428–431 ff.

Hare, B. A., and Hare, J. M. Learning disabilities in young children. In S. G. Harwood (Ed.). *Educating young handicapped children: A developmental approach*. Germantown, Md.: Aspen Systems Corp., 1979.

Hart, V. *Mainstreaming children with special needs*. New York: Longman, 1981.

Jacobs, L. B. Providing balanced contacts with literature for children. In L. B. Jacobs (Ed.), *Literature for children*. Washington, D.C.: Association for Childhood Education International, 1972.

Johnson, W., Brown, S. F., Curtis, J. F., Edney, C. W., and Keaster, J. *Speech handicapped school children*. New York: Harper and Row, 1967.

LeBlanc, J. M., Etzel, B. C., and Domash, M. A. A functional curriculum for early intervention. In K. E. Allen, V. A. Holm, and R. L. Scheffelbusch (Eds.). *Early interven-*

tion: A team approach. Baltimore, Md.: University Park Press, 1978.

Lebrun, Y., and Van de Craen, P. Developmental writing disorders and their prevention. *Journal of Special Education*, 1975, *9* (2), 201–207.

Scheuerman, N., Cartwright, S., York, R., Lowry, P., and Brown, L. Teaching young severely handicapped students to follow verbal directions. *Journal of Special Education*, 1974, *8* (3), 223–236.

Eleven

TEACHING SOCIAL STUDIES, SCIENCE, AND MATHEMATICS

Social studies, science, and mathematics are generally presented to handicapped pupils by the teacher in a regular class. As with all aspects of mainstreaming, however, responsibility must be shared by both regular and special teachers. This chapter discusses strategies for modifying instruction in these areas for handicapped children.

SOCIAL STUDIES IN EARLY CHILDHOOD EDUCATION

Young children need to be helped to understand themselves, the world around them, and their relation to it. As children receive feedback from the outside world they also learn about themselves. They need to develop knowledge and skills that are essential both for their everyday life and for future learning. Young children have direct access to the physical world, learning about physical things by touching them, listening to them, or viewing them. Social phenomena are less directly accessible. Although young children have direct contact with people and can observe their behavior directly, they need to learn to interpret these observable behaviors. The social studies program should be composed of four processes: intellectualization, socialization, and development of values and self-awareness (Spodek, 1978).

Intellectual Processes

Piaget (1970) stresses the significance of continued interaction with the environment to facilitate the development of logical reasoning. Children act on the world, experiencing it and abstracting information from these experiences through their senses. New experiences are related to prior experiences and to concepts previously attained. Prior concepts are expanded as new information is *assimilated* or added to the child's existing store. When prior concepts no longer fit, they are modified through the process of restructuring called *accommodation*. These two processes, assimilation and accommodation, create continual changes toward a balance or *equilibrium* in understanding. This equilibrium process takes place in relation to social studies knowledge as it does in other areas of knowledge. Piaget speaks of different forms of knowledge including physical knowledge, social knowledge, and logico-mathematical knowledge. Physical knowledge is knowledge of the physical attributes of things. We can provide such knowledge through direct experiences, such as field trips, observations, and interviews. Once children gain a sense of the world we can substitute indirect sources such as texts, audiovisual material, and simulations for direct experiences in the same vein.

Social knowledge—the knowledge of social conventions, symbols, values, rituals, and myths—relates to right and wrong social behavior and rules. It cannot be discovered easily; thus it must be taught to children either directly or indirectly. Logico-mathematical knowledge consists of intellectual processes that are used to organize and make sense of information; these include classifying and ordering objects and events, quantifying objects and events, observing and identifying relationships, and placing things into the proper time/space context. We represent our ideas and feelings through pictures, maps, play activities, and stories. In an inquiry-oriented social studies program, children gather social data, arrange that data, interpret it, and represent the products of their inquiry.

Although some handicapping conditions make it more difficult for children to use their intellectual processes in certain subject areas, they should not be avoided. Some children may have language or reading problems. Others may have trouble remembering content and deriving generalizations. Nevertheless, all should be encouraged to continue to work in all subject areas and should be provided with additional necessary resources. If children learn slowly, the pace of instruction should be modified and a greater variety of experiences provided to illustrate the same ideas. If children fatigue easily, instruction should be reorganized into smaller units that take less time. Class organization can provide individual, small group and whole class activities. Learning centers can be established where individuals or small groups of children can work at their own pace. A range of audiovisual media can be used, including pictures, charts, films, filmstrips, and records. Braille atlases, textured relief maps made of molded plastic, and talking books can be made available. These written materials should be at the children's reading level and should be supplemented by other materials, including tapes of the text, maps, charts, newspapers, and magazines. Group projects can be used to allow children to help one another and provide opportunities for informal peer tutoring.

Mentally retarded children usually take longer than their normal peers to learn concepts and may need to attain concepts at a simpler level. Mentally retarded and learning-disabled children can be helped by being provided information in small, manageable steps and by being offered concrete representations of ideas. The teacher can identify problems that arise and provide for the missing links in the learn-

ing chain, retracing each step to determine what help is needed for those
who failed to learn a concept. Active
involvement in inquiry activities as op-
posed to passive sitting, looking, and
listening facilitates concept learning.
Once children have learned a concept,
they need to practice it.

The motor problems of cerebral palsied children may restrict their capacity
to process information. The effects of
the disability depend on the location of
the affected areas and the severity of
the handicap. Cognitive learning becomes a problem when organic or
functional language disabilities restrict
children's access to information or
their capacity to make experiences
coherent. Teachers can provide language experiences in a meaningful
context to these children while using
prompting, fading, and modeling to
help them assimilate language learning.
Cueing techniques employing verbal
instruction along with gestures or other
physical means of prodding can also
help children remember responses.
Selecting appropriate cues to use with
individual children requires that
teachers analyze which cues work.

Sociodramatic play helps children
process information and generate concepts. For example, children can play at
shopping in the grocery store with a
large number of grocery items (e.g.,
empty coffee cans, fruit cans, cereal
boxes) displayed on a table. Some
children can be shoppers and buy
groceries in the store while others are
grocery workers helping with the selection and tallying the cost of what is
bought. Shoppers can place their selections in a large paper sack to take
home. The children can unpack their
groceries and place them on sections

of the table labeled *breakfast, lunch,*
and *dinner.* Discussion can follow
about the process of shopping, what
foods are eaten at which meal, and
what constitutes a balanced meal. Similar activities can be designed with other
objects that can be categorized and discussed. For example, toy cars, boats,
and airplanes can be grouped as means
of land, sea, and air transportation.
Dollhouse furniture can be classified
into kitchen, bedroom, and living room
furniture (Walsh, 1980).

Children need to adapt to, relate to,
and interpret their environment.
Visually impaired children may need a
greater variety of experiences with objects than other children do. Although
the visually impaired develop intellectually in the same way as sighted
children, they cannot use vision to
gather information. A social studies
curriculum that focuses on concrete
experiences is probably more important for visually impaired students than
for sighted students.

Socialization

In socializing children, the teacher
helps them learn their roles in both the
school community and the larger
community and helps them develop
social skills. Children must learn the
way society is organized and the shared
values, rituals, symbols, and myths of
the larger community. Children learn
these through holiday celebrations,
stories about historic figures and
heroes, and traditional stories and
songs. Experiences that permit students
to inquire about social phenomena
provide the children with an understanding of the organization of society
and the expectations of their role.

Children need to learn the rules, expectations, mores, and values of the school. The rituals of daily life and the teacher's classroom organization, mode of enforcing rules, provisions for independent activity, and selection of experiences are all related to children's socialization and are an important part of social studies.

The social needs of handicapped and nonhandicapped children are similar, although handicapped children may have special problems that affect their rate of social development. Children's social interaction patterns can be influenced in several ways by their handicaps. In some settings a handicap is a social disturbance, especially when people react negatively to a perceived handicap. Society tends to punish handicapped children, restricting their social contacts and impairing their normal social development. Such children may encounter problems in expressing anger, hostility, guilt, and frustration appropriately. They may be highly introverted and fearful. They may also fail to enjoy their achievements and become increasingly dependent on others. Socially incompetent children are often mistreated by their classmates, causing them to withdraw even further from social situations. Withdrawn children need to learn to offer positive social reinforcement to their peers in order to become socially accepted (Charlesworth & Hartup, 1967). In learning social skills, Keller and Carlson (1974) suggest symbolic modeling—showing appropriate behavior with pictures or stories—as a way to decrease fear of interaction with peers.

Social development can be enhanced if the negative aspects of the handicap and its related coping factors are explained and discussed with those who know and care about handicapped children, helping them learn self-control. A positive, trusting relationship between a child and the important adults in that child's life can provide the foundation for developing trust. Children who mistrust adults are continuously testing them to discover the status of their relationship. A positive relationship avoids irritation and frustration and can help handicapped children cope with their disabilities.

An accepting relationship is essential in a least restrictive environment. Most handicapped children will probably never be completely normal, and parents and teachers need to accept handicapped children's limitations and maximize their capacities for the best possible social development. These children need to function in as normal a social environment as possible, and to this end teachers need to promote active social involvement. Handicapped children need to learn manners they can apply in different learning situations and settings. Acceptable social behavior learned in the classroom can be used at home, on the playground, or in community settings. Children's interactions affect their social awareness. Appropriate curriculum content and teaching methods can support the socialization processes in early childhood development.

Values

Values are principles or standards that are part of an individual's code of living and are employed daily in regular life patterns. They are an integral part of life (e.g., religion, traditions, sense of responsibility, and sexuality) and define the person's thoughts and feelings about components of the social world. A person selects a value after considering possible alternatives and the consequences of each alternative, assessing the value, appreciating the choice that was made, and publicly taking stands to defend it. The basic values of early childhood social studies education relate to the worth of the individual, to concepts of freedom and responsibility, to the importance of democratic decision-making, and to a concern for the safety of persons and property. While these values may be taught in different subject matter areas, the social studies have particular responsibility for them.

Teachers are always transmitting their values to children. Children learn the values reflected in the behavior of significant adults including teachers by imitating their behavior and assimilating their perceived values. The pattern of classroom management, decisions about classroom activities, and rules about permissible behavior also influence children's values, as do the types of questions teachers pose to children for they can either further inquiry or lead to stereotyped responses. If a teacher arbitrarily establishes rules for behavior, children may learn not to value rational decision-making.

Valued behavior can be taught through imitation, role-playing, creative dramatics, literature, and art experiences. Young children learn from imitating others. Careful planning for modeling can help young handicapped and nonhandicapped children acquire acceptable behaviors and the values that underlie such behaviors.

Open-ended stories provide a useful medium for exploring values with young children. The stories should be realistic so that children can identify with the characters. For example, an appropriate story for second or third graders could be about two children, Johnny and Ralph, who take a difficult test. Johnny, the school's bully, cheats, and Ralph sees him. Johnny gets a high score while Ralph and the rest of the class fail. What should Ralph do? If he does not report Johnny, everybody will fail and Johnny will be reinforced. If Ralph does report Johnny, Ralph may be accused of jealousy and Johnny might beat him up. Children can provide alternative endings for such a story based on their own values.

Literature can be effective in changing children's values. Stories that can help nonhandicapped children value handicapped children include:

Brightman, A. *Like me.* Boston: Little, Brown & Co., 1976.

Caudell, R. *A certain small shepherd.* New York: Holt, Rinehart & Winston, 1965.

Charlie, R., and Miller, M. B. *Handtalk: An ABC of finger spelling and sign language.* New York: Parents Magazine Press, 1974.

Heide, F. *Sound of sunshine, sound of rain.* New York: Parents Magazine Press, 1970.

Keats, E. J. *Apartment 3.* New York: Macmillan, 1971.

Keats, E. J. *My sister is deaf.* New York: Macmillan, 1971.

Klein, G. *The blue rose.* Westport, Conn.: Lawrence Hill, 1974.

Ominisky, E. *John O: A special boy.* Englewood Cliffs, N. J.: Prentice-Hall, 1977.

Parker, M. *Horses, airplanes, and frogs.* Elgin, Ill.: Child's World, 1977.

Peterson, J. W. *I have a sister, my sister is deaf.* New York: Harper & Row, 1977.

Pursell, M. *A look at physical handicaps.* Minneapolis, Minn.: Lerner Publications, 1976.

Rinkoff, B. *The watchers.* New York: Knopf, 1972.

Robinet, H. *Jay and the marigold.* Chicago: Children's Press, 1976.

Sobol, H. L. *My brother is retarded.* New York: Macmillan, 1977.

Stein, S. B. *About handicaps.* New York: Walker & Co., 1974.

Tester, S. R. *Tell me a tale about the trolls.* Elgin, Ill.: Child's World, 1976.

Wolf, B. *Anna's silent world.* New York: Lippincott, 1977.

Wolf, B. *Don't feel sorry for Paul.* New York: Lippincott, 1974.

Mentally retarded children develop reasoning ability at a slow pace and take longer to distinguish between right and wrong and to develop internal controls. The teacher may need to remind them more often than other children about class rules and restrictions. Class rules can be posted for joint reference when needed.

Teachers need to be less concerned about teaching moral values directly and more concerned about establishing a classroom atmosphere that permits children to evolve through stages of moral development. A concern for moral development in the classroom should extend beyond the social studies and be integrated throughout all aspects of the classroom.

Self-Awareness

Early childhood educators have always been concerned with the affective aspects of children's development. Many goals of early childhood education focus specifically on the affective domain. Children are helped to explore and enhance their self-concepts, cope with feelings about themselves and others, and learn appropriate ways to express their feelings and interact appropriately with others. Social studies should include a concern for affective goals. Experiences must be provided to strengthen children's self-concepts—experiences that help individuals develop a unique set of perceptions, ideas, and attitudes of themselves. Personal experiences and interaction with others can develop a positive or a negative self-concept. Individuals with a positive self-concept view themselves as important, being able to perform at a normal or superior level; those with a negative self-concept lack the ability to employ learning experiences. An individual's self-concept is usually constant over a wide range of situations and for a long period (Saracho, 1980).

Young handicapped children need to develop realistic self-images (how they view themselves) and positive self-concepts (how they value themselves). Children with physical and emotional disabilities, developmental delays, divergent language patterns, and other types of handicaps need special attention. Discussions, role-playing, storytelling, and similar experiences can be effective in helping children gain a sense of themselves. Children can draw pictures of their homes and have their addresses and telephone numbers printed by themselves or the teacher at the bottom of the paper. The teacher can then take a full-length photograph of each child with a Polaroid camera, and attach these near the children's pictures of their homes. These pictures and photographs may then be displayed on the wall or bulletin board to help children relate home to school.

Recording and then listening to children's voices can develop their sense of identity and contribute to their self-images. The teacher can ask the children to sing a song or tell a story and record it on tape. The recordings can then be played back to the children. These are stored in the listening area for children to listen to independently during the day. A full-length mirror in the classroom allows children to examine themselves from head to toe, contributing to self-image and promoting children's self-concept. A valid self-image, however, is not enough to ensure a healthy self-concept. Emotional stability is also essential in acquiring a positive self-concept.

To develop the children's positive self-concepts the teacher must do more than just help them feel good about themselves. A realistic, positive self-concept needs (1) a strong foundation from which to be able to make decisions about interacting with the world; (2) a feeling of competence or mastery; (3) a belief in being able to perform to the limits of one's potential; (4) a sense of social responsibility and a sense of self-sufficiency or self-direction; and (5) an appreciation and enjoyment of oneself along with an appreciation of and respect for others. Individuals who appreciate themselves have a comfortable sense about all components of the self while simultaneously feeling eager to expand their horizons (Peters & Raupp, 1980).

Handicapped children need activities to promote an awareness and understanding of the parts of the body and of the body as a unified entity. Teachers can plan group experiences such as songs, action plays, art activities, and other improvisation activities. Action games such as "Simon Says," "Hokey Pokey," or "Put Your Finger in the Air" are valuable. Children can also trace each others' bodies on large strips of brown wrapping paper. The children can then add and color in the rest of their features including their clothes. Children's works can be displayed in the classroom with their names on it, helping them become aware of themselves as individuals and as members of a group. The teacher may need to provide some children with special help with their tracing, showing them, for example, the way the legs and arms can be traced.

Asking children to draw their own faces on newsprint paper can also help develop body awareness. Children can later talk about facial features and about the fact that some children need to use eyeglasses and hearing aids to help them see and hear. Children can become aware of the need for other prosthetic devices such as wheelchairs or braces. This activity offers a good opportunity to observe the children's reactions to handicaps, and how they cope with them. Children must learn to deal with their emotions and develop a heightened awareness of themselves, but teachers should not establish unrealistic expectations.

Another facet of self-awareness is that of self-help skills and independence routines. Such skills as grooming, eating, toileting, and dressing play a critical role in helping handicapped children function independently. The more proficient children become in self-help skills, the less likely they will be placed in special segregated classes. Moreover, handicapped children who function independently can have more instructional time available in subject areas.

It is important to remember that there are many ways to develop most self-help skills. For example, a coat can be put on in various ways: (1) one arm at a time from the back, (2) arms placed in the sleeves of a coat laid out on a table in front of the child and lifted over the head, (3) a coat laid behind the child into which the child places both arms and then the coat lifted onto the child's shoulders. If one approach is not successful, the teacher should work with the child to develop another (Alberto, 1979).

In most preschools, children are expected to spend time working and playing independently. Clearly, independence training is an important developmental task. Some handicapping conditions, such as physical disabilities, can limit a child's opportunities to function independently. Preschool materials may need to be modified so that children with limited independence skills can use them. Materials, for example, can be stored in containers that are low, unbreakable, and easy to open and close so that all children can use them independently. Children who lack independence are dependent on adult feedback and reinforcement. By adapting materials for corrective feedback (e.g., color coding, sorting materials, accompanying puzzles with pictures of the completed work), the teacher can help these children become less dependent on social feedback (Neisworth et al., 1980).

Although most children use their sight to acquire self-help skills, visually impaired children must be taught many of these skills directly including turning their head toward the speaker, holding eating utensils properly, and not engaging in distracting behaviors when someone is speaking. The teacher also needs to coach these children on their personal appearance, dress, and mannerisms. Physical guidance along with modeling and demonstration is often used in teaching these skills. Wehman and Goodwyn (1978) suggest a basic sequence in teaching a self-help skill:

1. The teacher gets the child's attention.

2. The teacher offers instruction including demonstration, encouragement, or imitation.

3. The teacher helps the child respond correctly by prompting, cueing, modeling, and repeating instructions.

4. The teacher manually guides the child through the response if the child proves unable to perform the desired skills.

5. The teacher rewards appropriate responses immediately.

6. The teacher corrects inappropriate responses immediately.

This sequence can be used to teach a number of self-help skills. Oversized buttons can be used at the beginning and these gradually reduced in size to minimize errors in dressing. Color-coded shoe eyelets can help children lace their shoes (Gold & Scott, 1971). Practice in each specific skill is important.

Children must develop positive relationships with others in their social environment. Children develop basic ideas about themselves and others through these relationships. Teachers should help them develop a basis for personal and social understandings. Thoughts that are formed at an early age persist as the nucleus of a life-long system of developing social relationships.

The residual effects of handicapping conditions often affect children emotionally. They may become lonely, have a negative self-image, or perceive themselves as being unable to meet their parents' expectations. These self-perceptions can make even four- and five-year-old children feel ashamed and guilty and impair their relations with peers. A child's inability to meet unrealistic demands can increase the sense of self-pity and frustration that a disability imposes (Draper, Garner, & Resnick, 1978). The problem can be alleviated if handicapped children understand how others feel, and vice versa.

Sometimes pictures can help children understand other people's feelings. A photograph, cartoon, illustration, or other visual presentation can depict a situation important to the child. For example, children presented with a magazine picture depicting children climbing a chain-link fence on which there is a sign saying, "Danger. High Voltage. Keep Out," can use that picture to discuss feelings of danger or fear. A picture, illustrating a mother holding a broken vase and sternly staring at her three- or four-year-old son who is standing before her with an apprehensive look on his face, can serve as a springboard for a discussion to help children understand the way their behavior affects others. Such pictures allow children to identify with other persons and situations and perceive the world from another person's point of view. Such activities also help children develop critical social skills as they analyze situations, identify problems, and predict outcomes (Walsh, 1980).

The self-concept begins to develop during infancy when children begin to differentiate themselves from their mothers and the rest of their environment. Children who do not have volitional control over parts of their own body, who may not be able to move a limb, or move it only with great difficulty, or must wear a prosthesis need guidance in developing feelings of autonomy and independence. Handicapped children must also develop a realistic sense of themselves in relation to their physical environment, even if it is a difficult task for them.

Thus, a social studies program in early childhood education should help young children acquire a better understanding of themselves and their social world. It also must offer children reasonable and verifiable knowledge and understanding of their social and physical world that they can use to help make rational decisions.

MAINSTREAMING HANDICAPPED CHILDREN INTO A SCIENCE PROGRAM

Science is composed of facts, concepts, and generalizations. These are arranged systematically into a science curriculum that allows children to integrate information and generalize about their world. Science helps children discover and create order out of their daily experiences. As part of the science program, children need to generate and verify knowledge through observations of phenomena, testing hypotheses, and carefully reporting and describing science experiences.

An early childhood science program can be built around children's everyday experiences when they observe and describe physical objects, differentiate between groups of objects based on observable attributes, and categorize objects based on these attributes. Activities should allow free exploration of scientific materials and their use as well as provide more formal learning opportunities. A flexible classroom arrangement and a supportive social climate are essential to stimulate all children's exploration to meet the goals of the science program.

In the past schools often limited the science curriculum of handicapped students. Blind or spastic students, for example, were often seen as being incapable of handling science materials. Handicapped children have as much need for a science program as other children, and programs can be adapted to their handicapping conditions and presented within the regular classroom. Thompson (1979) suggests that these erroneous decisions of the past were based on myths about handicapped students' ability to function in the regular science curriculum.

Scientific knowledge is essential for understanding our existence and coping with modern technological living conditions. It also provides individuals with enjoyment, understanding, improved health, and often, an occupation. Teachers do not have the right to withhold these opportunities from

either handicapped or nonhandicapped students. Handicapped students may need more instructional and practice time and more varied experiences to master science skills or concepts— hearing-impaired students, for example, may require more time to learn the technical vocabulary of science, and that vocabulary may need to be presented differently.

Science for preschool children is mainly focused on having children experience physical and natural phenomena and develop ways of organizing the information that results from these experiences. In primitive ways, the techniques young children use to make sense of the world are not too much different from those used by mature scientists.

When teachers have handicapped children in their classes, they must be concerned about whether these children can gain the same sensory experiences as their nonhandicapped peers and whether they have the ability to process the information gained through their experiences. If there are sensory deficits, then the teacher needs to accommodate for them in planning the program, providing substitute experiences when appropriate and helping children build upon the sensory capacities they do have. Providing sensory experiences alone is not enough to help children learn to understand their physical world. They have to be helped to make sense of the world. Children do this by ordering their information. Children develop concepts as a result of what they come to know. They categorize information based upon these concepts and fit new information into the category system already developed, expanding and modifying the system as needed. They can order objects by some quantifiable attribute and put their understandings into a framework of time and space. Causality, for example, results from placing incidents into a time frame with incidents occurring earlier seen as causing those that follow in time.

Handicapped children in preschool can be offered a wide range of science experiences, although they may have to be modified for each child's specific handicap. While blind children may not have visual sensations available to them, they can experience the world through their other senses. Orthopedically handicapped children may require that the physical environment be adapted so that they can deal with things in a way as similar as possible to those of their normal peers. Learning-disabled children may have to have experiences simplified for them and cues provided to signal the activities in which they will engage. With such modifications, the basic processes of science can be approached by every child.

Preschool children, for example, can be given a wide range of objects to sort and classify. Leaves collected in fall can be viewed by the children, and their color, shape, texture, and other attributes discussed (and similarities and differences among the leaves identified). They can then be sorted by configuration. The teacher might later label one set of leaves as oak, another as maple, and so forth, possibly showing the children the trees from which they dropped.

A variety of similar experiences requiring observation of physical attributes of phenomena and categorization of objects by attributes can be pro-

vided. Different colors and sizes of beads or blocks or other small objects that can be grouped by size, shape, color, weight, or some other observable attribute can be grouped in the same way. Sighted children might be asked to order these materials by color, while blind children could be asked to order them by texture or shape.

Young children can also be given objects that differ by size or weight and asked to order them from the heaviest to the lightest or from the largest to the smallest. These activities provide practice in seriation skills.

Children can be helped to perceive that they can cause things to happen. A wheel toy that is pushed and continues to roll, for example, can be discussed in terms of cause and effect. Conditions can be varied to modify the consequences of children's action—the toy can be pushed for example, down a ramp, along a smooth surface of the floor, or along a carpeted section of the floor—and children can begin to see that the consequences of their actions will change depending upon conditions in the environment.

Children who are hyperactive or have temper tantrums may have to be controlled in such activities. They should not be allowed to destroy property or use materials in ways that may harm themselves or others. If a pet is abused or another child harmed, the experience can become a miseducative one. Thus, teachers may have to establish and adhere to special rules with some children or modify the activity to allow all the children to participate. If children are prone to throw containers around the room, the containers used for sorting activities might be fastened to a table board. A simple change in the environment may allow the child to participate more fully in learning activities.

In adapting the science program for handicapped children in kindergarten and the primary grades, individualized instruction must be provided, along with more demonstrations and discussions, perhaps pairing a nonhandicapped child with a handicapped partner. The attitude of the teacher is still the most important attribute of a successful class. The desire to teach both nonhandicapped and handicapped students, regardless of their learning needs or difficulties, will lead to programs appropriate for both groups.

Four basic types of instructional methods in science for learning-disabled children are: reading, doing, media, and discussion. Reading involves using a variety of printed materials, such as textbooks, information books, and children's magazines. Doing involves engaging children in hands-on learning activities and experiments (discussed later in this chapter). Media include use of a range of audiovisual materials.

Probably the most commonly used instructional method in early childhood education involves discussion, or talking with children. Handicapped students who have a short attention span, memory problems, language delays, and inappropriate behavior may have difficulty with learning through discussion. Students with short attention spans tend to have difficulty staying in their chairs and/or listening for more than a short period of time; such students may "tune out." Along with discussions the teacher must provide a variety of active learning experiences

including conducting experiments, completing prescribed activities with materials or learning activity packages at a learning center, using audiovisual aids, playing games, working with peer tutors or volunteers, and writing or illustrating stories about the concept being studied. Students with short attention spans should be seated close to the teacher during discussion periods. Writing a discussion outline on the board, and calling upon these students frequently to answer questions can also help.

Students with memory problems tend to forget important information. Teachers need to provide handicapped students with a summary of key points to remember and a set of exercises and activities to help them recall the critical elements of a discussion. These students can also be given opportunities to associate new information with concepts previously learned. Students with language delays may have problems understanding the technical language of science and comprehending words the teacher uses to define these technical terms. Teachers may need to introduce such new words carefully in context, first writing the definition on index cards in isolation, then presenting the words in a sentence, along with some form of illustration.

Students who have language delays may need systematic instruction in developing higher levels of thinking. These thinking processes include:

○ *Memory:* recalling or recognizing information

○ *Translation:* transforming information into a different symbolic form or language

○ *Interpretation:* discovering relationships among facts, generalizations, definitions, values, and skills

○ *Application:* solving a lifelike problem that requires identification of issues as well as selection and use of appropriate generalization and skills

○ *Analysis:* solving a problem by identifying its component parts

○ *Synthesis:* solving a problem that requires original and creative thinking

○ *Evaluation:* making a judgment of good or bad or right or wrong based on standards designated by the student (Bloom, 1956)

Children who are competent at the memory and translation levels can be helped to move to the interpretation level and beyond through the use of structured questions and activities.

Audiovisual materials, including pictures, charts, films, filmstrips, maps, and graphs, can be used effectively with many handicapped students. Mentally retarded and learning-disabled students with low reading levels can especially profit from using audiovisual materials since they make information available without the need to read.

Hearing-impaired students can be helped hear the audio portion of films, filmstrips, and videotapes by being seated close to the machine. Students who are severely hearing impaired, however, may need to be provided with captioned films that present written content on each frame or in each sequence. Students who can speech read or read sign language can make use of films in which an interpreter appears on a designated portion of the picture.

Many handicapped and nonhandicapped children tend to think in nonverbal terms. Logical thinking requires more than language, although language is a vehicle for abstract thinking. Language usage occurs after the children's development of logical relationships between concrete experiences and objects and events. Handicapped and nonhandicapped children gradually make the transition from concrete to abstract thinking. Science experiences should assist children with this transition without frustrating them with activities that require difficult language and reading skills. Children can be successful when learning is on their terms, and this success will promote further success.

Developing Learning Activities

Creating a science activity center within the classroom where children can work in small groups can enhance a science program. The science center should have adequate equipment and materials for children to examine and explore, and an abundant supply of paper towels and water should be available. All materials should be labeled in print and in braille if visually impaired children are in the class. Handicapped and nonhandicapped children should work together in small groups. The teacher needs to know which children may need assistance and plan to provide for it in as unobtrusive a manner as possible. Peer tutoring and social interaction among handicapped and nonhandicapped children may be all that are necessary.

Science experiences that cannot be adapted for children with a particular handicap should be alternated among different groups in the program. Each group can work independently, later joining together to share their findings to promote interaction within the class. The entire class should be together for science demonstrations and discussions. Lengthy discussions or long dull reports should be avoided and reports on observations or experiments should be accompanied by demonstrations.

Experiments

Most science experiments can be adapted for children with different handicaps.

For the Hearing-Impaired.   Science experiments for hearing-impaired children should provide written labels or language cards that identify the mate-

rials in each experiment. These vocabulary cards should be displayed during discussion or demonstration periods and referred to when appropriate. Only a few language cards should be used at one time.

Word cards or charts can be prepared ahead of time using questions and directions such as

○ Observe carefully.

○ What do you think will happen?

○ What did you see?

○ How are they the same?

○ How are they different?

○ What caused the differences? (Hadary & Cohen, 1978).

For the Visually Impaired.   Teachers should carefully select words used in experiments when visually impaired children are involved. Phrases such as *blue water* or *green leaves* have no meaning to them for they lack the visual referents. In conducting science experiments with the visually impaired, Hadary and Cohen (1978) recommend the following modifications:

1. When real objects cannot be directly observed, models should be employed in their place.

2. Equipment should be anchored in place so children can find them without knocking them down.

3. The exact location of displayed materials should be identified.

4. Objects should be described to the visually impaired so they know what is available.

5. Paired grouping—a visually impaired child working alongside a sighted partner—is effective. The sighted partner can help the visually impaired child with what cannot be seen.

6. A large quantity of paper towels and sufficient water should be accessible in case of spillage. Visually impaired children, particularly, seem to dislike a mess.

For the Emotionally Disturbed.
Science often can serve as therapy to the emotionally disturbed, providing rational, logical explanations and offering control over what is otherwise a confusing world. Science facilitates cause-and-effect observations of behavior, separates facts from feelings, and teaches problem-solving strategies that can be used to resolve conflict. Science can offer the emotionally disturbed child an understanding of life events and reality principles. Exploring and

investigating help such children acquire feelings of autonomy, develop self-confidence, and become more comfortable with themselves and their world. The following adaptations in conducting science experiments with emotionally disturbed children have been suggested by Hadary and Cohen (1978):

1. Experiments should be intellectually stimulating.

2. Experiments should be presented in sequential order.

3. Discussions of discoveries should be encouraged.

4. Emotionally disturbed children can be paired with visually impaired children.

5. Thinking about observed processes before responding actively should be encouraged.

Malone and Lucchi (1979) provide the following examples of life science activities for handicapped children:

1. *Studying Seeds:* Students can remove seeds from fruits and vegetables to compare the amounts and sizes of these seeds. They can (1) dry and plant the seeds, (2) investigate the types of seeds that can be used for food, and (3) make collages with different kinds of seeds.

2. *Observing Snails:* Large snails can be used as classroom animals. They are easy for young children to care for. Students can tape a wire harness to a snail to discover the amount of mass it can pull (students might be surprised). Visually impaired students can touch the load on the snail

gently with one finger to find out whether the snail has moved its load. Students can measure the snail's traveling speed. (For younger children simply setting up an eco-system with a snail, plants, and water in a jar may be enough.)

3. *Studying Crayfish:* Young children can learn about the structure, function, behavior and environment of the crayfish. Crayfish are easy to handle. Students can carefully place rubber tubing on their pincers. An aquarium plant (anacharis) can be measured to find out how much of it one crayfish will eat in a specific period of time. Follow-up activities can include composing stories about crayfish, reading books about crayfish, and preparing reports on crayfish. Students will enjoy becoming experts on crayfish and sharing their knowledge with others.

In addition, *Batteries and Bulbs, Mealworms, Mystery Powders* and other units of the Elementary Science Study science experiments for normal children (developed by the Education Development Center, Newton, Massachusetts) can be adapted for mentally retarded or learning-disabled students.

Most handicapped students, with the exception of the seriously hearing-impaired, can use a tape recorder effectively for science instruction. Children can also dictate the results of experiments on tape. The tape recorder is helpful as a memory bank since students are able to move it forward or backward until they find the information they need (Eichenberger, 1974).

Children can gain their own sense of order and beauty from their science discoveries. Hadary and Cohen (1978) describe a blind girl observing seeds grow through her sense of touch and writing about her experience, "I made a greenhouse, a home for a seed; it wasn't just science, it was science and art. The seeds grew and made lines through space" (p. 10).

Science instruction is an important part of the early childhood curriculum. It requires children to act upon materials and experiences and think about their experiences with physical and natural phenomena, creating their own conclusions. Teachers should not spend a great deal of time telling children science facts but should provide them with opportunities to seek out answers. If an atmosphere of inquiry pervades the classroom, it will support the increasing autonomy of children. The significance in science learning is not the product of scientific inquiry (the conclusions the children make or the different categories they develop) but the processes by which they arrive at them.

MATHEMATICS IN EARLY CHILDHOOD EDUCATION

Mathematics programs in early childhood education vary greatly. Some programs emphasize proficiency in counting, in writing numerals, and in other mathematical skills, while others focus on generating meanings. Some provide systematic, isolated lessons while others use children's everyday experiences as the bases for developing competency. Young children naturally search for meanings their world and in this search have many varied contacts with a world of quantity, space, number, shapes, time, and distance. Teachers need to help children become aware of and understand the numerical, spatial, and measuring aspects of their world.

Young children already have a repertoire of mathematical concepts when they enter the elementary school. Suydam and Weaver (1975) have summarized these for five-year-olds:

1. They are able to count the number of objects to 10, and some have the ability to count to at least 20.

2. They can name the numbers for tens in order (such as 10, 20, 30, 40), and some can tell the number names when counting by twos and fives.

3. They know and understand the meaning of *first* and are able to identify ordinal positions through fifty.

4. They can identify and write the numerals from 1 to 10.

5. They can answer simple problems with addition and subtraction combinations presented verbally and may or may not use manipulative materials.

6. They know about coins, time, and other measures; about fractions; and about geometric shapes.

This suggests that a considerable amount of mathematics learning takes place during the preschool period.

Early childhood mathematics programs must (1) provide a rich environment in which children can accumulate sensory data about quantity; (2) use a range of teaching techniques for children to develop mathematical concepts; (3) demonstrate the relationship between mathematical experiences and mathematical language; (4) present problems that require children to understand the meaning of situations and apply their mathematical understandings, and (5) focus on methods that promote both computational skills and problem-solving ability.

Helping Young Children Develop Mathematical Concepts

Handicapped children develop quantitative concepts in the same order as do nonhandicapped children, but retarded children will develop them later, and children with sensory disorders may have a diminished understanding of the relationships among objects. The ability to understand mathematical concepts is achieved as a result of a combination of learning and maturation. Even repeated drill in the performance of quantitative tasks will not substitute for maturation in the development of these understandings. This does not mean that learning experiences should be withheld from those who are developing less normally; rather it means that readiness activities in mathematics have to be consistent with what the child can understand.

At the preschool level, mathematics activities can focus on:

o experiences with object permanence and conservation of number

o seriation, classification, and equivalence experiences

o combination and identification of sets of various objects

o one-to-one correspondence

o rational counting

o number recognition, matching numbers and numerals, and ordination (Alberto, 1979)

Teachers can use many naturally occurring classroom incidents to teach these concepts. This would require the teacher to systematically analyze daily activities to identify those elements that can help children develop mathematical meanings. Snack time, for example, could allow children to match one cup of juice or one cracker to each child, a way of developing the concept of one-to-one correspondence. In addition, specially planned experiences using manipulative materials can be used. Insert puzzles that require the child to put one puzzle piece into one space provide an experience to help acquire the same concept.

Other activities that can be used include providing children with written numerals and having them match a number; ordering blocks, beads, or other objects according to size; matching patterns of beads on a string to various models the teacher provides; or pointing out groups of two objects or three objects that exist in the classroom or surrounding area.

Teachers need to select for mathematics teaching materials that are appropriate to each child, no matter what the handicap. In addition, they can modify classroom materials. Wooden domino pieces, for example, can have felt dots pasted over the painted dots, so that visually handicapped children can feel the numbers. Cues for putting together puzzles can be created by marking the back of each piece and matching it with a similarly marked space in the puzzle.

In teaching mathematics teachers will find that some children may need a great deal of practice in order to learn and apply mathematical principles while others will grasp them easily. Many young handicapped students have difficulty with mathematics. Characteristics that may cause difficulty in mathematics include:

1. *Poor Self-concept.* Some handicapped children learn to accept failure at an early age. They do not attempt new tasks because they are afraid to fail. Teachers have to provide experiences in which these children can succeed and help them understand that failure is sometimes a step toward learning. Children who perceive themselves as worthy and who approach problems with confidence have a better chance at success (Cruikshank, Fitzgerald, & Jensen, 1980).

2. *Poor Self-control.* Some children are unable to control their behavior and may exhibit explosive, hyperactive, and/or erratic behavior. They are constantly in motion, rarely sit still, and wander aimlessly around the room. Hyperactive children need an environment that limits distractions (Cruikshank, Fitzgerald, & Jensen, 1980).

3. *Specific Mathematics Disability.* Children with minimal brain damage often cannot learn quantitative concepts. Perceptual problems such as inability to define a position in space (e.g., near, far, up, down, left, right), inability to distinguish a figure from its background, and poor eye-hand coordination may affect the learning of spatial concepts. Students may be easily distracted by extraneous stimuli, such as too many problems or pictures on a page, or too many objects or people in a classroom. Children with perceptual problems need simple worksheets and a relatively uncluttered classroom environment (Cruikshank, Fitzgerald, & Jensen, 1980).

4. *Brain Dominance.* It has been suggested that some children's brains are dominated by the left hemisphere, while other children's are dominated by the right hemisphere. The left hemisphere affects verbal, numerical, and logical functions while the right affects visual, spatial, perceptual, intuitive, and imaginative functions. Teachers usually focus their lessons on skills related to the left hemisphere when they ask children to read, listen, think, and write. This procedure, while appropriate for children whose thinking is dominated by the left hemisphere, may create difficulties for those whose thinking is dominated by the right hemisphere. Some educators suggest providing learning activities that strengthen both hemispheres of the brain and the bonds between

them (Cruikshank, Fitzgerald, & Jensen, 1980).

5. *Language Problems.* Many children who have language difficulties also encounter problems in learning mathematics. They may have trouble understanding common mathematical terms such as up, down, in, two, or plus and may not be able to communicate concepts they understand. For these children, the language of mathematics needs to be kept as simple as possible, and any misunderstanding of terms must be clarified immediately. Concepts may be more easily developed by relating physical objects to language (Cruikshank, Fitzgerald, & Jensen, 1980).

6. *Poor Memory.* Some children who have difficulty recalling information perceived or learned a few moments before may need to overlearn to ensure retention of information. Practice, drill, and repetition within context is effective in improving recall. Retarded children may remember and may be able to apply skills if transfer is practiced with understanding. Complex problem-solving is probably difficult; however, simple rote learning of factual materials such as basic facts can be learned, memorized, and applied (Cruikshank, Fitzgerald, & Jensen, 1980).

7. *Short Attention Span.* Children with short attention spans can have difficulty with problems that are too elaborate, too long, or not interesting enough. Many children can work for relatively long periods of time if problems are interesting and challenging. Filtering out extraneous information and focusing on pertinent facts can help to sustain a child's attention (Cruikshank, Fitzgerald, & Jensen, 1980).

8. *Visual and Auditory Discrimination Disabilities.* Children who have difficulty recognizing that two separate auditory or visual stimuli or patterns of stimuli are the same or different have problems in comparing like and unlike elements. Almost all mathematical tasks require these types of discrimination. Such a disability is a threat to success in mathematics (Johnson, 1979).

9. *Visual and Auditory Association Disabilities.* Children who have difficulty relating separately perceived visual or auditorial stimuli or sets of stimuli to each other will have difficulty with mathematics. Visual and auditory association is essential in coping with abstractions and elements of mathematics (Johnson, 1979).

10. *Perceptual-Motor Difficulties.* Children who have difficulty with eye-motor coordination or who cannot relate visual stimuli to motor responses or motor cues to visual stimuli will have problems in mathematics. Most of the performance skills in mathematics, from writing numbers to moving decimal points, require development of perceptual-motor skills (Johnson, 1979).

11. *Spatial Awareness and Orientation Disabilities.* Children who cannot recognize or adequately employ temporal or spatial relationships between objects (difficulties related

to perceptual motor problems) will have problems with the mathematics curriculum. Telling time, learning simple geometry, and developing the vocabulary of position will be particularly difficult (Johnson, 1979).

12. *Verbal Expression Disabilities.* Children who cannot communicate information to others (either through speaking or writing), are unable to communicate or request mathematics information. These children have trouble selecting the appropriate operations needed to solve mathematical problems (Johnson, 1979).

13. *Closure and Generalization (Convergence and Divergence) Disabilities.* Some children encounter difficulty interpolating parts from wholes or wholes from parts, a requirement of mathematics. Closure or generalization problems (sometimes called convergence and divergence) prevent children from moving beyond a direct use of mathematics information and ideas. These children are restricted to the demonstrable present. Abstract information creates difficulty for them as do the analytical processes of mathematics (Johnson, 1979).

14. *Slow Development Through Intellectual Stages.* Children who are slow in mathematics may be at an earlier developmental stage than their age-mates. Children at different stages need to learn different concepts and have topics presented in different ways. For instance, a preoperational child who cannot conserve numbers is not ready to learn the numbers from 1 to 10. (Cruikshank, Fitzgerald, & Jensen, 1980).

Adapting Experiences to Various Handicaps

Some handicapping conditions interfere more with learning mathematics than others. Instructional adaptations should be added according to those characteristics that interfere with mathematics learning. Children who learn more slowly than their classmates may need special attention in developing early number awareness. Students who suffer from cognitive impairment, learning disabilities, and visual and hearing disadvantages need to have the mathematics curriculum adjusted for them. Most students who are low achievers in mathematics will probably never completely catch up with grade-level expectations. Thus, the mathematical concepts and skills that retarded students master in mathematics tend to be less than those of nonhandicapped classmates. Teachers need to identify the parts of the mathematics curriculum most relevant to daily living situations and to focus on them for these children (Turnbull & Schulz, 1979). The physically handicapped, on the other hand, will probably not need any special curriculum adjustment in the content of their mathematics program. Less emphasis may be placed on the use of manipulative material, however.

The performance deficits found in learning-disabled children may be grouped into categories of intellectual, spatial, and verbal reasoning ability. Many mathematics dysfunctions have underlying language deficits such as lexical dyscalculia, verbal dyscalculia, and ideognostic dyscalculia. Lexical dyscalculia is a disability in reading mathematical symbols (e.g., digits, numbers, or operational signs) (Kosc, 1974). Verbal dyscalculia is the inability to label mathematical terms verbally (e.g., misnaming numbers of items, numerals, and operational symbols). Ideognostic dyscalculia or semantic aphasia is a disability in understanding mathematical ideas and relations required for mental calculation. Students cannot calculate even the easiest sums and cannot clearly read or write numerals. This mathematical dysfunction also affects children's ability to develop ideas (Blackwell, 1976).

Students with brain injuries may be unable to solve simple mathematics problems or comprehend logical relationships. Such injuries can also disturb pupils' ability to solve verbal problems, especially those requiring a change from one operation to another or those requiring solution of mathematical equations within a complex structure. Children with such problems need an appropriate remedial program. Learning-disabled children can work with materials such as *Tangrams, Pattern Blocks, Mirror Cards, Attribute Blocks,* and *Geo-Boards,* all of which are manipulative materials designed to develop general skills and teach children about shapes.

Emotionally disturbed children who have difficulty in mathematics also benefit from working with manipulative materials that offer immediate feedback and opportunities for success. Individual work with manipulative materials also limits competition. Physically handicapped, visually handicapped, and multiply handicapped students should be provided with similar materials.

Visually impaired students, for example, can work through mathematical problems using a braille abacus. Teachers who do not have access to a braille abacus can make a memory-assistance device by stringing beads with holes through the center on thin wire. Three or more columns of ten beads each can be made in this fashion and placed in a wooden frame or attached to the edges of a cardboard box. The beads help students remember intermediate steps in their mathematical operations. The beads are arranged to represent specific numbers and can be separated into groups by attaching small alligator clips to the wire (Eichenberger, 1974).

Learning Activities for Handicapped Children

There are a variety of activities teachers can provide to allow handicapped children learn difficult mathematical concepts. For example, children who do not understand the *-er* and *-est* comparatives can be allowed to compare actual objects to determine the relationships between them. By comparing two objects they can determine if one object is heavier, lighter, smoother, smaller, or shorter than the other. Specific language can be taught later and comparisons can be developed into precise measurements (Knight & Hargis, 1977).

Balance beams and seesaws help children use their own bodies to develop concepts of weight, equivalence, and balance. They can pretend to be tightrope walkers and use their ex-

FIGURE 11-1

FIGURE 11-2

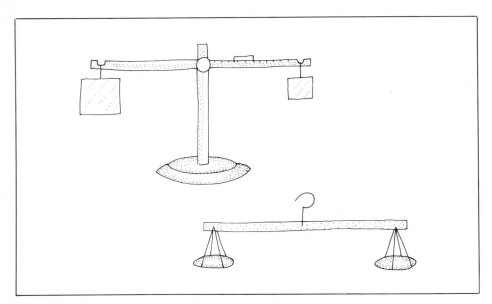

FIGURE 11-3

FIGURE 11-4

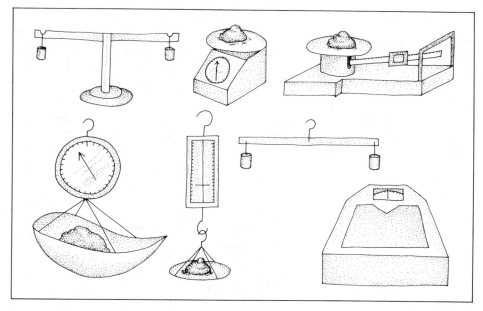

FIGURE 11-5

tended arms to balance themselves. They can also carefully tread a crack in the sidewalk, a line between tiles in the classroom, or a long strip of masking tape attached to the floor (see Figure 11-1).

Children on a treasure hunt, can collect objects of varying weights and discuss the objects they collect in terms of *heavy* and *light* . When students understand these terms, they can learn to compare *heavier than* with *lighter than*. By lifting heavy and light objects, the children sense the meaning of these comparative terms (see Figure 11-2).

Children can construct simple balance scales using a plunger as a base and a notched dowel stick, two pails, two washers, and a pivot screw. Crimping plasticine on the light side will help

balance the scale. Children can build individual balance scales, drilling three holes in a ruler; one on each end and one in the middle. Again, plasticine can help maintain the balance (see Figure 11-3).

Children can understand the movement of the scale. They can simulate the action on the balance by holding two pails of different weight on each hand (see Figure 11-4).

Children can then learn to read the dials on simple and one-arm balance scales and check their readings by weighing the same objects in their two-pan balance scales where they employ their own set of standard weights. Other scales can also be used (see Figure 11-5). These activities help children understand the term *weight* and the meaning of the numbers they see on

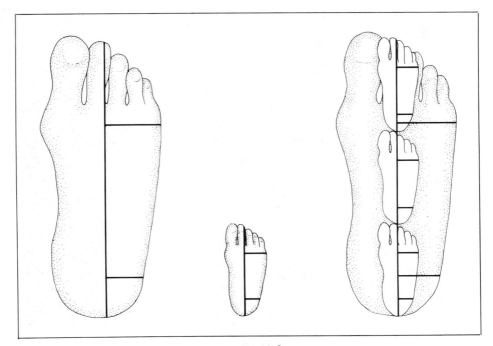

FIGURE 11-6

the scale. A variety of balancing and weighing experiences can help children create the necessary mental picture.

Linear measurement can also be learned through concrete experience. Young children are not aware that linear measurement is continuous and that a unit of measure is repeated. Nonstandard units of measure can introduce young children to linear measurement. Bruni and Silverman (1976) suggest using nonstandard units of measure such as a "baby foot" (4 inches long) and a "giant foot" (three baby feet or 12 inches long). The teacher draws a line in the middle of each baby foot and each giant foot to help children focus on a continuous straight line as they employ several units of measure. An arrow indicating direction can be drawn near the toes to enable the children to utilize the baby feet and giant feet the same way each time. If slits are cut on the feet, the children can string the feet along a rope, being careful to avoid overlapping, and use the rope as a measuring instrument (see Figure 11-6).

The ratio of the giant foot's length to the baby foot's length (3 to 1) will allow children to gain a sense of the standard length of *foot* and *yard*. This activity can be varied by using the children's own footprints. A child and a partner can trace each other's feet and can use this as a pattern for duplicating more feet. More durable feet can be made from oaktag, felt material, air conditioner filters, or styrofoam.

Before making their measuring ropes, the children should compare lengths of two feet. Feet of different lengths can be stored in cigar boxes. Children can compare two feet, aligning them to find out which one is longer or shorter or if they are the same size. Charts can be made to reinforce these concepts. After a child has compared the lengths of two feet, they can tape the feet in the appropriate space.

Children who are able to compare the lengths of two feet can make measuring ropes by stringing baby feet on a string and then begin measuring objects in the room with the rope. They can guess how many baby-feet-long objects are and then measure the objects by laying the measuring rope across them. Children should be sure that their ropes show a continuous line before they count the number of baby feet to the nearest baby foot. Children should be encouraged to use terms such as *about*, *a little longer than*, and *a little shorter than*.

These experiences can be repeated using giant feet. After the children have measured objects using baby feet and giant feet separately, they can measure the same objects using both nonstandard units. Children take two ropes that are the same length and string baby feet on one rope and string giant feet on the other. Before stringing the baby feet or the giant feet, the children should be encouraged to estimate the number of feet that will be needed.

Following such measurement experiences with nonstandard units, children should be introduced to standard

units of measure including English and metric units. Teachers can introduce these units of linear measurement (such as inches, feet, and yards) by providing children with both oaktag strips that are one inch wide and one foot long and a supply of one-inch-by-one-inch gummed stickers in two colors. Children can glue the stickers on the oaktag strip, alternating the colors. Before they glue the stickers, have them estimate and then count the number of stickers that will be required. Numbering each sticker in the upper right hand corner helps children keep track of the count as they glue them down.

Children can then measure the baby feet and the giant feet with their standard foot rules. Before measuring, children should estimate how many gummed stickers long each one is.

The words *inch* and *foot* can then be introduced.

Games that repeatedly use the same numerical language help teach mathematics. Play and movement activities that provide children with the opportunity to manipulate objects and build their mathematical language should also be used. It is also important to consistently use the same mathematics vocabulary. For example, in referring to regrouping, renaming, and carrying, which are comparable processes, the handicapped student's confusion will be reduced by consistently using only one of these terms (Lowenbraum & Affleck, 1976).

Visual prompts or demonstrations are often more effective in teaching mathematical language than lengthy verbal explanations. Children need to see what happens to understand a computation. Cawley and Vitello (1979) suggest a comprehensive model of visual prompts or demonstration for mathematics instruction. Their model consists of three cells: "Do," "See" and "Say". The "do" cell includes manipulation of objects and pictures in tasks employing constructing, ordering, arranging, and other similar skills. The "see" cell consists of responding to pictures or to a visual model by pointing or marking; the "say" cell focuses on spoken or written language. This model has been an effective framework in teaching mathematics concepts to handicapped students. Basically, the sequence of difficulty is from the "do-do" combination (at the easiest level) to the "see-see" and then "say-say."

Children's errors provide clues to their level of understanding. There are common types of errors made by students. Many computational errors are the result of not knowing basic facts. A basic fact is a combination of two- or one-digit numbers that has a sum (for addition) or subtrahend (for subtraction). For example, the following are basic facts:

$$5 + 6 = 11$$
$$17 - 9 = 8$$

Addition has 100 basic facts while subtraction has 55. Children who make systematic errors in solving the problems for a particular basic fact are making systematic basic-fact errors. For example, if a child always says that $8 + 5 = 14$, this mistake is a systematic basic-fact error rather than a systematic computational error (Cox, 1975).

Children's mathematical errors can be recorded and analyzed to identify patterns. Recognizing patterns in these errors is the first step toward remediation. Without proper instruction many children will continue to make the same errors. The appropriateness and effectiveness of various manipulative aids and instructional strategies must be assessed to remediate the errors (Cox, 1975).

General principles of good teaching are important for all children, including those with special needs. Cruikshank, Fitzgerald, and Jensen (1980) developed the following teaching principles for handicapped children:

1. All children are able to learn if they are taught at their level.

2. Learning should be planned to ensure some success. Immediate feedback is effective.

3. A positive self-concept affects success. Young children must perceive themselves as being important to themselves and to others.

4. Practice is important to develop concrete concepts. Practice provided in practical situations allows for transfer of learning to new situations.

5. A variety of alternative teaching strategies should be planned. If one approach fails, others can be attempted. Sensory approaches can meet each child's individual learning style.

6. Children who have a mathematics handicap tend to work slowly and at a concrete level. They may be incapable of performing abstract work; therefore, they may need to fully develop their concrete levels.

7. Children's errors should be carefully analyzed to understand their thinking processes and to provide clues about ways to clarify their concepts.

8. All children learn differently. An instructional mathematics program should be planned based on careful diagnosis and evaluation.

SUMMARY

When difficulties arise in education, there is always the tendency to narrow the focus of the curriculum and give greatest priority to the basic skills. There is no denying the importance of the basic academic areas of reading, writing, and arithmetic for all children including the handicapped. However, if we want handicapped children to live as normal a life as possible, we need to be careful that the educational experiences we provide them are not too restrictive. Mathematics, science, and social studies provide a framework through which children can organize their perception of the physical and social world. These areas allow them to understand their inner world and relate it to the outer world they share with other people.

There is a broad range of activities that teachers can use in providing handicapped children with experiences in mathematics, science, and social studies. Whenever we deal with individual differences in the classroom we must modify the basic assumptions we hold about what all children should come to know and how all children learn. When handicapped children are concerned, we must accept the need for such modification as a matter of course. We should be willing to find ways in which each child can be a competent learner in the classroom and then adapt these learnings to the outside world. Then subject matter areas have a particularly strong contribution to make in normalizing the lives of handicapped children.

REFERENCES

Alberto, P. A. The young mildly retarded child. In S. G. Garwood (Ed.). *Educating young handicapped children: A developmental approach.* Germantown, Md.: Aspen Systems Corporation, 1979.

Blackwell, J. H. When 2 + 2 ain't 4. *Language Arts,* 1976, *53,* 422–424.

Bloom, B. S. (Ed.). *Taxonomy of educational objectives. Handbook I: Cognitive domain.* New York: David McKay, 1956.

Bruni, J. V., and Silverman, H. An introduction to weight measurement. *The Arithmetic Teacher,* 1976, *23* (1), 4–10.

Cawley, J. F., and Vitello, S. J. Model for arithmetical programming for handicapped children. *Exceptional Children,* 1972, *39* (2), 101–110.

Charlesworth, R., and Hartup, W. W. Positive social reinforcement in the nursery school peer group. *Child Development*, 1967, *38*, 993–1002.

Cox, L. S. Diagnosing and remeding systematic errors in addition and subtraction computations. *The Arithmetic Teacher*, 1975, *22* (2), 151–156.

Cruikshank, D. E., Fitzgerald, D. L., and Jensen, J. R. *Young children learning mathematics*. Boston: Allyn & Bacon, 1980.

Draper, W., Garner, H. G., and Resnick, R. J. Emotional and social development. In N. H. Fallen (Ed.). *Young children with special needs*. Columbus, Ohio: Charles E. Merrill, 1978.

Eichenberger, R. J. Teaching science to the blind student. *The Science Teacher*, 1974, *41* (19), 53–55.

Gold, M. W., and Scott, K. G. Discrimination learning. In W. B. Stephens (Ed.). *Training the developmentally young*. New York: John Day, 1971.

Hadary, D. E., and Cohen, S. H. *Laboratory science and art for blind, deaf, and emotionally disturbed children: A mainstreaming approach*. Baltimore, Md: University Park Press, 1978.

Johnson, S. W. *Arithmetic and learning disabilities: Guidelines for identification and remediation*. Boston: Allyn & Bacon, 1979.

Keller, M. F., and Carlson, P. M. The use of symbolic modeling to promote social skills in preschool children with low levels of social responsiveness. *Child Development*, 1974, *45*, 912–919.

Knight, L. N., and Hargis, C. H. Math language ability: Its relationship to reading in math. *Language Arts*, 1977, *54* (4), 423–428.

Kosc, L. Developmental dyscalculia. *Journal of Learning Disabilities*, 1974, *7* (3), 164–177.

Lowenbraun, S., and Affleck, J. Q. *Teaching mildly handicapped children in regular classes*. Columbus, Ohio: Charles E. Merrill, 1976.

Malone, L., and Lucchi, L. D. Life science for visually impaired students. *Science and Children*, 1979, *16* (5), 20–31.

Neisworth, J. T., Willoughby-Herb, S. J., Bagnato, S. J., Cartwright, C. A., and Laub, K. W. *Individualized education for preschool exceptional children*. Germantown, Md.: Aspen Systems Corporation, 1980.

Peters, D. L., and Raupp, C. D. Developing a self-concept of the exceptional child. In T. D. Yawkey (Ed.). *The self-concept of the young child*. Provo, Utah: Brigham Young University Press, 1980.

Piaget, J. *Science and education and the psychology of the child*. New York: Orion Press, 1970.

Saracho, O. N. The role of the teacher in enhancing the child's self-concept. In T. D. Yawkey (Ed.). *The self-concept of the young child*. Provo, Utah: Brigham Young University Press, 1980.

Spodek, B. *Teaching in the early years*, 2nd ed. Englewood Cliffs, N. J.: Prentice-Hall, 1978.

Suydam, M. N., and Weaver, J. F. Research on mathematics learning. In J. N. Payne (Ed.). *Mathematics in early childhood*. 37th Yearbook of the National Council of Teachers of Mathematics. Reston, Va.: National Council of Teachers of Mathematics, 1975.

Thompson, B. Myth and science for the handicapped. *Science and Children*, 1979, *17* (3), 16–17.

Turnbull, A. P., and Schulz, J. B. *Mainstreaming handicapped students*. Boston: Allyn & Bacon, 1979.

Walsh, H. M. *Introducing the young child to the social world*. New York: Macmillan, 1980.

Wehman, P., and Goodwyn, R. L. Self-help skill development. In N. H. Fallen (Ed.). *Young children with special needs*. Columbus, Ohio: Charles E. Merrill, 1978.

Twelve

PLAY IN THE INTEGRATED CLASSROOM

Play has always been an important component of early childhood programs. It can support the social, emotional, physical, and cognitive development of children, since all areas of development are influenced by play. Play gives children an opportunity to express their ideas and their feelings as well as to symbolize and test their knowledge of the world. This is as much a need for handicapped children as for normal children. While much of the education of handicapped children is addressed to providing direct supports for academic and preacademic learning, play should not be denied its rightful place in their education. In fact, the integrated setting of a mainstreamed class provides the ideal support for play-learning activities.

Play is a form of behavior that is intrinsically motivated, is performed for its own sake, and is conducted in a relaxed way producing a positive affect. Play is free from concern with end products, and interference with the spontaneity of play can destroy its essential character.

Weisler and McCall (1976) describe the characteristics of play:

1. Play is different for each individual and in each situation. Even though play, especially the thematic play of young children, is well organized, its content and sequence may differ drastically from situation to situation and from child to child.

2. Play does not depend on appetitive drives or extrinsic goals. It does not follow the principles of simple drive reduction nor does it indicate an obvious task orientation, goal, or purpose. Many believe that play does not have a purpose or an apparent goal and is performed for its own sake.

3. Play does not take place if an individual is in a condition of high subjective uncertainty or fear. Play tends to occur only when individuals sense security and respect for their basic needs.

4. Play is pleasurable. Individuals usually smile, laugh, and relax at play. For example, young children can be almost debilitated in their play-fighting by their giggling and laughter.

5. Play helps individuals assimilate information from the environment.

This chapter presents various theories of play and discusses the importance of play in the education of handicapped children. It also contains suggestions for adapting different kinds of educational play, including manipulative play, physical play, dramatic play, and games for children with varying handicapping conditions.

THE ROLE OF PLAY

Play is difficult to understand and hard to define, although play can usually be identified during observations. Play is evident in adult, child, and animal behavior. There are three major theories of play. These are the psychoanalytic, cognitive, and arousal-seeking theories.

Each of these explains why children play though it fails to offer teachers a guide for action. Understanding of these theories, however, does help teachers generate guidelines for the different types of play (manipulative, physical, dramatic play, and games) used in educational settings.

The Psychoanalytic Theory

The psychoanalytic theory of play was founded in the early work of Freud. Children's play is viewed as intrinsically motivated, with playful acts intended to reduce accumulated tension and to provide pleasure. According to Freud, play serves two roles. First, it is a vehicle children use to master their own covert thoughts and overt actions. Children's active participation or passive observation controls their internalized thought processes and their voluntary physical movements.

Activity, the second role of play, is related to the individual's socio-emotional development. Pain or unpleasantness tend to affect the establishment of social relationships or interpersonal exchanges. Play activities and exploration help children understand painful situations and substitute pleasurable feelings for unpleasant ones. Play involves interpretation of a situation and might include symbolic properties of people and objects in the present and past. Thus, children are able to express their feelings through play behavior (Wehman & Abramson, 1976).

Play therapy, an application of psychoanalytic theory, uses play to permit children to naturally express themselves and to act out feelings of tension, fear, and insecurity. This process helps children control their feelings and become more secure (Axline, 1974). The play therapist's responsibilities are to draw out children's feelings through play while communicating at the children's level. Play therapy is a clinical method of treatment that has been used extensively with emotionally disturbed children.

The Cognitive Theory

The cognitive theory of play, based on Piaget's work, suggests that children gain knowledge through the dual processes of assimilation and accommodation. In assimilation, children model reality to meet their needs, integrating information into existing mental structures. In the process of accommodation, children mold their behavior to meet the reality of given circumstances, thus changing their mental structures. Normally, these opposing forces join to reach a state of balance or equilibrium. When assimilation assumes primacy over accommodation, as it occurs in childhood, the product becomes spontaneous play.

According to Piaget (1962) there are three developmental stages of play, (1) sensory-motor play, (2) symbolic play, and (3) games with rules. Each stage evolves in a sequential order, and the mental structures of each are progressively integrated into later stages. For example, playing games with rules always occurs after symbolic play, while symbolic play occurs after sensory-motor play. As a new stage of play develops, the previous stages become subsumed but are always accessible to the child or adult.

In the first stage of play, the repetitive nature of children's actions focuses the play on physical activity. In the second stage, make believe or symbolic play evolves. This begins when children are approximately 18 months of age and continues until they are about seven years old. Symbolic play does not require the presence of the actual object being represented. Any object can take the place and characteristics of the original item. For example, wooden boxes can be used to represent cars and trucks in this stage.

The final form of play, games with rules, occurs through social convention and interaction. This play evolves after age seven and always includes activities involving two or more children. As rule games become established, practice play and symbolic play diminish, although they continue to be accessible to individuals throughout their life span. Examples of games with rules include checkers, chess, and card games.

The Arousal-Seeking Theory

The arousal-seeking theory is founded on the assumption that people play to maintain an optimal arousal level. Ellis (1973) suggests that people constantly strive for sensory variation. Research shows that if sensory input remains constant, individuals cannot pay attention to it for very long. A variety of information is needed. When not enough information is available, individuals search for additional stimulation; if there is too much information available, they avoid more stimulation. Individuals think best in situations that provide novelty, uncertainty, and complexity, and play provides this.

PLAY WITH YOUNG HANDICAPPED CHILDREN

The available research on play with handicapped children is limited both in scope and comprehensiveness. This may be the result of the problems in defining play, the difficulties in identifying optimal instructional play strategies,

and the lack of a theory of play that impacts on handicapped children. Play for such children needs to be rigorously examined to develop a theory of play in which postulates (1) are synthesized for the purposes of explaining and predicting play behavior, (2) are clearly specified and directly related to the learning characteristics of these children, (3) are facilitated through the prediction of children's play behavior under specific conditions (such as with a variety of toys, models, or instructions), and (4) explain and account for play behavior in a parsimonious fashion (Wehman, 1975).

The play of handicapped children has attracted attention in recent years. Educational play can improve such children's performance in language, motor, cognitive, and social skills (Strain, Cooke, & Appolloni, 1976; Wehman, 1977), and can positively influence their adaptive behavior.

Mehlman (1953) and Leland, Walker, and Taboada (1959) found play correlated with increases in personality adjustment, social behavior, and intelligence in mildly retarded children, although such increases were small and a cause-effect relationship was not established. The positive influence of play on the development of fine motor, language, and personal-social skills in handicapped children has also been found (Morrison & Newcomer, 1975). Cooperative and competitive play behavior directly affect social behavior. Cooperative play teaches children acceptable modes of socialization such as sharing, taking turns, responsibility, and others that young handicapped children often lack. They usually play independently for long periods of time and may not cooperate with their peers unless they receive verbal encouragement or physical guidance (Whitman, Mercurio, & Caponigri, 1970). Play also develops other types of social behavior. Children who become involved in spontaneous play rarely display aggressive behavior. In addition, severely handicapped children's stereotypic rocking behavior and bizarre vocal sounds may be reduced or eliminated during play (Wehman, 1978).

Play has at least four major values for handicapped children: (1) it develops gross or fine motor skills, language, and a higher level of social behavior; (2) it employs activities to achieve educational goals; (3) it reduces socially unacceptable behaviors; and (4) it provides enjoyment (Wehman, 1978). Play should not be restricted to nonhandicapped children, but should include all children. Play methods and materials for young children must be carefully selected for their learning and behavior outcomes and the degree to which they need to be changed for a particular limitation.

Mentally Retarded Children

Mentally retarded children lack spontaneity in play (Paloutzian, Hasazi, Streifel, & Edgar, 1971). Toys and play materials must be carefully selected to promote and stimulate the mentally retarded child's play behavior. The following criteria can be used in selecting appropriate toys and materials:

1. *Toys and materials must be durable enough to hold up for a long period of time,* otherwise they will collapse quickly.

2. *Toys should promote concrete experiences.* Young mentally retarded children are usually not at the symbolic or abstract level. Mentally re-

tarded young children may ignore houses or dolls or transportation vehicles that promote symbolic and imaginative play since they do not know how to use them.

3. *Toys should provide a positive psychological effect.* Some mentally retarded children may have the mental age of very young children. Toys for these children should be appropriate for their mental age.

Mentally retarded children are not radically different from nonretarded children in their play needs and interests. They need to be part of a social group even though they often play in isolation and encounter problems in group cooperation. Retarded children with experience and perseverance can participate in social activities. These children want social approval, and social success encourages them to participate socially. Since competition is difficult for them to deal with and they may become aggressive when they lose, the cooperative aspects of play should be emphasized (Wehman, 1977).

Emotionally Disturbed Children

Play can help emotionally disturbed children control their behaviors. If children become aware that they are capable of controlling materials, they will realize they are capable of controlling themselves and their interactions with others (Bernhardt & Mackler, 1975). Play is the child's natural medium of self-expression and provides opportunities to act out feelings, just as talk provides adults with similar opportunities (Axline, 1974).

Group play improves emotionally disturbed children's relationships with peers thus increasing their social acceptance. These children need to identify themselves with a group, and earning admiration provides a sense of security. Group play experiences can provide the emotionally disturbed with a common bond for continuous interaction with others during the day. Those who have a restricted repertoire of experiences may be deficient in their social skills and their ability to socialize, a deficiency often evident during play activities.

Play for the emotionally disturbed can release or curb their emotions, provide emotional self-gratification, and reduce their inhibited hostility and anger as they express their emotions through play. In play, emotions need not be misdirected in destructive acts toward themselves and others. Play also allows emotionally disturbed children to express themselves through their actions, making play emotionally self-gratifying.

Hearing-Impaired Children

Spontaneous play experiences can help hearing-impaired children develop normal movement potential. Obstacles that restrict their freedom of movement become social rather than physical restraints. Social play provides them with the greatest opportunities for social development.

Play can also promote the hearing-impaired child's speech. Play experiences include many sounds (human, mechanical, and natural) that can stimulate hearing. Hearing-impaired children want to communicate their interests, and play words become action words. In early childhood classrooms, although speech is often secondary to action during play, play situations can lead to extended vocabulary. Hearing-impaired children tend to have play interests that are similar to those of children younger than themselves. Usually these immature interests indicate a deficiency in psychosocial maturation. These children generally have a restricted repertoire of experiences that make them seem more socially deficient than they actually are (Hunt, 1955).

Visually Impaired Children

Visually impaired children have the same play needs and interests as their sighted peers. They may be afraid to move freely, although they have the necessary movement skills. They need to develop self-reliance and acquire courage to offset their physical insecurity.

The visually impaired can succeed with play activities when they can use their other senses. Young visually impaired children, like seeing children, enjoy tactile games with blocks, toys, and materials made of different textures and forms. Most visually impaired children select play objects that have a definite shape and are easily identified through touch. Complicated forms and soft, somewhat diffuse objects such as those made of fur or cotton are difficult for the visually impaired to understand and may be disliked. Games can be used to develop kinesthetic sense and provide opportunities to move flexibly—by changing direction, stopping, and starting. Games and other physical activities are generally better for developing visually impaired children's movement skills than are gymnastics and apparatus work. Some visually impaired children encounter problems with balance activities but they are usually able to climb ropes or play with push toys, swings, seesaws, parallel bars, rings, and other equipment that primarily uses the sense of touch (Wehman, 1977). Dramatics, mimetics, art, and dance can be used to promote their creativity through body and facial expressions.

Visually impaired children enjoy socializing with other children, often developing close-knit relationships with small groups within larger groups. This can slow their socialization process. The visually impaired must extend their social contact to larger groups of children to be able to play successfully with their peers. They need the security of knowing that they are socially accepted and that their impairment does not restrict their enjoyment of play. They need to have personally satisfying play activities that they enjoy both with others and by themselves.

Orthopedically Handicapped Children

Some play needs of the orthopedically handicapped are difficult to satisfy and may be exaggerated by the large number of hours spent in treatment or in the resource room. Seriously orthopedically handicapped children are limited in their involvement in active games because they cannot stand without support, walk or run with ease, or coordinate their hands and arms easily. Since the orthopedically handicapped are not able to produce movements easily, tensions may be higher for them. Orthopedically handicapped children who move and enjoy active play can usually reduce their tensions. Many refuse to play in groups because they feel inferior, become self-conscious, and are afraid of competition or self-testing.

EDUCATIONAL PLAY

There are four major types of educational play: manipulative play, physical play, dramatic play, and games. Each needs to be included in the program of a mainstream class.

Manipulative Play

In manipulative play children handle small pieces of equipment such as puzzles, cuisenairie rods, and pegboards. Most of the actions are self-contained and there seldom is a dramatic quality to the play activity. Using Montessori materials is a good example of educational manipulative play. Children may play with a set of wooden cylinders, comparing their lengths or diameters and fitting them into a specially designed case. This activity teaches children to compare sizes and to seriate.

Manipulative materials can teach self-care skills. Young handicapped children might experience difficulty in

FIGURE 12-1

dressing. Dolls and dressing frames can be provided for the children to dress. Children can use these to practice their dressing skills as preparation to dressing themselves. Commercial doll clothes tend to be too small and their fastenings can be fragile for handicapped children to handle. A large, two foot tall, stuffed doll can be provided with a wardrobe that requires snapping, buttoning, zippering, buckling, hooking, and lacing. Clothes can be made with large heavy-duty fasteners, large hooks and snaps (such as those found on pants), large, flat rather than domed buttons about one inch in diameter, and heavy zippers with a zipper-pull ring. The teacher could create an octopus that has a different type of fastener or part of a fastener at the end of each tentacle (see Figure 12-1). Various fasteners can also be sewn to pieces of material and attached to frames or incorporated in pillows and other articles.

Boards with shoelaces attached that require lacing and knot-tying can take the children through part of the process of putting on shoes (see Figure 12-2). The children learn to put the string through the holes, crossing the middle in proper sequence and lacing the strings alternatively into the next holes. In tying knots, children learn to cross the midline and make an X with the strings. Clues on how to perform

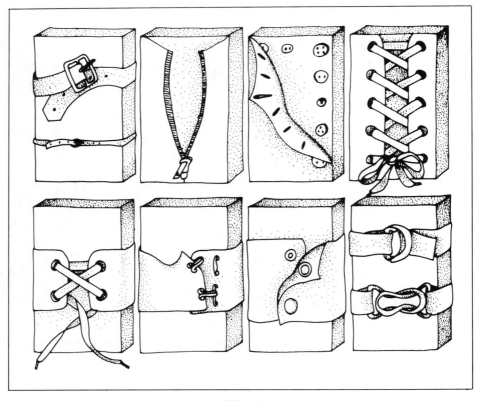

FIGURE 12-2

the task can be presented to the children. Other kinds of dressing frames can also be made, as shown in Fugure 12-2. Different types of manipulative play might be needed by children with different types of disabilities. Boxes can be used in place of boards or frames (see Figure 12-3).

Mentally Retarded Children. Mentally retarded children often interact with the materials by using repetitive manual manipulations and physical contacts, some of which may be stereotypic in nature. They may also pound, push, pull, or throw the materials,

much like children at a less mature stage of development. Sensory feedback gained from using manipulative material helps such children move on to the next stage.

These children may push, pull, and throw manipulative materials in an attempt to explore them. They may put a puzzle together or put the pieces of the puzzles in their mouth. As their play behavior becomes more organized the children slowly acquire manipulative skills with materials—spinning the wheels of a truck, turning a nut on a bolt, or placing pegs into a pegboard. Once the children achieve a simple

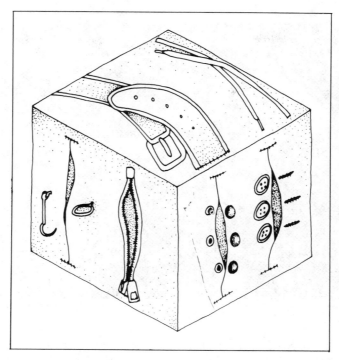

FIGURE 12-3

level of manipulation they can learn to classify different materials, eventually combining the various uses of the materials. For example, children can disconnect cars from a train, undress a doll, or untie a knot. Later, they can dress the doll and use blocks to make different objects (Goetz & Baer, 1973), or include toy cars and buses in their block play (Wehman, 1977).

Manipulative materials can be used to teach number concepts and a variety of academic tasks to mentally retarded children. The Pacemaker Games Program, for example, teaches mentally retarded children concepts of shape and color (Ross, 1969). The program consists of five simple games using cards, dice, dominoes, and shape and color

counters, as well as puzzles, checkers, and other table games that promote socialization and develop competitiveness.

Visually Impaired Children. Visually impaired children need manipulative materials to help them understand their environment and to promote cognitive concepts paralleling those of their sighted peers (Guthrie, 1979). Manipulative materials should offer visually impaired children basic concrete experiences so they can develop cognitive skills. Manipulative materials should have easily identified shapes and a variety of textures, and if possible, they should provide auditory stimulation. Smell is also important.

Children who have some residual vision should be provided with colorful materials. Visually impaired children should be helped become aware of the qualities in manipulative materials, either visually or through their other senses. The materials should require a variety of actions such as holding, tasting, smelling, shaking, and perhaps dropping or throwing. They should stimulate sensory awareness as well as promote developing concepts and skills. These materials can often be used for more than one purpose. A set of rubber squeak-toy creatures made out of pliable, lightweight rubber, for example, can be squeaked with a light touch to encourage repetitive hand activities such as tapping, squeezing, and touching. Each toy can be composed of several textures and bright colors and can have a whimsical face and a soft squeak. Textures encourage exploring

the creatures' surface, leading the children to develop their pincer grasp reflex. The creatures' facial attributes (such as eyelashes and noses) should be identifiable by touch alone. The tactile attributes should also be evident in the other parts of the creatures' bodies, as in a ten-legged bristly caterpillar or a spiny porcupine (Guthrie, 1979).

The teacher can place a variety of objects in a box, allowing the children to put their hands in and use their tactile sense to identify the objects. Initially, common objects that are familiar to the child should be used. A similiar activity can require visually impaired children to match various pieces of material according to texture. Two different sets of cardboards with material of various textures glued to each (e.g., rough, smooth) can be provided. Children can match the cardboards that have identical pieces of textures. A texture book in

FIGURE 12-4

which each page is made of material of a different texture can also be used. Pieces of each textured material can be glued on pieces of cardboard the same size as the pages in the texture book to allow the children to match textures.

Teachers can collect different sized boxes and can nest boxes within boxes. A noisemaker or flashlight (if the child has light perception) can be placed inside the center box and the children can manipulate the boxes to find the object. The degree of difficulty planned into these activities should be based on the children's ability levels. Manipulative materials that permit the visually impaired to judge weight are also valuable. Children can be asked to judge the weight of materials placed in small containers and arranged in order from lightest to heaviest. Teachers can help visually impaired children discriminate using clues from their environment. They can learn to use their hearing

through materials like the Montessori sound boxes (Taite, 1974).

Orthopedically Handicapped Children. Manipulative play may need to be adapted for orthopedically handicapped children. Those who cannot sit well, even with adapted furniture, can lie down on the carpet to acquire the advantages of eye-hand positioning. Children with poor muscular control throughout their bodies can have a foam rubber roll put under their chests while sitting at a table or lying on the floor (see Figure 12-4). The foam roll lifts their body weight from the floor, lets them get their hands out in front of them, and positions their heads in such a way that they are able to view their hands and the objects in front of them. This position also helps them control their head and shoulders. The roll can be made firmer by rolling corrugated cardboard along with the foam rubber. Larger rolls can be made by taping or tying several additional layers of cardboard together or by using a hollow plastic pipe. The rolls must be firm and strong enough bear the children's weights. Canvas bags used to cover the rolls can be removed to be washed as often as required (Fallen, 1978). If tables are high enough for a wheelchair, wooden or rubber stops can be used to stabilize wheelchairs without locks so that individuals can use their arms in manipulative play. Tables can also be built with recesses and supplied with strap harnesses for children who are not able to stand or sit without support. Wooden or metal poles can be strapped to an orthopedically handicapped child's body to free the hands, allowing him or her to become involved in manipulative play (Hunt, 1955).

Physical Play

During physical play, children engage in large actions such as running, jumping, or riding a tricycle. Physical play helps children develop physical skills and use them under new circumstances. Physical play includes outdoor and indoor play as well as block play.

Mentally Retarded Children.

Although some mentally retarded individuals are more limited in their physical skills than normal individuals, they may appear more normal in physical ability than in intellectual ability. Hopping, skipping, and galloping are learned by some much later than is normal while others never learn these skills. They may catch a ball with their wrists and arms instead of using their poorly functioning hands. Some of these children require larger, softer balls as well as extra opportunities for catching practice. Most mentally retarded children are able to perform primary reflex motor activities such as jumping, running, throwing, and climbing.

Mentally retarded children may have low stamina, tiring easily. During physical play, teachers need to observe and help those children who show signs of excessive fatigue. They might be encouraged to rest or to play with toys of interest to them. Mentally retarded children are interested in concrete items they are able to handle. They can manipulate simple toys without engaging in make-believe. For example, they will explore attributes of a new ball instead of its use. They may become frustrated if they cannot play with it immediately (Hunt, 1955).

Emotionally Disturbed Children.

Physical play directly enhances the functioning of emotionally disturbed children as they become stimulated, relaxed, and emotionally satisfied. In some cases, however, fear of failure may prevent a child from participating in an activity. The teacher may then need to develop strategies to promote participation at some level that will ensure success. Hyperactive children may respond positively to large motor activities (Hunt, 1955).

Visually Impaired Children.

Physical play activities for the visually impaired should be as broad as those for their normally sighted peers, although these children may not be able to engage in some activities enjoyed by seeing children. The visually impaired may sometimes refuse to participate in an activity because they are afraid to fail. Physical activities that demand a great deal of skill may be of little value to them and may need to be adapted to be fun.

Visually impaired children can feel the different shapes of building blocks and build with them. They may need to develop a sense for balance as they build so that their structures do not collapse. Water play, which teaches children to pour from one container to another, is a good physical activity for these children. The ability to pour is important because it relates to practical life skills such as pouring juice or milk into a glass. Auditory discrimination exercises such as the sound of liquid pouring into a container, and concepts of full, and half-full are important for them. They need to learn to judge the depth of the liquid by sound to avoid spilling. This type of activity can be varied by pouring sand or beans from one container to another rather than water. Children can pour sand instead of water and learn that all of the sand in a small jar can be poured into a large jar but if all the sand in a large jar is poured into a smaller one, the sand will spill (Taite, 1974).

Visually impaired children may enjoy outdoor play since the trees, wind, rain, and other natural features are exciting. They may also enjoy seasonal activities such as kite flying and snow games and learn about the seasonal changes in nature. They can use swings, slides, ropes, rings and seesaws outdoors.

Other physical skills visually impaired children can learn include bouncing a ball, skipping, and hopping. They can also learn to roller skate by using one skate first and then two.

Orthopedically Handicapped Children. Safety should not be taken for granted in activities with orthopedically handicapped children. The extent of the handicap and the different areas of the body involved must be considered when planning physical play. Play experiences, however, should be restricted only by limitations imposed by a physical handicap.

Individuals with orthopedic disabilities tend to have difficulty running fast, yet running should be a component of any physical program. Running can be slow or very active. Orthopedically handicapped children can wear small football helmets or felt headbands during active play time to protect them from falls. Some difficulties can be alleviated if players are paired so that each child completes a part of a task

but both are able to achieve the entire act together (Hunt, 1955).

Depending on the level of their handicap, the physical features of the classroom, the outdoor play area, and the school may need to be modified in the following ways for orthopedically handicapped children.

1. Buildings may need more entrances and exits.

2. Doors and halls must be wider and without thresholds to allow for more expansive movements and for wheelchairs to pass through.

3. Rest rooms may need to include beds and reclining chairs.

4. Toilet facilities must be close to classrooms and playing space.

5. Ramps must be substituted for stairs.

6. Chairs should be sturdy with rubber crutch tips under the legs so they will not slip when a child with a leg brace sits down.

Sand pits instead of dirt or asphalt should be provided under playground equipment. The playground for the orthopedically handicapped should be surfaced with a combination of grass, asphalt, and dirt. Asphalt has the best friction for moving but it is hazardous in a fall, while grass is safest for falling but is slippery. Hard dirt is an excellent surface for bouncing games and for sliding equipment and if there are no soft surfaces, sand and pebbles can provide good traction for running, jumping, and supporting crutches (Hunt, 1955).

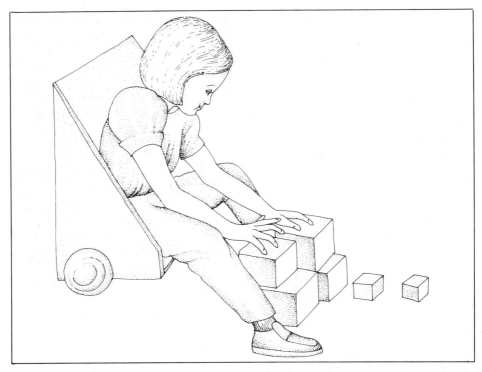

FIGURE 12-5

Children in wheelchairs who cannot work on the floor to build with blocks can use a scooter board (belly board or crawler) in various ways (Fallen, 1978). The scooter board is a rectangular board of 3/4-inch plywood with heavy duty casters attached to each corner. The board can be padded with a layer of foam or some other type of cushion and covered with vinyl. Orthopedically handicapped children can lie on their stomachs on top of scooter boards while raising their heads, and can propel themselves using their hands or elbows, reach around themselves, and use blocks or manipulative toys.

Orthopedically handicapped children who can partially maintain a sitting position can be helped sit close to the floor for block building. A large cardboard box, plastic trash can, or laundry basket can be cut on one side while the other side is left intact providing minimal support (Fallen, 1978). A strap can be buckled under the arms to help the children sit up. Casters attached under the can, box or basket help children move by pushing off with their hands (see Figure 12-5).

Dramatic Play

In dramatic play, children assume and act out a role, generally in relationship to their classmates who are playing other roles. These informal dramatic situations often represent the children's life experiences. Dramatic play permits

children to develop a sense of self-regard and self-confidence as they interact with their environment. Dramatic play helps them familiarize themselves with their motoric, sensorial, and intellectual apparatuses as they become involved in self-stimulatory activities. This form of play helps children create their own world and, through it, discover the real world. As they continuously manipulate and manage their surroundings, children develop confidence in their own capacities and a realization that they live in a cause-effect universe (Wehman, 1977).

The dramatic play area (usually the housekeeping corner) is where children assume the roles of their family members and act out their home situations. Teachers need to vary this area and provide other dramatic play situations so children can learn about many different roles. Prop boxes that are easy to store and use can contain material

representing different themes such as hairdresser, post office, restaurant, or grocery store. In block building, children participate in miniature dramatizations. This type of activity requires children to use block accessories in order that their play can evolve beyond building. Sometimes children can assume roles in a dramatic play situation through puppets.

Mentally Retarded Children.
Mentally retarded children have difficulty maintaining an interest in dramatic play over a long period of time. Their imagination usually leans toward simple make-believe activities such as cowboys and Indians, cops and robbers, playing house, and dolls. They chase and capture, shoot and escape, avoiding any complications of right and wrong, trials, or ceremonies. They love to play with dolls, manipulate dishes, and maneuver furniture. Their make-

believe is composed of nonverbal roles that are simple and are related to their experiences. Mentally retarded children seem to enjoy repeating these roles daily. Dramatic play can be made more imaginative by furnishing the environment with suggestive equipment and by stimulating these children with stories, pictures, and interesting excursions (Hunt, 1955).

Some experts (e.g., Paloutzian, Hasazi, Streifel, & Edgar, 1971; Wehman, 1977) feel that mentally retarded children have limited imitation skills and need to be trained in this area. Strategies for imitation training include:

1. using an adult to train a mentally retarded child in different play situations

2. pairing a mentally retarded child with a higher functioning peer who will participate in dramatic play

3. grouping two equivalent mentally retarded children with one or more adults for training

4. integrating the mentally retarded child into a group of nonretarded peers

5. using reinforcement such as points, edibles, or praise

6. modifying the environment before the onset of play through toy selection, room size or background, and music

Emotionally Disturbed Children.

Play therapists set up dramatic play situations, often in miniature, to allow disturbed children opportunities to act out conflicting situations in miniature. Such play may serve as a catharsis, allowing children to rid themselves of feelings with which they cannot cope. More often the play serves to communicate to the therapist the nature of the conflicts with which the child is struggling. Because the communication may be in idiosyncratic symbolic form, it is often difficult for a nontherapist to understand. In addition, therapists tend to be careful in allowing the child to expose feelings only to the extent that the child is capable of managing them.

While teachers are not child psychotherapists, they can learn a great deal by observing the play of children, although they need to be careful in the interpretations they make. They can also provide play activities that will allow children to work through some of their own problems on their own.

The value of dramatic play for emotionally disturbed children depends on their peers' enjoyment, their expressive ability, and the meanings derived from it. Emotionally disturbed children unconsciously act out their problems. Psychiatrists affirm that a person can modify behavior by assuming the role of another person who has different attributes. Such role taking is used in play therapy (Axline, 1974). The projective and creative components of dramatic play can be promoted through puppets, pantomimes, and charades and through excursions to places of interest such as art exhibits, museums, and libraries.

Visually Impaired Children.

Visually impaired children tend to spend most of their dramatic play time in a world of fantasy. As they act out roles in dramatic experiences, their imaginations are enhanced, they gain enjoyment, they lose their self-conscious-

ness through projection, and their understanding is increased. Visually impaired children need to be encouraged to project themselves into different roles. They can pretend to be the wind, a growing flower, or a lively kitten as authentically as their seeing peers (Hunt, 1955).

Visually impaired children can also act out live situations, such as setting the table or baking a cake, though they may encounter difficulty in assuming roles dealing with everyday subjects or imaginative circumstances. Teachers need to plan such activities carefully, making sure that all children participate (Taite, 1974).

Games

Games are structured rather than spontaneous activities and include specific rules to follow. Simple games or musical game-like activities can be used with young children. Children should learn the techniques for game playing. This may require teachers to guide the game to help children understand and follow the rules.

Mentally Retarded Children.

Games help mentally retarded children acquire and retain knowledge. A mentally retarded child may be able to perform simple addition if it is part of a game she or he enjoys, such as keeping score at a baseball game. Children enhance their sensory awareness by singing, playing games, telling stories, pantomiming, and taking field trips and field walks. The play equipment required for games also stimulates their senses through brightness of color, texture, and shape (Hunt, 1955).

Games for the retarded should have few simple directions, require little remembering, possess attractive names, and utilize interesting equipment. Some mentally retarded children might have difficulty understanding a game at the start, although they can perform parts of the game such as ball throwing, running, and tagging, which eventually can be combined. Movements such as running, climbing, turning, and jumping are fun and make it possible for them to learn games and stunts. Throwing can continue for some time (with and at different objects, at different levels, and over various sizes of objects). Games that include singing, dancing, and storytelling promote reasoning and memory in mentally retarded children and should be scheduled early in the day and in an area where distractions can be avoided (Hunt, 1955).

Emotionally Disturbed Children.
Although games with rules enhance competitive and cooperative play skills, they may be difficult for some emotionally disturbed children. Special educators often recommend structured learning in teaching games to these children (Wehman, 1977). Simple games are useful with emotionally disturbed children because of their short interest span. Games that are intellectual or competitive or that require separate score-keeping may be too stressful for some children. Contests that require physical contact between players should also be avoided.

Hearing-Impaired Children. Hearing-impaired children can easily play active games with other children in the primary grades, although imaginative language games present some difficulty. As they encounter problems learning new games, these children may cling to the old ones, preferring not to change or modify games or make up new ones.

Hearing-impaired children should be encouraged to experiment with different types of games common to their age group (Hunt, 1955). Often these children prefer contact and aggressive games. Games like tug-of-war, relay races, and other team games give them the opportunity to learn about sportsmanship, to develop social skills, and to compete successfully. Although some speech is required to play such games, this is often secondary.

The hearing-impaired need to understand the instructions given in a game. The teacher must provide instructions at the onset of play because these children do not readily learn them from other children. Once learned, they rarely forget a game, skill, or dance, possibly because the teaching methods used for the hearing-impaired are especially thorough.

Since hearing-impaired children appear normal, their hearing peers may not tolerate mistakes they would excuse in other handicapped children. Teachers may need to help normal children understand the difficulties incurred by the hearing-impaired. However, singling the hearing-impaired out for special consideration can be demeaning and embarrassing to them.

Visually Impaired Children.
Games for visually impaired children should be neither so difficult they cause frustration nor so simple as to

cause resentment. Visually impaired children need encouragement, a permissive approach, and stimulation of their imagination, but they do not need to be pampered. The fun of the game is lost when there is no challenge (Hunt, 1955). Their interest in game activities generally develops at a later age then in their sighted peers. Since visually impaired children need to memorize the game and their surroundings, games should be simple when first introduced; complexities can be added later. Play groups for visually impaired children should be small so the teacher can assist children individually. As soon as these children thoroughly learn a game, they should have the opportunity to enjoy their new skills with sighted peers.

The visually impaired need to be aware of the size, shape, and composition of the area in which they play in order to feel secure; however, games should be presented in more than one place. Tours and contest games can orient the visually impaired to an unfamiliar place by helping them explore it themselves as well as having teachers describe it. Since the visually impaired must memorize everything in a play space, including equipment and movable facilities, nothing should be changed without informing the child.

It is important that the visually impaired child know exactly where the teacher and other players are as well as what is happening during a game. Sighted children and the teacher should talk to each other and use names to help identify themselves. Also, visually impaired children are unable to read the nonverbal messages (such as glances and facial expressions) players send to one another during a game, so there is increased reliance on verbal, auditory, and tactile clues.

Orthopedically Handicapped Children. Orthopedically handicapped children can play basic childhood games through vigorous, skillful movements of their arms and by moving objects through space. Easy-to-handle game equipment with projectiles that automatically return to the players, either by means of tilted playing surfaces or by a string or elastic attached to the projectile, can be provided. Many orthopedically handicapped children have little experience in childhood games and must depend on their teachers for guidance. Like the visually impaired they prefer not to move on to new games or modifications of old ones. They need to avoid strong competition but can be involved in controlled competition in group games.

Orthopedically handicapped children may need larger and lighter balls (such as a 17-inch softball) or alternatives for throwing (such as beanbags, balloons, and cloth bags stuffed with paper). The play space for the orthopedically handicapped is usually smaller and the equipment is lighter to restrict the area of movement. Crutch and wheelchair users can enjoy playing circle toss or volleyball games with a rubber balloon, because the balloon travels and falls slowly. A light tap is enough to maintain the balloon in the air, yet a forceful hit will not knock it out of bounds (Hunt, 1955).

SUMMARY

Play is an activity that is independent of rewards or goals, is pleasurable, and is useful for children in developing understandings. Various theories have been developed over the years to explain play; among the most significant are the psychodynamic, cognitive, and arousal-seeking theories. Each of these can illuminate the way in which play serves basic human needs and can help teachers develop guidelines for modifying play to make it serve educational purposes without distorting its essential nature. Among the various forms of educational play are manipulative play, physical play, dramatic play, and games. Each can be modified to help children with particular disabilities become involved in play activities.

In creating a play environment, teachers can establish various play centers to support both handicapped and nonhandicapped children's play.

A play environment needs to be safe for all children. Some situations that do not present a hazard to normal children, however, may be hazardous to a child with a handicapping condition.

Concern for the safety of play materials and settings must be as important as a concern for their developmental appropriateness.

Boundaries must be clearly indicated and rules need to be established for what can go on within the play centers. Dramatic play centers should be provided with props for play, including dress-up clothing and various artifacts related to other play themes. Manipulative play centers need to have tables and chairs that accommodate handicapped and nonhandicapped children. Manipulative materials should be provided in ways that promote easy access for children and easy return of materials for storage and cleanup. Physical play, either indoors or outdoors, requires sufficient space and appropriate equipment as well as a concern for child safety. Games can be provided in various settings, depending on the nature of the game. Each child's capacity must be considered as the teacher creates a play environment and adapts active play activities in an integrated setting.

REFERENCES

Axline, V. M. *Play therapy*. New York: Ballentine Books, 1974.

Bernhardt, M. and Mackler, B. The use of play therapy with the mentally retarded. *Journal of Special Education*, 1975, 9 (4), 409–414.

Ellis, M. J. *Why people play?* Englewood Cliffs, N.J.: Prentice-Hall, 1973.

Fallen, N. H. Motor skills. In N. H. Fallen (Ed.). *Young children with special needs*. Columbus, Ohio: Charles E. Merrill, 1978.

Goetz, E. M., and Baer, D. M. Social control of form diversity and the emergence of new forms in children's blockbuilding. *Journal of Applied Behavior Analysis*, 1973, 6 (2), 209–217.

Guthrie, S. Criteria for educational toys for pre-school visually impaired children. *Journal of Visual Impairment and Blindness*, 1979, *73* (4), 144-146.

Hunt, V. V. *Recreation for the handicapped*. Englewood Cliffs, N.J.: Prentice-Hall, 1955.

Leland, H., Walker, H., and Taboada, A. Group play therapy with a group of post-nursery male retardates. *American Journal of Mental Deficiency*, 1959, *63* (5), 848-851.

Mehlman, B. Group play therapy with mentally retarded children. *Journal of Abnormal and Social Psychology*, 1953, *48* (1), 53-60.

Morrison, T., and Newcomer, B. Effects of directive versus nondirective play therapy with institutionalized retarded children. *American Journal of Mental Deficiency*, 1975, *79*, 666-669.

Paloutzian, R. F., Hasazi, J., Streifel, J., and Edgar, C. Promotion of positive social interaction in severely retarded young children. *American Journal of Mental Deficiency*, 1971, *75*, 519-524.

Piaget, J. *Play, dreams and imitation in childhood*. New York: W. W. Norton and Co., 1962.

Ross, D. *Pacemaker games program*. Palo Alto, Calif.: F. E. Peacock, 1969.

Strain, P. S., Cooke, T. P., and Appolloni, T. *Teaching exceptional children: Assessing and modifying social behavior*. New York: Academic Press, 1976.

Taite, P. C. Believing without seeing: Teaching the blind child in a "regular" kindergarten. *Childhood Education*, 1974, *50* (5), 285-291.

Wehman, P. Establishing play behaviors in mentally retarded youth. *Rehabilitation Literature*, 1975, *36* (8), 238-246.

Wehman, P. *Helping the mentally retarded acquire play skills: A behavioral approach*. Springfield, Ill.: Charles C. Thomas, 1977.

Wehman, P. Play skill development. In N. H. Fallen (Ed.). *Young children with special needs*. Columbus, Ohio: Charles E. Merrill, 1978.

Wehman, P., and Abramson, M. Three theoretical approaches to play. *American Journal of Occupational Therapy*, 1976, *30* (9), 551-559.

Weisler, A., and McCall, R. B. Exploration and play. *American Psychologist*, 1976, *31* (7), 492-508.

Whitman, T. L., Mercurio, J. R., and Caponigri, V. Development of social responses in two severely retarded children. *Journal of Applied Behavior Analysis*, 1970, *3*, 133-138.

Thirteen

FOSTERING CREATIVE EXPRESSION

The creative arts, long a part of early education for normal young children, should also be part of handicapped children's educational programs. Movement, music, and art provide young children with opportunities to create and appreciate unique products. They can also serve a compensating function for the handicapped. Creative experiences promote new perceptions of and responses to the world around them. Through various art media, children explore ways to express themselves better and develop self-discipline, developing expressive modes that might offer them new outlets. Thus a language-disabled child may learn to use art media to express ideas that cannot be put into words. This chapter explores movement, music, and art, the three most widely used expressive media in early childhood education.

MOVEMENT EDUCATION

Individuals vary in the speed, balance, precision, and efficiency of their own movement. Most individuals enjoy moving themselves and watching others move. Precision and grace are qualities people view as beautiful in activities such as dancing, skating, diving, or gymnastics. The essence of these activities is in the aesthetic quality of the movement itself.

Children use movement to make sense of their world, creating ideas through their actions. For example, a child who touches a hot iron and gets burned will pull away quickly and will be more cautious the next time in approaching an iron that may be hot enough to burn, recalling both the burning sensation and the body movement related to it.

Rudolph Laban, more than anyone else, has influenced movement education. Laban (1971) proposed having children explore body movement rather than having specific directions dictated to them. Open-ended problems of movement exploration with no right or wrong answers are presented for solution. Follow-up questions encourage children to explore additional alternatives. An understanding of the structure of movement education and of its process provides the foundation for physical education. Games, gymnastics, and dance promote children's physical and emotional development through such movement concepts as body awareness, space, qualities, and relationships. The parts of the body vary in their relationship to each other and to objects (e.g., near, far, on,

around, under), in the number and variation of actions (e.g., straight, curved, zigzag), and in a wide range of motions (from small to large). Speed and rhythm also affect movement. Their force fluctuates in a continuum from strong to weak and in quality from sudden to sustained, while the flow varies in the degree of its freedom (Copple, Sigel, & Saunders, 1979). These movement elements are the basis of Laban's framework for movement education.

The fun of discovering has replaced drill in movement education and invention and creativity have reduced competition. Enjoyment and satisfaction should be an integral part of the program for all the children as they achieve a higher level of physical skills through games, dances, and gymnastics activities. Students can acquire confident, positive attitudes and enthusiasm toward physical activity out of and in school.

Goals and Objectives

The goals of movement education, according to Kirchner, Cunningham, and Warrell (1978), include the following:

1. physical fitness and skills in a variety of areas

2. an understanding of the principles of movement

3. an awareness of what the body is able to do

4. increased self-discipline and self-reliance

5. modes of self-expression and creativity

6. increased confidence in meeting physical challenges

7. greater cooperation and sensitivity toward others

A number of goals can be achieved by centering on a variety of activities related to a theme. In the theme "moving at different speeds," knowledge objectives can include an understanding that movements differ in speed from very slow to very fast; thus movement is modified as the amount of time it takes to perform the movement is altered. Skill objectives can relate to ways of modifying the speed of movements, accelerating and decelerating slowly and quickly and consciously controlling the speed of body movement. In developing positive attitudes toward movement, children must want to listen,

think, and solve problems as well as have the desire to search for skillful, thoughtful, and original modes of movement exploration. Movement education can also teach appreciation of individual differences, task persistence, self-motivation, self-esteem, and enjoyment.

Activities in Movement Education

Activities in movement education at the early childhood level should be provided through games, gymnastics, and dance and should include movement experiences and body mechanics (which are locomotor, nonlocomotor, and manipulative), apparatus, stunts and tumbling, simple games, and sports skills and activities.

Games.   The main purpose of games is to challenge oneself or (for older children) an opponent. Competition is the essence of games, although it is only enjoyed when students have mastered the skills involved. Thus formal games are generally introduced in the kindergarten and primary grades. Skills, developed in the early years and fundamental to games, include visual perception (spatial body awareness, spatial relations, form constancy, figure/ground relationships), auditory discrimination (sound localization, rhythm discrimination, figure-ground selection), tactile-touch, kinesthetic, sensory integration (balance, exploration, eye-hand coordination), strength, endurance, flexibility, and motor ability (balance, power, coordination, speed, agility, rhythm). Specific movements include balancing, bouncing, catching, hopping, jumping, pushing, running, tagging, and twisting (Eason & Smith, 1976). Children can improve these skills by practicing them through play.

Individual and partner games can be used in the primary grades to develop individual skills and encourage cooperation. In partner games, the teacher should equalize the competition so that children have the greatest opportunity to develop their skills and experience both success and failure. Continuous failure lowers self-esteem while continuous success creates a false sense of superiority and conceit—all feelings children do not need to acquire.

Gymnastics.   Gymnastics help children learn to control their movements and work safely and aesthetically within their own restrictions. Gymnastics can be offered even in the preschool. Movement tasks and problems are individualized, and a concern for winning or losing becomes irrelevant. Individuals can be expected to work at near maximum capacity with high levels of effort and concentration.

Dance.   Dance is the most creative of the movement areas. It can be presented informally in the preschool and more formally in later grades. While not competitive, it requires a high degree of individual effort and concentration. Through dance, children experience, understand, and create the expressive aspects of movement, analyzing, selecting, and interpreting them. A movement idea can be explored through music, rhythm, and words. Children need to have the opportunity to enjoy all three. Music, provided through instruments or records, supports dance activities and should be available.

In order to provide the balance of games, gymnastics, and dance, movement activities may be developed around themes designed to teach specific concepts and skills. For example, flying may be the main theme for a series of activities focusing on jumping and landing in which children explore basic jumps such as jumping from one foot to another or jumping on the same foot. The theme provides a focus to clarify relationships between children and space and identify similarities and differences in types of movement.

An obstacle course provides a good example of a series of activities used in a movement theme. A series of obstacles can be created that require children to crawl under, jump over, climb through, or walk around them. Objects should be sufficiently spaced so that several children can work on them separately but sequentially. In the obstacle course illustrated in Figure 13-1, a child can move in various ways between the tractor tires on the ground—jumping on one foot, jumping on two feet, or turning in the air while jumping. Another child can balance on the balance beam, assuming different body positions while a third child climbs or runs through the ladder. Thus, several children can use the different pieces of equipment simultaneously, without waiting for or interfering with each other.

Movement Education for Handicapped Children

Carefully planned movement programs offer handicapped children opportunities for new experiences, enabling them to extend their horizons and to become a part of the class, school, and

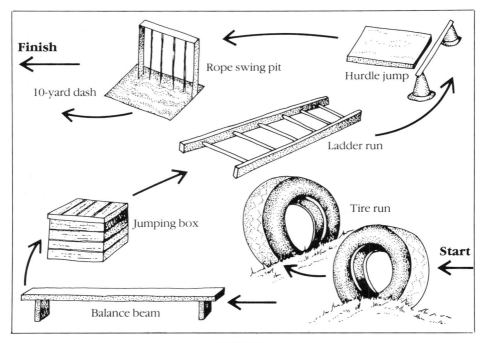

Finish

10-yard dash

Rope swing pit

Hurdle jump

Ladder run

Tire run

Jumping box

Start

Balance beam

FIGURE 13-1
An obstacle course for young children

community. Some handicapped children who have low opinions of themselves in relation to their academic and physical performance can be helped to develop self-confidence through physical activity. Every child, regardless of the severity of the handicap, should have the opportunity to succeed on the playing field, in the gymnasium, or in the swimming pool. Such success can carry over to the classroom and to other life situations.

Handicapped children who participate in individually tailored movement education programs will become increasingly aware of others and will learn to win and lose, succeed and fail through individual and group effort. Social interaction and awareness of

other children improves cooperation; thus children learn to respect one another.

Handicapped children, who may have a poor conception of time, of space, of body image, and of many other perceptual concepts, can benefit from a comprehensive movement education program that includes activities using balance boards, balance beams, obstacle courses, tumbling, and swimming. The following are realistic and attainable goals for handicapped children, according to Bucher and Thaxton (1979):

1. to understand, appreciate, and enjoy movement experiences

2. to experience a series of movement experiences

3. to develop body awareness

4. to improve physical skills

5. to understand and appreciate one's physical capacities and restrictions

6. to cultivate one's physical fitness within one's capacities

7. to promote a positive self-image

8. to foster effective interpersonal relationships

9. to become aware of safety precautions

10. to learn to protect oneself from injuries that can occur through engagement in physical activities

Since handicapped students have a variety of abilities and restrictions, the movement program should be modified to meet their individual needs. Bucher and Thaxton (1979) suggest these guidelines for a movement education program for handicapped children:

1. The school should cooperate with health service personnel (physicians and nurses) in planning each child's program.

2. The child's motor skill, ability, and physical fitness levels should be evaluated to develop a program that meets the student's needs.

3. The program needs to be constantly assessed and careful records kept including test scores, activities engaged in, and progress reports. This process keeps the parents, physician, and other involved persons up to date concerning the child's progress.

4. Challenges that are within the student's capabilities and limitations and that offer opportunities for success should be provided.

5. Instruction should be individualized and extra assistance made available.

6. Appropriate activities should be selected based on the individual fitness level of each student as well as the student's interests, ability, needs, sex, and age.

7. Activities should be modified for the student based on the child's handicap, capabilities, and restrictions.

8. Facilities and equipment need to be carefully checked for safety.

Movement education programs must be individualized to help children learn within their own capabilities and at their own rate without regard to any specified standards. Learning centers established in the gymnasium, playground, multipurpose room, or self-contained room provide a practical method for individualizing instruction. Figure 13-2 presents a plan to set up learning centers and includes skills to be learned and activities to develop those skills. Learning centers can be established in four general areas of activity with signs in each identifying the skill areas and tasks. Skill sheets related to the activity in the designated area can be provided as guidance for the children. Students can be allowed to move from one area to another before mastering all levels of a skill, so that a series of movement skills is taught and developed simultaneously. Several

LEARNING CENTER ACTIVITIES

Skill: balance

Activities:

balance beam
balance beam benches
balance boards
balance block
balance stunts
tumbling activities
balance activities
   on tumbling mats
balance touch
carpet squares
bango boards

Skill: space relations

Activities:

obstacle course
gym scooters
cargo net
mini gym
stepping stones
bounding boards
wands
horizontal ladder
exercise bar
jumping box
jump ropes

Skill: eye-hand coordination

Activities:

bean bags
hoops
appropriate balls
targets
tennis paddle and
   sponge balls
bowling pins and ball
scoops for catching
flying saucers (frisbees)
parachute play
geometric shapes

Skill: body image

Activities:

locomotor patterns
Simon Says (song)
rhythms
rope climbing
jumping boxes
magic rope activities
dances
horizontal ladder
axial movements (bend,
   turn, twist, fly stunts)

learning alternatives are provided for each skill, and activities within each area can be varied in complexity to help individuals progress at their own rate. For children who cannot read, instructions for developing a skill may consist of a series of pictures illustrating how a specific skill can be mastered and the types of activities that develop that skill.

Learning centers allow teachers to work with children on a one-to-one basis without taking time from the class. Burton (1977) has identified several ways of implementing learning centers:

1. The teacher presents different types of learning experiences.

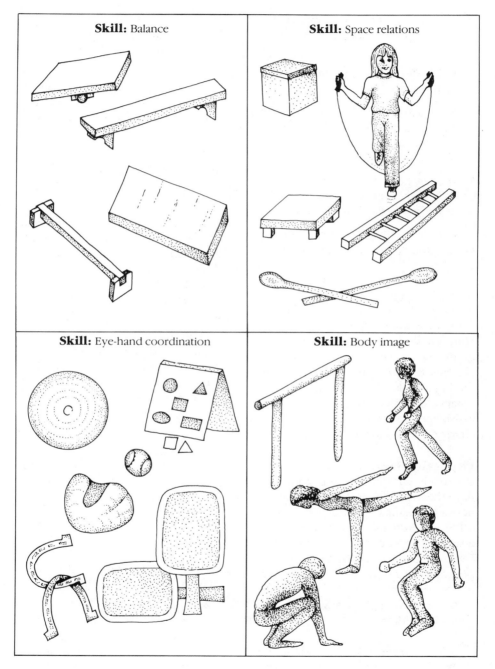

FIGURE 13-2
Diagram of learning centers with skills and activities

2. Children can select the skill(s) they wish to pursue.

3. The teacher discusses the process and performance objectives with each child.

4. The teacher provides instructions on how tasks can be completed, where equipment and supplies are located, and the time limit.

5. The teacher offers enrichment materials, such as pictures, posters, charts, records, films, and books.

An individualized instruction program can be planned so that students progress at their own pace while learning psychomotor skills and developing helping, caring behavior.

The teacher circulates around the room providing help and testing while children work on individualized programs. Skills that have been mastered are checked off on the skill sheet and filed in a folder. Children who need assistance can ask a teacher or peer for assistance or review the large wall charts provided for the specific skill.

Physically Handicapped Children.   Physically impaired students have the same drives, feelings, and needs for regular physical activity as other children and should receive adequate opportunities to participate in well-rounded movement education programs and movement activities. The following primary movements can be used with young physically handicapped children:

○ *Body Awareness.* Move head, neck, shoulders, arms, hands, trunk, legs, and feet.

○ *Spatial Relationship.* Use parts of the body in relation to objects in space; develop laterality and directionality.

○ *Balance.* Move in various directions and in different ways to develop dynamic and static balance; use activities that require balancing of objects.

○ *Axial Movement.* Lie on the stomach and raise the head; raise the arms and other parts of the body that can be raised.

○ *Swing and Sway.* Sit down and swing (or sway) as many parts of the body as possible; swing arm(s) in many directions—in circles, squares, triangles, rectangles, letter shapes, number formations.

○ *Pushing and Pulling.* Sit or lie down and use hands, elbows, arms, or trunk to push some object in as many directions as possible; pull it; pull and/or push in an upward or downward or sideways direction.

○ *Bending and Stretching.* Bend various parts of the body while sitting or lying down; bend or stretch parts of the body in as many directions as possible.

○ *Twisting, Turning, and Whirling.* Sit or lie down and twist, turn, or whirl as many parts of the body as possible; twist the body in one direction, then the other direction—to the right, to the left, and other ways.

○ *Shaking and Beating.* Sit, lie down, or stand and shake as many parts of the body as possible; shake the right (left) side of the body and beat a rhythm with the left (right) (Christensen, 1970).

Basic body movements for physically impaired children are first initiated on tumbling mats. The first movements are begun by placing the children in a lying position and having them pull themselves toward the teacher. At the beginning the arms do most of the work but gradually the use of the feet is encouraged. These movements can be done from prone, supine, side, or sitting positions. While it is difficult for a child in a wheelchair to perform on balance beams, balance boards, jump boards, sawhorses, stairs, stilts, tables, and tires, the physically handicapped child can be successful with other pieces of apparatus. The following equipment can be used with such children:

○ *Balls.* Throw the ball up and catch it; let it bounce before catching it; throw the ball in many different ways to a partner.

○ *Beanbags.* Experiment with the beanbag; throw it up high and catch it; close your eyes and throw (toss) it alternating from hand to hand.

○ *Deck Tennis Rings.* Throw a ring up in the air and catch it with one or two hands; clap hands before catching it; catch the ring in such a way that it slides over one arm or both arms.

Christensen (1970) describes Mickey, a kindergarten boy afflicted with cerebral palsy. Mickey, in his wheelchair, could use his arms, chest, shoulders, trunk, neck, and head. During Mickey's primary years, his movement education program was adapted to his handicap. In self-testing activities, Mickey was able to conduct a leg roll, seal walk, and wheelbarrow (Mickey is the barrow); to grasp the horizontal bar; to travel on the horizontal ladder; and to perform some balancing activities with a wand. Rhythms allowed Mickey to perform modified imitations and any rhythmic activity using hand, shoulder, head, arm, and trunk movements and to play rhythm sticks or other instruments. During softball, Mickey practiced throwing, catching, fielding, and batting.

Movement education activities can be adapted for children in wheelchairs by using ropes that are inexpensive and versatile. An activity that improves extensor and flexor muscles of the arms and legs uses ropes in conjunction with weights and a pulley. A simple eyelet can be made in the wall with a wooden pin or weight attached to the rope can give the effect of a weight and a pulley, as the rope is pulled through the eyelet against the weight. Two students in wheelchairs, each holding one end of the rope, can face each other with the brakes on one chair to hold it still. The student in the other wheelchair pulls himself or herself toward the student in the stationary wheelchair. The student in the moving wheelchair experiences a hand-over movement while the one in the stationary wheelchair encounters tension. This activity can be facilitated by tying knots one to two inches apart in the rope (Frederick, 1971).

Devices added to ropes provide mobility in learning activities. The teacher can tie a rope tightly on one side of the room and give the other end of the rope to a child in a wheelchair at the other side of the room. The child then uses the rope to pull the wheelchair across the room. This activity can be varied by tying the rope to different stationary objects in the room such as door knobs, other wheelchairs, or windows. Mobility activities can develop other learnings as different numbers, colors, shapes, forms, or pictures are placed at different points in the classroom. An obstacle course can be created with barriers for students in wheelchairs to cross by going around, over, or through them.

Ropes can also be used in conjunction with balls. The teacher can tie a rope to a whiffle ball or to a rubber ball with a hole in it. The other end of the rope is tied to a stationary object or to the student's wheelchair. The student throws or hits the ball with a bat and uses the rope to recover the ball. Other movement experiences can also be adjusted for physically handicapped children in regular classes, permitting children to use and explore different movements at their own developmental level without any pressures from their peers or inappropriate performance standards.

Visually Impaired Children. Visually impaired children need higher levels of physical fitness than persons with normal vision because they use more energy to perform, achieve, and succeed at their sighted peers' level. In addition to increasing physical fitness, group physical activities teach responsibility, consideration, cooperation, unselfishness, and courtesy and social awareness, all of which enhance their interpersonal relationships.

Visually impaired students can be successfully integrated into regular activities with only minor modifications. Simple procedures can help them use their other senses. A severely impaired child can work together with a classmate who can see normally. Both can run together, with the visually impaired student grasping the normally sighted student's arm just above the elbow. This places the child approximately one-half step behind and one-half step to the side of the sighted student. In this position the visually impaired student can anticipate the sighted student's movements better than through joined hands (Buell, 1970).

Visually impaired students can take short runs using some type of device to direct them. A good guide is a piece of cord stretched from the start to finish line and marked at the beginning and at the end with knots. Children can run holding the cord until they feel the knots (Buell, 1970). A ring that slides along the line will allow children to grasp the line but not be slowed down by the friction of hand on the rope. They can also touch another person as that person goes through movement activities. Success in this activity will encourage them to attempt other types of activities such as tumbling, jumping rope, playing games, and climbing. Then the teacher guides the visually impaired children through the same motions while they touch themselves to feel the movement and to recognize when and where emphasis needs to be placed on speed or strength.

Tumbling is also a good activity for visually impaired students. It helps them develop equilibrium, poise, and trust in themselves when their feet leave the ground. Tumbling requires the ability to relocate in the environment, especially after a series of forward rolls. Visually impaired students must learn to fall safely to prevent serious injuries.

Jumping rope fosters coordination, muscular strength, and cardiorespiratory endurance, as well as a sense of timing and adeptness of performance. Visually impaired children can learn to jump rope by first learning to jump high and low without a rope, distinguishing the different jumps, and feeling the jump required. A normally sighted peer can jump in tandem to give the severely visually impaired child the feel of jump rhythm. By placing hands on the partner's shoulder, the visually impaired child can gain a sense of the jump rhythm. Once jump skills have been mastered, two turners can swing a long rope back and forth to give the child the feeling of jumping over a rope. When the child is ready, the turners swing the rope in a complete arc and when the rope is over the child's head, they say, "Jump!" The next skill to learn is to run into the long rope and jump. When the rope hits the floor, the turners say, "Run!" The visually impaired child who has mastered jump skills with the long rope can learn to jump on individual ropes.

Games help visually impaired children develop social and personal qualities such as leadership, followership, courtesy, respect, enthusiasm, cooperativeness, competitiveness, and faith in others. To avoid confusion, directions for games should be simple and concise. Teachers must wait until they have everyone's attention before giving directions. Games for the visually impaired should reflect skills they have mastered. In a game such as dodgeball,

visually impaired children need partners to help them dodge the ball when it is thrown in their direction and when it is their turn to throw the ball, the other players should clap their hands, sing, or make some kind of noise to place themselves (Johansen, 1971).

Volleyball can be modified for the visually impaired player by having the visually impaired players only serve their team by throwing or batting the ball or, when the ball goes in the direction of the visually impaired players, requiring it to bounce once before they toss the ball over the net. In softball, the ball can be placed on a tee for the visually impaired child to hit with a bat. When the visually impaired child hits the ball, a partner grasps her or his hand and they run together to first base. If a visually impaired fielder picks up a moving ball, the running player is out. Kickball requires using an audible ball or, for children who have a partial visual impairment, a light colored ball, preferably yellow. The visually impaired kicker places the ball on home plate, kicks it, and runs as in softball. Visually impaired players can pitch by rolling the ball to the batter while the catcher claps hands to guide the pitcher.

Mentally Retarded Children.
Movement education develops mentally retarded students' independence, helping them improve physical, mental, and social competencies. The teacher must be aware of the children's level of competency and degree of retardation and of any psychological, social, or behavior problems. Stein and Pangle

(1966) present the following basic constructs of psychomotor functions for the mentally retarded:

1. At any specific age, normal children tend to perform higher than mentally retarded children on most measures of motor proficiency.

2. Although mentally retarded children have a low achievement level, they are closer to the norm physically than mentally.

3. Planned and systematic programs in movement education can develop physical proficiency in the mentally retarded.

4. Mentally retarded students enrolled in the public schools have higher physical abilities than those in institutions.

5. Mentally retarded students learn better with activities that require simple skills rather than complex neuro-muscular skills.

6. Mentally retarded children's physical development has no effect on their sociometric status.

7. Educable mentally retarded students can achieve significant IQ gains by participating in planned and progressive movement education activities.

8. Retarded students exhibit a stronger relationship between physical proficiency and intelligence than normal pupils.

Mentally retarded children are often more poorly coordinated than non-retarded children. Skills can be learned through repetition, using activities these children enjoy, activities that allow them to develop at their own rate. The teacher should provide assistance or support to these children as needed during activities (Oliver, 1966).

Emotionally Disturbed Children.
Emotionally disturbed children are usually not physically retarded; some may have outstanding coordination and physical fitness. Goals for these children are similar to those established for nonhandicapped children. Gymnastics, games, and dance experiences offer vehicles whereby emotionally disturbed children can develop body awareness and become physically fit. These programs should focus specifically on socialization, development of coordination and movement exploration, and positive redirection of energy.

Emotionally disturbed children may need different strategies in order to achieve the goals in movement education, to increase their attention span, and to develop self-discipline. Teachers should be aware of each child's pathology and select appropriate techniques. Before making program decisions, teachers should examine each child's psychological records as well as staff recommendations and past experiences in similar situations. Individualized programs can help emotionally disturbed children progress at their own rate. Activities must be challenging but

not so challenging the child becomes frustrated and gives up. On the other hand, activities that are far too easy insult their abilities.

Many emotionally disturbed children have difficulty hitting or catching a ball, jumping high, playing games requiring considerable organization, and following rules (Waggoner, 1973). Some emotionally disturbed children remain passive and have short attention spans. Alternative activities must be planned for times when such a child's attention begins to decline. Such activities should not all be new because presenting many new activities can be upsetting. Since emotionally disturbed children have difficulty waiting, remaining quiet, or listening to long explanations, teachers should prepare the environment before the children arrive so that activities can be introduced quickly.

Equipment should be colored brightly enough to attract the children's attention, but not be so gaudy that it frightens them. The children's short attention span also requires that equipment be available for their use throughout the period since they may not be able to stand in line and wait their turn. It helps if an aide is available to work on a one-to-one basis with each child.

MUSIC EDUCATION

Children are exposed to a wide range of sounds throughout their lives. From infancy, they hear vacuum cleaners, airplanes, dogs, doorbells, thunder, rain, and human voices. They learn to discriminate differences in volume, rhythm, tempo, and pitch in speech or

music. Music provides pleasure and an outlet for expression during the early years. As children mature, knowledge, concepts, and skills in relation to listening, singing, playing, moving, and reading and writing music develop. Music experiences can teach concepts, develop motor skills and music appreciation, and provide enrichment.

A music program in the preschool, kindergarten, and primary grades is mainly composed of singing, playing simple instruments, listening, and creative rhythms. Each of these areas is discussed below.

Singing

Music is based on three elements: intensity (soft and loud), pitch (high and low), and tempo (fast and slow) that can be illustrated through singing. Almost all children love to sing. They like a song with a good melody, easy words, and possibilities for action play. The melody in the song should be pleasant, the range limited, and the intervals easy to attain.

The first musical experience in school programs is usually singing together in a group. Most preschool children know nursery rhymes and will sing them with enthusiasm. Young children integrate movement, speech, and singing to develop chants that correspond to their melodramatic configurations, repetitive character, and rhythmic movement (McDonald, 1979). The teacher can use such chants to describe daily situations and facilitate transitions. Learning to sing requires a combination of words and vocal pitch. Teachers need to initially use songs that are within the children's range and gradually present other songs that extend that range. Somewhat older children can be taught concepts about melody through singing. Appropriate teaching techniques include both using physical movements of the hand or body that correspond to the direction

of movement of a song's melody and presenting visual cues such as dashes or musical notes, which indicate high-low, same, or up-down tones. These visual cues can be augmented with an accompaniment on song bells, a piano, or step bells. The children's cultural backgrounds can suggest a variety of sources for songs besides the music textbook. Children can also compose new songs or adapt familiar ones and the teacher can record them on a chart or a tape recorder.

Musical Instruments

Musical instruments can be played independently by young children or in a group. Instruments to be used can include drums, tambourines, gourds, maracas, metal triangles, a variety of bells (jingle bells, dainty table bells, cow bells), xylophones with good musical quality, and cymbals that vibrate when clashed. Durable instruments that produce good sounds can be made by the teacher or by the students. Commercially made instruments should also be provided, since many homemade instruments do not achieve a high quality of tone. Only instruments with good sound attributes should be bought and toy instruments should be avoided. Opportunities to explore instruments will help children discriminate the quality of pitched and non-pitched sounds. Children can use their imagination to produce original tunes, rhythms, and sounds.

Drums can be made out of coffee cans by removing the lid and covering one end with plastic. A more authentic drum can be made by removing both ends of the coffee can and stretching sheet rubber or animal hide across the openings. A garden-hose flute can be made out of a foot-long piece of garden hose closed at one end with a cork and with holes bored down one side. This can be played much like a recorder.

Experiences with instruments appropriate for young children include experimenting with sounds, joining in a rhythm band, observing older children or adults play instruments, creating original tunes, and spontaneously playing instruments. Children can use instruments to experiment with new ideas in sound as well as to refine the skills they develop.

Listening

Listening, one of the basic skills in the music program, is also important in other parts of the program. Children listen to the world around them and abstract sounds to learn about the world. Listening to music helps children learn to discriminate between qualities of sound (e.g., pitch, intensity, rhythm, and patterns). Attentive listening is a prerequisite for learning to sing. Children must remember the song and accurately reproduce its pitch and rhythmic pattern. Children also listen to the music when they create movements.

Young children are most interested in active listening. They are responsive to music with movement, creative dance, or with appropriate instrumental accompaniment. Children need to listen to a wide variety of music including classical, jazz, and popular music; music from diverse cultures; and avante-garde and twentieth-century serious music. The types of music favored by children should be played most often, but children need to be encouraged to listen to other styles of music as well. Since children imitate the teacher's behavior, the teacher should model an interest in listening to all types of music. Teachers can invite parents, older children, or community members to share their musical tastes and talents in making music with the class.

Rhythms

Young children become aware of rhythmic patterns in music as they match movement with music. They gradually learn to keep time with music as they listen to recordings, sing songs, and recite nursery rhymes or chant. Exploratory and imitative experiences with rhythm help children gain a repertoire of both musical and nonmusical rhythmic movements.

When children create informal and spontaneous rhythms, teachers can add a chant, a hand-clapping, or an instrumental accompaniment. Opportunities to move spontaneously to music, speech rhythms, and movements that are synchronized with a beat assist children in controlling their rhythmic responses. An awareness of the beat and the synchronizing of movement with that beat can be developed through playing action songs and games that use instruments, visual devices such as clocks and metronomes, and recordings with a predominant rhythmic character. Older children, with better motor coordination than younger ones, can test out rhythmic patterns through clapping and chanting word rhythms of poetry, chant, and

song. They should be encouraged to improvise, to share ideas, and verbalize their rhythmic understandings through basic musical terms such as fast-slow, long-short, and even-uneven.

Music Education for Handicapped Children

The basic elements of a music program—singing songs, playing instruments, listening to music, and rhythmic movement—can widen the horizons of the handicapped child. Music can draw shy, withdrawn children into a group; encourage spastic children to control their movements; increase hyperkinetic children's involvement in learning movements such as acting out a character while sitting quietly for long periods of time; and reduce language problems for children through singing. Musical experiences also help hand-

icapped children come into closer contact with their peers and support social relationships.

Children with physical and mental handicaps can learn to play in a rhythm band. There are several pieces of music that are particularly effective and easy to adapt to these children's needs including "Shoemaker's Dance," "The Xylophone Dance," "Tambourine Waltz," and "Drums of Parade" (Schattner, 1967). Teachers need to experiment, trying any piece of music or technique that can help the children realize themselves fully. Children can share a joyous and enriched experience performing for others.

The music goals for handicapped children are similar to those for non-handicapped children and include participating in all forms of music activities, appreciating music, and developing musicianship. The extent to which handicapped children achieve these goals depends on their capabilities and limitations. Ganato (cited in Bayless & Ramsey, 1978) suggests using the following guidelines for musical activities for handicapped (and nonhandicapped) children:

1. Teach through creativity.

2. Teach through multisensory perception.

3. Teach at the appropriate developmental level and rate.

4. Repeat in a variety of ways.

5. Avoid drastic changes of gears.

6. Exclude distractions.

7. Provide instruction in small steps.

8. Offer success-assured activities.

9. Avoid overstimulation with too loud and/or rhythmic music.

10. Consider the children's level of social and language development.

11. Consider children's short attention span and/or other handicapping conditions.

12. Repeat songs until children have learned them before attempting any variations.

13. Expect small successes; be ready for changes; be flexible.

14. Wait until the children have learned a song before accompanying it with instruments.

15. Share ideas with and seek them from others who work with and care for handicapped children.

In music, there is no right or wrong and there is no competition. Handicapped children can feel comfortable with music. They can sing songs about familiar persons or objects such as names, family, pets, and others; sing popular songs such as "Happy Birthday," "Good Morning," "I'm Pleased to See You"; sing television jingles, nursery rhymes, and family favorites; action plays; circle games; listen to music that has humor or an element of surprise; and sing songs that use props (e.g., scarves or puppets), songs that repeat words or phrases, and songs that are used to follow directions.

Physically Handicapped Children.
Physically handicapped children who are bound to a wheelchair need to become aware that their bodies are instruments for joy and that they can express movement and respond to rhythm. These children can move naturally and joyously to music, compose their own music, and create their own movements. They, also, have the urge to move when they hear music and need to learn to use their bodies for this purpose. Musical experiences should be provided to help physically handicapped children acquire enough confidence in themselves to move freely to music.

Music activities should be modified for physically handicapped students, allowing them to crawl, roll over, clap their hands, or respond in any way they can. These children can also listen to music, learn to sing and hum, and play rhythm instruments. During rhythm periods, they can sway to music, move their arms, and turn their bodies from side to side. For dance periods, they can watch and clap out rhythms as other children learn the steps of a dance. The teacher or a peer can move a child's wheelchair in time to music, beginning with a simple waltz rhythm, humming with the child as the chair is moved—back and forth, to the right and left, and in circles. When able, physically handicapped children can move their own wheelchairs propelling them in time to the music—back and forth, around in circles, to the right and left, or in several directions. Children in wheelchairs enjoy this experience as a form of dancing since their wheelchairs become extensions of themselves. A wheelchair dance need not be restricted to one child as shown in the following steps for at least two children:

1. Wheelchairs are placed facing each other.

2. Wheel back for one measure, then forward for one measure. Repeat four times.

3. Each wheelchair circles in place.

4. First wheelchair circles the second.

5. Second wheelchair circles the first.

6. Both return to the first position and bow from the chairs (Schattner, 1967).

A solo wheelchair dance can be largely self-inspired, while a wheelchair dance for two may need assistance and structuring.

Physically handicapped students can observe dance or gymnastic activities as well as use rhythmic activities during their physical therapy sessions. When the music activity requires instruments,

the extent of their coordination and their ability to move must be matched with their instruments. Students with primarily gross motor skills can play drums or tambourines. Sand blocks or rhythm sticks or sleigh bells can be tied to a part of the body the child is able to use (Turnbull & Schulz, 1979). Rhythmic experiences usually improve children's muscles as they develop coordination and control. Singing relaxes tight muscles and offers an opportunity to share, participate in, and enjoy music.

Visually Impaired Children.
Visually impaired children also need modified musical experiences. These children may have a distorted awareness of space and may need to develop spatial boundaries. They are often physically insecure and may have poor coordination and balance in rhythmic movement. Such students need assistance in exploring movement.

Rhythmic activities can foster the visually impaired student's mobility skills. Music or activities requiring large movements can be used at the beginning of a lesson, then gradually refined. The child listens to the teacher and feels the movement of the teacher as directions are provided along with demonstrations. Rhythmic movements can include "rocks rolling," "swings," "swaying," and "walking in the rain." Circle games such as *Skip to My Lou, Looby Lou,* and *London Bridge* can also build the children's feelings of security and help them achieve social recognition.

Visually impaired children's rhythmic ability helps them respond well to percussion instruments. They easily acquire and create rhythmic patterns. Sounds made by bells, tambourines, or other similar instruments allow visually impaired children to become aware of other classmates' positions so they can avoid collision during movement activities.

Children enjoy using several instruments to complement the quality of sound and movement. They examine and experiment with the instruments to learn how they are played. They feel and hear the vibrations of the lasting sound of a gong long after it has been struck. Many characters, events, and dramas can be created with a gong, a tinkling bell, or a drum. Children can integrate these sounds into dances as they move to the whistling and flow of the wind over them, as they run to the sound of waves and passing trucks, or as they move to the sounds made by voices, words, and music.

Hearing-Impaired Children. Music can be amplified and played through headphones to allow hearing-impaired children to hear and enjoy music. These children can play and feel a wide range of musical instruments. Playing instruments develops eye-hand coordination, helps children feel the various sensations created by sounds, and increases muscle strength, joint motion, and coordination. Hearing-impaired children can enjoy humming and clapping along with the other children during music. They can use movement to learn rhythms while observing the rhythmic sequence in different meters and reproducing the pattern through clapping or playing instruments. This kinesthetic approach is a valuable technique in teaching rhythms.

Nursery rhymes help hearing-impaired children acquire rhythm. They can also learn rhythm through tactile sensory perceptions, placing their fingers on a drum or another instrument playing the nursery rhymes. Much repetition is essential for them to feel the rhythm. Nursery rhymes can also help the hearing-impaired children's speech rhythm.

Children with peculiar breathing patterns, poorly developed voices, and language problems have difficulty with singing. They can participate in rhythmic activities through movement or instruments. Marching, hopping, skipping, and other strong rhythmic actions develop hearing-impaired children's speech rhythm and bodily coordination. Together, movement experiences and music improve a hearing-impaired student's ability, posture, and physical fitness.

Mentally Retarded Children. Music experiences help mentally retarded children develop listening skills, increase their attention span, develop coordination through rhythms, and create spontaneous interest. Young educable mentally retarded children can learn to sing simple songs some time after their fourth birthday. Although they may have pitch problems, they often can listen for short periods to music that interests them (Graham, 1972).

Mentally retarded children are usually monotone singers. They have short attention spans, often lack auditory perception, and are sometimes unable to understand what is required of them in music. Singing songs can help reduce these deficiencies. One technique for teaching them songs is for the teacher to sing simple songs repeatedly to the children using a variety of illustrative materials. Such songs as *A Little Teapot, Eency Weency Spider,* and various nursery rhymes can be introduced with colorful illustrations and movements to facilitate learning and can strengthen mentally retarded children's memory and concentration. Moving the body to music, clapping, and brisk stepping can be taught to mentally retarded children through action songs like *Row, Row, Row, Your Boat.* The large-muscle movements, used in this song, provide additional reinforcement for memory.

Musical experiences for the mentally retarded should include playing instruments. The Center for Development and Learning Disorders (n.d.) offers the following steps for playing musical instruments with mentally retarded children:

1. The children explore the musical instruments alone.

2. The teacher and a child play instruments together, labeling the sounds (e.g., This is a drum—boom! This is a bell—jingle, jingle!).

3. The teacher asks the children to close their eyes and questions them ("What's this sound?" or "Is this a drum?").

4. The teacher taps a rhythm and asks the child to play that rhythm with her or him.

5. The teacher plays or sings a simple rhythm and then the child taps the rhythm.

6. The teacher plays increasingly difficult rhythms and asks the child to play them.

Since retarded children's rate of development is often uneven or slow, musical experiences must be repeated in a variety of modes. Handicapped children's musical achievement is often higher and with more depth than the teacher might expect.

ART EDUCATION

Art serves as a means of nonverbal communication for young children. In the primary grades children respond more to visual and tactile experiences than they do in the earlier years. As they mature, they can continue to work with the same art media in a more sophisticated way, making prints, constructing, modeling, painting, stitching, and weaving.

Children's art abilities progress through a series of stages characterized as: the preschematic stage (4 to 7 years), the schematic stage (7 to 9 years), and the stage of drawing realism (9 to 11 years) (Lowenfeld & Brittain, 1970). These stage distinctions are based on the characteristics of children's art products, including representation of the human figure, space, color, design, motivation, topics, and materials. For example, a child's work in the preschematic stage may be characterized as follows:

1. general characteristic—discovery of relationship between drawing, thinking, and environment

2. presentation of human figure—circular motion for head, longitudinal for legs and arms

3. use of space—self as center with no orderly arrangement of objects in space

4. use of color—no conscious approach

5. motivation topics—activating of passive knowledge related mainly to self-body parts

6. use of materials—crayons; clay; tempera paints; thick, large bristle brushes; large sheets of absorbent paper

Lowenfeld's stages of art expression parallel Piaget's stages of intellectual development. Children's drawings also indicate their style of thinking. Children who draw details usually perceive objects as separate from the field, can abstract an item from the surrounding field, and are analytic individuals. Those who omit details tend to rely on the surrounding perceptual field, experience their environment in a relatively global fashion by conforming to the effects of the prevailing field or context, and are social individuals.

Lowenfeld's art stages provide an index teachers can use to evaluate children's art abilities. For example, during a cutting activity the teacher can record which children hold scissors properly, are left- or right-handed, cut in an upward rather than downward direction, and which are able to state what form they wish to complete before cutting. Clay modeling, playdough modeling, paper tearing, and different forms of painting can all be evaluated this way. Having a sense of the children's stages allows teachers to appropriately direct and plan classroom activities in the motor, affective, perceptual, cognitive, and aesthetic domains.

Art Education for Handicapped Children

Teachers can use art as a way of helping handicapped children develop an awareness of their surroundings, building bridges for communication and motivating them to relate to others. Children who have a consuming anger can use art to express those feelings without fear of retaliation. Self-destructive children can find something in their art products that is worthwhile. Children with delayed speech development can gradually explore complex nonlinguistic symbolic forms. Art experiences are also beneficial to physically handicapped, visually impaired, and neurologically damaged children who have distorted sensory perceptions that produce bizarre responses of fragmentation and disorganization of cognitive processes.

The art curriculum for handicapped children must be modified in content, methods, materials, timing, and sequence and must be presented in a climate of acceptance, openness, and empathy. Challenging experiences can help these children explore ideas, resolve intense feelings, and become less dependent. Some handicapped children become easily disoriented and

upset; some lack self-motivation; some have learned to expect failure; some have limited receptive and expressive abilities; and some have short attention spans. Some handicapped children also lack self-confidence, have a poor self-image, and expect to fail. These students need successful experiences that make them comfortable with the materials and allow them to express their thoughts and feelings.

Children who lack self-direction need an enthusiastic presentation to help them become interested and involved in art activities. Visual aids (such as films, slide presentations, prepared motivation boards or charts, pictures from magazines, and demonstrations) that capture their attention and provide stimulation can be helpful.

Easily understood instructions must be provided to children with limited receptive abilities. These should be supplemented by demonstrations so those who cannot fully understand the teachers' words will be able to follow their actions. Teachers may also stand behind the children and move their hands in the same direction as the children's hands (Hollander, 1971). Encouraging questions allows children to indicate any confusion they might have.

Physically Handicapped Children.
Physically handicapped students who can only move their arms, hands, and fingers can still participate in the art program. Students with limited fine motor skills may need help holding pencils, crayons, or paint brushes. A ball of clay or a foam rubber sponge wrapped around a pencil, crayon, or brush can help. Students with jerky or uncoordinated movements may knock

the paper from the easel or table, spill paint, or knock other supplies to the floor. These students may need a separate work area with sturdy holders in which to snugly insert paint jars. Students' papers can be taped to easels or to the surfaces on which they are working. Students who cannot manipulate small objects may have to use large objects for their art work. If they cannot use paint, they might work with crayons or collage. Felt-tip pens, soft-lead pencils, and ball-point pens are good drawing tools that require little pressure and do not have to be refilled.

Visually Impaired Children. Often visually impaired children are not included in the art program. These children appreciate art tactually and enjoy a variety of textures and forms. They need opportunities to actively partici-

pate in the creative process and discover their own place in the world of art. Art activities appropriate for the visually impaired depend on the degree of the handicap, their perceptual experiences, and their age. These children need to be encouraged to become involved, but they should not be too overwhelmed.

Visually impaired students learn through multisensory instruction, combining auditory, tactile, and kinesthetic experiences. Teachers can provide verbal instructions while allowing the students to feel the texture of the material. For example, in tying a knot, the teacher guides the student's fingers and hands through the sequence of steps while giving directions verbally. A variety of materials including boxes, balls, cups, different types of paper, wood, textiles, sand, yarn, pipe cleaners, wires, rubber, and plastic can be provided. The children will begin to work with just a few materials and gradually extend their repertoires.

Visually impaired students enjoy art experiences modelling with clay, making prints, pasting collages, and fingerpainting. They can explore a wide range of textures and refine their tactile sense.

Hearing-Impaired Children.   Art activities for the hearing-impaired should be initiated with concrete subjects, providing pictures along with manual communication to help them acquire a sense of the visual representation they will produce. Hearing-impaired children are keen observers, which can help them excel in art (Krone, 1978). Art can do little for the children's hearing loss, but can help them resolve their emotional detachment caused by a lack of environmental awareness and interaction. The teacher should offer art experiences that allow them to symbolize their feelings through art; three-dimensional art such as modeling or carving is helpful.

Since hearing-impaired children's experiences are diminished and distorted by their handicap, they need many experiences to help them develop greater environmental and body awareness. They need a variety of sensory experiences in order to acquire knowledge about themselves and the surrounding world and to substitute for information they are unable to hear. Art experiences can help them identify and interact with the world of space and motion.

Mentally Retarded Children.   Educators often disregard the value of art for the mentally retarded, considering it a frill or a fill-in. However, art experiences are educationally valuable as well as personally satisfying for these children. Mentally retarded children often have normal patterns of growth in art expression, although they may develop at a slower rate. The artistic abilities of mentally retarded children are characterized as follows (Uhlin, 1979):

1. slow rate but a normal pattern of growth

2. simple or primitive forms but good motor coordination

3. lack of experiences expressed in perseveration of form and subject

4. poor spatial Gestalt features indicating a lack of energy expended for association in the perceptual task

5. haptic-type, or tactile experiences expressed in
   a. a body-self centering of viewpoint concerning the space of the drawing or painting
   b. piece-method approach to modeling
   c. lack of spatial depth in drawing or painting
   d. bold, continuous-line character in drawing
   e. emotional exaggeration, deletion, or distortion of form when motivated with a particular experience
   f. emotional employment of color
   g. expression of tactual kinesthetic awareness

Mentally retarded students need to develop a sensitivity to form and space, increased intellectual flexibility, greater emotional sensitivity, an enriched con-

ceptual repertoire, and more social confidence. In view of these needs, teachers should (1) design structured activities, starting with shape, (2) select activities that have display possibilities, (3) direct children to discovery of new forms, (4) use activities that the children may have engaged in at home such as cutting, pasting, or assembling, (5) demonstrate art projects clearly in a step-by-step progression, (6) select materials a size larger than the hand, and (7) include many three-dimensional activities (Lovano-Kerr & Savage, 1972).

Mentally retarded children are able to express themselves and are capable of learning restricted art concepts through systematic teaching and through the use of specific instructional materials. Drawing with a heavy crayon helps develop kinesthetic skills and provides the teacher with an indication of progress. Making simple puppets is also a good activity. Puppetry helps these children identify roles and respond to them as they create conversations among their puppets. Young children can make jewelry, rolling a salt-flour playdough mixture into beads, puncturing them with toothpicks, and laying them out to dry. After the beads are dried, they can be painted, varnished, and strung to wear as a necklace.

Emotionally Disturbed Children.
Art activities, much like play activities, have long been used as a form of therapy for emotionally disturbed young children (see, for example, Kramer, 1971; Naumberg, 1973). Art allows children to express ideas and feelings in nondiscursive ways. The graphic symbols of art may represent

unconscious and often repressed elements of a child's personality and communicate elements of that child's affect, mood, and private fantasies (Kramer, 1971).

The teacher, while not an art therapist, can use elements of the art program to reach disturbed children and help them deal with themselves in the context of the school setting. Often with a young child the opportunity to express a feeling may provide enough of a catharsis so that that child will not be troubled by disturbing feelings. The expression of feeling is also a step in the development of ways of understanding and coping with feelings. Sometimes, however, art can be used to hide feelings, providing a defense against apparent exposure through stereotyped products.

Care must be taken that art materials provided for the emotionally disturbed child are appropriate. Materials that are easily controlled, such as crayon and chalk are best for some children, since they may have difficulty coping with freedom of other materials. Malleable materials such as clay may be best for others. Some children will be fearful of new and unfamiliar material. Others will take pleasure from the tactile and kinesthetic sensations derived from a range of material. It is helpful for the teacher to approach art with these children tentatively, offering a choice of materials and taking cues from their responses rather than prescribing the same art experiences for these children as for others.

The teacher must also be careful in interpreting the art products of children. Often meanings that are expressed in children's artwork are symbolized in strange ways. The children themselves may not be aware of the meanings expressed and may be unsure as to the nature of the representation. Their level of development will also place limits on their artistic productions, which can further complicate interpretation. From the classroom teacher's point of view, art experiences for these children, as for all children, should be concerned with providing pleasure and satisfaction along with increased skill in using the material.

Learning-Disabled Children.
Learning-disabled children are often unable to sequence events. Initial art products can include two-step situations, integrating the children's personal experiences. For instance, the children might draw a story in two parts: the first picture indicates that a girl was given a piece of candy while the second picture indicates what she did with the candy (ate it, gave it to someone else, lost it). The children can gradually work with more complicated stories until they are able to sequence a story with many parts. Sequencing is also important in other art experiences (such as sculpture and printmaking) that require that a large number of directions be followed in order.

Learning-disabled children may become upset when they think they have made a mistake on a project. They can be provided with projects using material that can be reshaped or changed often. For example, children who draw on the blackboard or use fingerpaint can easily erase and start a new drawing. Clay can be molded and remolded into many different shapes, allowing children to work over a clay project

until they are satisfied. More advanced children can weave, creating a more structured product that can also be easily modified. After experience with these materials, children will realize that it is possible to alter one's plans and that it is not necessary to develop the object exactly the way they wished the first time (Krone, 1978).

Language-Disabled Children.
Art is an important means of communication for children who have difficulty expressing themselves in language. Children with language problems usually have receptive and expressive communication gaps. They often have an impaired sensory system. Communicatively handicapped children may hear or see words but not derive meaning from them. Art reinforces their language concepts and develops

visual symbolism. For example, children may draw a kite after seeing one, naming and describing the qualities of the kite (shape, color, texture, weight) and identifying these quality words as they reproduce the kite. Pictures or slides of a variety of kites can be shown and discussed as their similarities and differences are compared. Then the children can fly the kite they used as a model or watch others fly it, observing and describing the manner in which the kite flies, the importance of the wind (cause and effect), the sound of the wind as it blows the kite, the way the kite moves, and the importance of the string. Children can recapture this experience as they draw or paint. This procedure encourages children to use their sensory capacities to better understand and express themselves verbally and artistically (Krone, 1978).

SUMMARY

Children express their thoughts and feelings in many ways. While language is the predominant mode of expression for most people, movement, music and art are also important, especially during childhood. These forms of expression should be accessible to all children, including the handicapped, for they extend the child's way of understanding the world as well as allow for the creation of unique creative communications. Personal ways of knowing related to art, music, and movement are highly satisfying to young children and may be especially important to children who are less successful in using conventional forms of expression.

Teachers working with handicapped children need to know the basic elements of each expressive mode as well as how children develop in their ability to use each mode. They need to be aware of the skills and competencies of each child in relation to their expressive abilities. By meshing the knowledge of the child with the knowledge of the media of art, movement, and music, teachers can develop activities that are satisfying to children and also allow them to extend their abilities beyond stereotyped forms into true forms of personal expression. These activities need to be designed so that they are free from hazards and safe for children. Teachers must be especially cautious when handicapped children are involved.

REFERENCES

Bayless, K. M., and Ramsey, M. E. *Music: A way of life for the young child.* St. Louis: C. V. Mosby, 1978.

Bucher, C. A., and Thaxton, N. A. *Physical education for children: Movement foundations and experiences.* New York: Macmillan, 1979.

Buell, C. The school's responsibility for providing physical activities for blind students. *Journal of Health, Physical Education and Recreation*, 1970, *41* (6), 41–42.

Burton, E. C. *The new physical education for elementary school children.* Boston: Houghton Mifflin, 1977.

Center for Development and Learning Disorders, 1720 Seventh Avenue, South Birmingham, AL 35233.

Christensen, D. Creativity in teaching physical education to the physically handicapped child. *Journal of Health, Physical Education and Recreation,* 1970, *41* (3), 73–74.

Copple, C., Sigel, I., and Saunders, R. *Educating the young thinker.* New York: Van Nostrand, 1979.

Eason, R. L., and Smith, T. L. A perceptual motor program model for learning disabled children. *Physical Education Research Journal,* 1976, *33* (1), 4.

Frederick, J. Ropes for wheelchairs. *Journal of Health, Physical Education and Recreation*, 1971, *42* (3), 50.

Graham, R. M. Seven million plus need special attention. Who are they? *Music Educators Journal*, 1972, *50* (8), 22–25.

Hollander, H. C. *Creative opportunities for the retarded child at home and in school*. New York: Doubleday, 1971.

Johansen, G. Integrating visually handicapped children into a public school physical education program. *Journal of Health, Physical Education and Recreation*, 1971, *42* (4), 61–62.

Kirchner, G., Cunningham, J., and Warrell, E. *Introduction to movement education*. Dubuque, Iowa: Wm. C. Brown Company, 1978.

Kramer, E. *Art as therapy with children*. New York: Schocken Books, 1971.

Krone, A. *Art instruction for handicapped children*. Denver: Love Publishing Co., 1978.

Laban, R. *The mastery of movement*. London: Macdonald and Evans, 1971.

Lovano-Kerr, J., and Savage, S. Incremental art curriculum for the mentally retarded, *Exceptional Children*, 1972, *39* (3), 193–199.

Lowenfeld, V., and Brittain, W. L. *Creative and mental growth*, 5th ed. New York: Macmillan, 1970.

McDonald, D. T. *Music in our lives: The early years*. Washington, D.C.: National Association for the Education of Young Children, 1979.

Naumberg, M. *An introduction to art therapy*. New York: Teachers College Press, 1973.

Oliver, J. N. Add challenge with variety in activities. *Journal of Health, Physical Education and Recreation*, 1966, *37* (4), 37–39.

Schattner, R. *Creative dramatics for handicapped children*. New York: John Day Company, 1967.

Stein, J. U., and Pangle, R. What research says about psychomotor function of retarded. *Journal of Health, Physical Education and Recreation*, 1966, *37* (4), 36–40.

Turnbull, A. P., and Schulz, J. B. *Mainstreaming handicapped students: A guide for the classroom teacher*. Boston: Allyn & Bacon, 1979.

Uhlin, D. M. *Art for exceptional children*. Dubuque, Iowa: Wm. C. Brown Company, 1979.

Waggoner, E. Motivation in physical education and recreation for emotionally handicapped children. *Journal of Health, Physical Education and Recreation*, 1973, *44* (3), 73–76.

INDEX

ABC Inventory. *See* Screening instruments
Accommodation, 223–224
Adaptive behavior, 17
Advisory councils, 171–172
Aggressiveness. *See* Behavior, aggressive
Alphabets
  braille, 196
  ita, 216
  special, 216
Alternative communications systems, 32
American Association on Mental Deficiency, 17
American Printing House for the Blind, 195
American sign language, 26
Antisocial behavior, 13
Appropriate behavior, reinforcement for, 15
Arousal-seeking theory of play, 256
Art abilities
  of mentally retarded, 302
  stages of development of, 298–300
Art activities, as therapy, 303–304
Art education, 299–306
  for emotionally disturbed children, 303–304
  function of, 298
  for language-disabled children, 304–305
  for learning-disabled children, 305
  for mentally retarded children, 302–303
  for physically handicapped children, 300–301

for visually impaired children, 301–302
Art, preschematic stage, characteristics of, 298–299
Assessment
  in design of IEP, 108
  direct observation in, 109
  of handicap, 8
  of handicapped children, 61, 62–63, 108–133
  initial, 108
  observations, 108–109
  ongoing, 108
  of reading abilities, 196–197
Assessment instruments. *See* Assessment inventories
Assessment inventories
  definition, 116
  list of, 124–133
  potential problems of, 116, 118
  sample inventory, 117
  sources of content, 116
Assessment team, 108
Assessment techniques, 109

Balance scales, 247
Bank Street Readers, 194
Basal readers, 193–195
  advantages of, 193–194
  characters as role models, 194–195

308